most baseball fans, the summer of 1981 is a void, an absence, a
k hole. Jeff Katz has finally illuminated that dark space, showing
what we going on behind the scenes of the sports world's most
longed labor action."   —Paul Lukas, ESPN.com and *Uniwatch*

going behind the scenes to reveal the game-changing labor
gotiations of 1981, and also bringing to life the thrills on the
ld—the unforgettable Fernando Valenzuela, and the last Yankees-
dgers World Series among them—Jeff Katz has delivered a worthy
k about a crucial season. Three cheers."   —Kostya Kennedy

t *Season*, Jeff Katz makes the business of baseball as fascinat-
he game afield, as the contentious 1981 season and the stun-
nges it brought to Major League Baseball come to life all
rs later . . . at its heart, *Split Season* is about American
its prime movers, capitalism and the battle for wealth.
st pitch of 1981 is thrown, and the wrappers and beer
and the game changed forever, you will be far wiser
before. And not just about baseball."
lander, senior sports columnist at the *Chicago Sun-Times*

favorite kind of book: an informative, historical
of one of the most pivotal baseball seasons over
on and off the field, but also funny. In an age
it reminds us the game is played by human
antics are far more interesting than on-base
g such a book sounds easy. Jeff Katz has
st me, it isn't."
thor of *The Last Hero: A Life of Henry Aaron*

brought life to the events of 1981 when
es were cancelled because of a player's
this fast-moving narrative is Katz's
and insight to both fields of play—
her at the bargaining table."
                                        —Paul Dickson

Split Season: 1981

Split Season: 1981

Fernandomania, the Bronx Zoo, and the
Strike That Saved Baseball

JEFF KATZ

THOMAS DUNNE BOOKS
ST. MARTIN'S PRESS
NEW YORK

THOMAS DUNNE BOOKS.
An imprint of St. Martin's Press.

www.thomasdunnebooks.com
www.stmartins.com

Designed by Omar Chapa

The Library of Congress Cataloging-in-Publication Data is available upon request.

ISBN 978-1-250-04521-8 (hardcover)
ISBN 978-1-4668-4377-6 (e-book)

First Edition: May 2015

10 9 8 7 6 5 4 3 2 1

To the players who play the game we love

Contents

x | Contents

Prologue

Bob Boone spun around and sprinted toward the home-team dugout, head up to follow the flight of Frank White's foul pop, head down
to find the dugout, head back up to find the ball. With one out in the
top of the ninth inning of Game 6, and the Philadelphia Phillies on
the verge of their first World Series championship, Boone knew how
important it was to make this catch. The bases were loaded, and
though the Phillies were leading the Kansas City Royals 4–1, anything
could happen. The ball, now high above the dugout, kept wafting its
way toward first base.

"Where the hell is Rose?" catcher Boone wondered. This was
becoming a play for the first baseman, but Pete Rose was nowhere
to be found. Charlie Hustle, my ass! The ball descended quickly, and
Boone, now under it, reached out for the grab. The ball squirted out
of his mitt.

Before the Philadelphia fans had time to curse their historically
miserable fate, Rose, suddenly on the scene, stuck out his glove below Boone's mitt and snagged the ball. Boone pumped his right fist
as Rose quickly turned to face the infield. One more out to go, but,
really, it was over right then.

As the Philadelphia K-9 corps entered the field in anticipation of
the riot to come, reliever Tug McGraw made quick work of Willie

Wilson, striking him out for Wilson's record-breaking 12th time. Arms extended high in the air, McGraw was mobbed by his teammates. The Phillies had won the 1980 World Series; they could never have done it without the free-agent signing of Pete Rose, who played with the energy of a man half his 39 years.

It had been a terrific season. The Yankees, led by Reggie Jackson and harassed by owner George Steinbrenner, won 103 games, tops in all baseball, only to be swept in the playoffs by the Royals and George Brett, now a certified superstar. Brett had nearly passed the magical .400 batting mark, ending the regular season at .390, but his most prodigious clout was a monstrous 3-run home run off Yankee closer Rich "Goose" Gossage, way up to the third deck at Yankee Stadium, that sent the Royals to the World Series and Steinbrenner on a tantrum in front of a national television audience. For his troubles, Yankee manager Dick Howser was forced to resign. If not for Brett's monumental year, Jackson would have won his second Most Valuable Player Award. For the first time in his career, "Mr. October" hit .300 and for the third time led the American League in home runs, with 41. Reggie was riding high, at 34 the undisputed number one Yankee.

It was a season of hotly fought, down-to-the-wire pennant races. In the National League East division, the Montreal Expos lost out on a postseason appearance for the second straight season, this time in the final week at home against the Phillies. The Expos were a much-talented, much-injured team, and though center fielder Andre Dawson pushed through horrendous knee injuries, made worse by the pounding he took on the thin artificial turf laid over concrete at Olympic Stadium, and pitching ace Steve Rogers overcame a reputation for failing under pressure by tossing back-to-back September shutouts, it wasn't enough to get the first Canadian team into the playoffs.

Out West, the Oakland A's staged a huge comeback behind Billy Martin, who came home to the Bay Area the long way, after being fired as Yankee skipper in October 1979 by Steinbrenner, for punching out a marshmallow salesman in a Minnesota hotel. And after resigning in 1978 for calling Jackson a liar and Steinbrenner a convicted felon (which he was, for illegal campaign contributions to Richard Nixon's reelection campaign in 1972). And after being fired from the Texas Rangers in 1975 for criticizing owner Brad Corbett. And after being fired in 1973 by the Detroit Tigers for ordering Tiger pitchers to throw spitballs. And after being fired by the Minnesota Twins in 1969, when he brought a division title to the Twins and a knockout punch and 20 stitches to his own pitcher, Dave Boswell. "Billy the Kid" brought a new brand of play, BillyBall, to Oakland and a second-place finish in the American League West.

Down I-5 in Los Angeles, the Dodgers forced a one-game play-off against the Houston Astros, sparked by a 19-year-old who looked 30, a hefty left-hander who, from the side, looked like a lowercase q. Fernando Valenzuela, the young man with an ancient face, a bad complexion, and hair that crossed the Beatles '65 with an Elvis pompadour, had been unknown in spring training at Vero Beach, but had turned into the organization's number one prospect over the summer. Minor league pitching coach and ex-Dodger reliever Ron Perranoski taught him how to set up his pitches—fastball, screwball, changeup—and Valenzuela caught fire. Over his next eight games with San Antonio of the Double-A Texas League, he was 7-0, with an earned run average of 0.87. That was enough to earn him a trip to the majors for the final two weeks.

"This kid is special," manager Tommy Lasorda was told. "Don't be afraid to use him in any situation." After watching his unlikely phenom strike out Johnny Bench in his second game for the Dodgers and, on the next night, with the team tied for first, pitch a scoreless ninth inning against the Reds, Lasorda knew he was told the truth. When it came time to pick a starter for a one-game, pressure-filled playoff at Dodger Stadium against the Astros, Lasorda thought long and hard about starting his teenager. He didn't, choosing disappointing veteran Dave Goltz, who was disastrously blown out early. By the time Valenzuela came to the mound and tossed two shutout innings of relief, it was too late. The Dodgers were on their way to a 7–1 shellacking and Tommy was headed for a winter of off-season agita and regret.

None of this would have happened if a strike had not been averted in May when Bowie Kuhn, the commissioner of baseball, stepped in at the 11th hour on May 23, 1980. By agreeing on all matters save one, compensation for free agents, management and players saved the 1980 season, but the underlying rift between the two sides on how to handle—in fact, how to interpret—the game's exploding salary structure was far from agreed upon.

From the fall day in 1979 when Kuhn called Marvin Miller, executive director of the Major League Baseball Players Association (MLBPA), asking to meet over drinks in advance of the 1980 expiration of the new Basic Agreement, which laid out the terms of the owner/player working relationship and the pension plan, a strike seemed inevitable. Miller entered the '21' Club via the 52nd Street entrance. Unctuously, in his anchorman baritone, the commissioner began by praising the great and undeniable strides the players' union had made under Miller's guidance since 1966 when he took on that role. When Miller arrived on the scene, players were powerless. No more. Salaries had skyrocketed after an arbitrator granted free agency in 1976. Since that ruling, all who qualified had the possibility of signing with the highest bidder, or forgoing top dollar to play in a city they desired to call home. Major league ballplayers now had the freedom in their jobs that all other workers in the United States had at theirs. Kuhn lauded the accomplishments he had fought to prevent.

The drinks were brought, but before they had a chance to leave a wet mark on the table, Kuhn cut to the chase.

"Marvin, the owners need a victory."

Miller knew immediately what Kuhn was driving at. It had been difficult for the commissioner to suffer defeat after defeat in these negotiations with the players. It hurt the office and it hurt the man, but reaching out to Miller for aid, as if he would be willing to bail out the commissioner and save the free-spending owners from their inability to control their own profligacy, was hard to believe. Unless you knew them.

"Are you asking me to throw the game?" Was Kuhn really asking, before negotiations began, that the players give up on free agency, that they give the owners a victory at the bargaining table they so desperately needed after years of nonstop losses? Kuhn most certainly wished for a return to the time when ballplayers' careers were still completely in the hands of their owners, when the athletes on the field were servants, like the lawn jockeys on the balcony that welcomed patrons to the '21' Club. Miller's winning streak against the owners had been easy to accomplish. It wasn't difficult to make major strides in a business 100 years behind in labor relations.

Returning to his office, Miller clearly wore the unpleasantness of the meeting on his face. Donald Fehr, counsel to the MLBPA, immediately asked, "What's wrong?"

"We're in for a hell of a fight," said a saddened Miller.

At the 1980 annual winter meetings, held in Dallas at the end of the year that had every American asking, "Who shot J.R.?" Kuhn strode to the podium on December 8, and faced an assemblage of owners, management, and assorted players to begin his state-of-the-game speech. While heralding the "golden age of baseball popularity that we are now celebrating," Kuhn cited a study his office had commissioned that explained that salaries were increasing far beyond the growth of revenues. In 1979, only 11 clubs operated in the black. Operating revenues simply would not grow fast enough to keep up with the cost of doing business. "Foolish player contracts signed by a few have aggravated the situation," and the commissioner projected player compensation by 1984 at $320,000 per man. Kuhn's speech presented the same old line—it was, wrote Red Smith in *The New York Times,* all the fault of "greedy, moneygrubbing players led by those bloodsucking vampires, the free agents."

What to do? "Barring the discovery of oil wells under second base," Kuhn continued, what was to become of franchises as costs for players rose higher? Besides financial woes, a "companion problem brought about by free agency is the threat to competitive balance." For troubles that a cursory look at bank books and standings would show were a fantasy, Kuhn warned that there was "no solution until the players" recognized the need for change. And they had better see it for there was now an "unprecedented unity among club ownership."

Miller was shocked by Kuhn's Dallas speech and the wild inconsistencies between statements coming from Kuhn and the owners he was supposed to represent. It was clear to Miller that Kuhn was asserting that the owners' compensation plan, which would penalize a team signing a free agent, would make great strides in addressing the concern over player salaries and would cause a drop in, if not an outright cap on, player salaries. The union would, under no circumstances, give in to the owners on this issue. The end of 1980 was filled with bad tidings for baseball's labor situation.

The stories that were reaped in 1981 were sown in the seeds of 1980. Nineteen eighty-one would be a story of traditions dying hard, of the old guard's pushing to reclaim what they'd lost, and of the new generation pushing back. It would be the story of rookies and veterans, of upstarts and old-timers, and it would end with a classic World Series between the Yankees and the Dodgers.

Nineteen eighty-one would be one for the ages: the first split season.

Chapter 1

Nineteen eighty closed on a somber note. John Lennon was dead, brutally gunned down in front of his New York City apartment. But with the martyred Beatle's "(Just Like) Starting Over" topping the charts, fans and nonfans rushing to buy the now-dead Beatle's latest single, January 1981 seemed a bit more hopeful. Though the economy fluctuated from mild recession to weak recovery, Americans hoped that better days were on their way. Ronald Reagan, delivering a smiley, positive message, trounced gloomy Jimmy Carter in the November election. Reagan seemed to be able to deliver immediately; the hostages in Iran, held captive since November 1979, were released hours after his swearing in.

It was a good time to be a conservative and a capitalist. The entire nation loved J. R. Ewing, the conniving, moneygrubbing oilman from the number-one-rated television show, *Dallas*. While the public worshipped J.R. and envied his rich and famous ways, that was fantasy. In reality, unemployment remained high and workers were under more and more strain. TV viewers watched *Dallas*, but moviegoers were flocking to see *9 to 5*, the box-office smash about everyday stiffs exacting revenge on a tyrannically evil boss. The gap between winners and losers seemed large and ever growing.

Dave Winfield was a winner. There he was, gripping a bat,

smiling widely, the picture of content in full Yankee splendor in front of a bloodred backdrop. In 1981, no one made a better fashion leap than Winfield, trading in the visually repugnant yellow-and-brown uniform of the San Diego Padres for Yankee pinstripes.

The first *Sports Illustrated* of the New Year heralded, "The Man Who Hit the Jackpot." The free-agent prize of 1980, David Mark Winfield, had signed a 10-year, $15 million deal on December 15, a pact that could, with inflation adjustments, climb as high as $22 million. At 6'6", 220 lbs., Winfield was an athletic dream, a former multisport star at the University of Minnesota, drafted by both the NBA Atlanta Hawks and ABA Utah Stars in basketball, the Minnesota Vikings in football, and the Padres, who selected him as a pitcher with the fourth pick in the first round. In 1973, with no minor league experience, he made his major league debut.

It didn't take long for Winfield to make an impact. By 1978, he was a star; by the following year a superstar and Most Valuable Player candidate. With his contract expiring at the end of the 1980 season, talks began between Winfield; his agent, Al Frohman; and Padres president Ballard Smith, son-in-law of Padres owner Ray Kroc, the man who created McDonald's.

The contract talks were brutal, and the negativity affected Winfield in 1980, for him a season of mediocre and, at times, lackadaisical play. He was hurt and felt unappreciated, vilified by Kroc: "I don't want him back. He can't hit with men on base. A dozen times he's come up with men on base and he hasn't done a damn thing."

Winfield declared himself a free agent at season's end. At the November 13 reentry draft, when major league clubs selected free agents they hoped to sign, Winfield was picked by 10 of 26 teams, including the Braves, Yankees, and Mets. Then the courting began.

At the winter meetings in Dallas, the buzz in the halls was about a Yankees-Mets bidding war. The Mets, losers for the last several years, were desperately trying to gain some kind, any kind, of leg up on the Yankees, who ruled New York and its press. The new owners at Shea Stadium were doing all they could to make themselves seem the winners of the Winfield sweepstakes, spreading word that they'd inked a deal, but they never had a chance.

Starting in the summer of 1980, Steinbrenner had prepared to make the hard sell. Smarting from his failure to convince erstwhile Dodger and now Houston Astros pitcher Don Sutton to join the Yankees, Steinbrenner, from his newly acquired racetrack, Tampa Bay Downs, told reporters, "We didn't need Sutton, but Dave Winfield is a different matter. He's the piece to fit into the puzzle. Don't count us out on Winfield." As he looked out to the paddock, Steinbrenner grew wistful. "Horses are great. They never complain. They can't talk to sportswriters and tell them what a bum the owner is."

Steinbrenner had had enough of that with Reggie Jackson, his first free-agent prize. George was fed up with Jackson, his controversies, his constant playing of the race card, his conflicts with teammates. The biggest sin was that Reggie let George down in the playoff loss to the Royals. With former Yankees team leader Thurman Munson gone, killed in a 1979 plane crash, a plane he piloted, Steinbrenner didn't want Reggie to be the face of the Yankees. Still, Steinbrenner was willing to toy with Reggie, bringing him close while privately planning to push him away.

Steinbrenner called Jackson to meet him for dinner at Elaine's. Just as George had sought Munson's feelings on bringing in Jackson, now Steinbrenner wanted Jackson's thoughts on Winfield. Jackson arrived in cowboy hat and sweater, the popularity of *The Dukes of Hazzard, Dallas,* and *Urban Cowboy* having set off a fashion frenzy of big-brimmed hats and giant belt buckles.

Although Jackson and Winfield shared the same position, right field, Reggie was all for signing the ex-Padre. A healthy dose of self-interest was at work. Reggie himself would be a free agent after the 1981 season. How much would Steinbrenner need to pay his reigning superstar if he was forking over millions to the new guy? "I'm not gonna be around forever," Jackson told Steinbrenner. He had no idea how true that was.

With Jackson on board, Steinbrenner flew to Minneapolis for a

University of Minnesota fund-raiser. Amid steaks and drinks with Winfield, Steinbrenner went into his spiel: "It's time you got with a winner."

Early December brought Winfield to New York for last-minute talks with both the Mets and the Yankees. Steinbrenner knew how to flirt, sending flowers, limos, and Broadway tickets to Winfield's hotel room.

"I like you a lot, Dave," Steinbrenner told Winfield in the limo. "I can take you places I could never take Reggie." Like a bored lover, Steinbrenner saw greener and more exciting pastures with Dave Winfield.

Winfield called his mother back in St. Paul on December 14 to tell her he'd made his decision—he was going to sign with the Yankees, a 10-year deal of up to $2 million per year. The next day, in front of a huge Yankee logo and behind a cluster of microphones, Winfield, dressed in an immaculate gray business suit, met the press. Jackson stood near the newest Yankee, smiling, thinking how much he'd be able to command. After the press conference, Steinbrenner invited Jackson up to his suite at the Carlyle Hotel. There, the boom was lowered. There would be no four- or five-year contract between the Yankees and Reggie Jackson; he was too old. Jackson was shaken.

As the New Year began and free-agent signings went on as usual, the baseball world eagerly awaited a report from a joint study committee set up in the agreement that forestalled a strike in May 1980 but left on the table the singularly explosive issue of free-agent compensation. There was no agreement between the parties on what, if anything, constituted a fair return to teams that had lost a player. Instead, an agreed-upon procedure was set in place—Attachment IX. Contained within, the owners had the option of implementing their compensation program, or one more beneficial to the players' association, between February 15 and 19, 1981. In their plan, when a free agent was selected in the postseason reentry draft by eight or more clubs and ranked in the top half of performance in their position (pitchers measured by starts or relief appearances, hitters by plate appearances), then the team who signed the free agent could protect 15 to 18 players on their major league roster, depending on whether the free agent was in the top one-third or one-half of the rankings. The team that lost that free agent could then pluck a major league player from the remainder of the signing team's roster. It was direct compensation, a punishment for teams signing a free agent.

If the owners adopted this direct compensation plan, the players had their own set of options. They could accept it, unlikely as that was, or ask the clubs whether the union might strike prior to the 1981 season or take one year under the clubs' plan and strike prior to the 1982 season. If the clubs elected for the players to strike in 1981, the players had to give notice by March 1 of their intent to strike and provide a date of no later than June 1.

But first, a joint study committee would be established to investigate the merits of compensation. There was always the outside chance that the committee would come up with something palatable to both parties. A 30-day period of bargaining would ensue between their findings and the playing out of the procedure.

The misrepresentation of this process had set Ray Grebey, the owners' lead negotiator, and Marvin Miller apart. On May 23, 1980, the day the new Basic Agreement was signed, Miller received a press release from Grebey that said that the players had agreed to the owners' compensation plan. Miller was irate; it was patently untrue. A procedure had been agreed to, that was all. Miller wondered whether Grebey, to soothe the owners, had told them he'd actually got the compensation terms they were after.

Announcing the plan the way Grebey did was purposefully misleading, to the public and the press, creating a situation where, if Grebey was to be believed, the players had already accepted something and any pushback was a betrayal. "They are lying," Miller said strongly.

In a matter-of-fact tone, Grebey said the players "knew compensation was important to us. They knew we cared because we didn't drop it."

Miller quickly countered, "It's not an agreed-upon proposal. It's an agreed-upon procedure."

The owners wanted a strike in 1981; it was, as they saw it, a way to force the players to give back on their free-agent rights. Kuhn admitted as much to himself as he scanned the 1980 Memorandum of Agreement. On the right-side margin of the section that gave players the right to strike, but only one time (if they did not choose to strike they could have "no further strike on this subject during the term of the Basic Agreement"), Kuhn wrote in pencil "one bite theory," and management was going to force the players to take it. Grebey, as Kuhn's proxy, became Marvin Miller's bête noire, an untrustworthy figure who made any kind of negotiations from here on out problematic.

Still, the joint study committee, composed of union representatives, Phillies catcher Bob Boone and Brewers third baseman Sal Bando, and management appointees, Brewers general manager Harry Dalton and Mets GM Frank Cashen, set out to work in good faith.

The players brought specifics—charts on increased attendance, tighter pennant races, club-by-club analyses of who gained free agents and who lost them, the changes in those teams' positions in the standings. Bando and Boone thought that thoughtful discussion would ensue, but since Grebey had expressed zero interest in a study committee before he ultimately agreed, the commitment wasn't there. At a Player Relations Committee meeting (the PRC being the designated bargaining arm of the owners) of Cashen, Dalton, Grebey, and American League president Lee MacPhail, when no players were around to hear the truth, Grebey convinced the others in plain language. "We don't have to prove need for compensation—it's already in the contract. We are not making the argument based on competitive balance. Our starting point should be that we now have compensation, and now we are here to discuss how we can make the system as good as possible."

As January came around, the joint study committee was obviously in tatters, going nowhere. At a PRC meeting on the 21st, the day after Reagan's inauguration, Cashen gave his assessment of what was to come.

"Miller will go to the brink but wants a settlement." Further,

Cashen reported that counsel James Garner "feels it is not imperative that we make concessions in the two-week period of negotiation." It was the very definition of bad-faith negotiating, but with Reagan in office, the owners felt the wind was at their back. The new president was pro-business, antiunion, and the country, after the Carter years, was with him.

To no one's surprise, two reports were issued, one from Dalton and Cashen, and another from Boone and Bando (written by Fehr). Player members knew compensation "would adversely affect the bargaining power of not only free agents, but also other players whose salaries are related to free agent salaries." In other words, everyone. Reagan's proposed trickle-down economics, unproven nationally, proved true in baseball. The big bucks commanded by free agents affected each and every player's contract. With no agreement on hand, the bargaining period was set to begin.

The first negotiating session took place at the PRC offices on January 29. Kuhn and the owners thought Miller's acceptance of the Attachment IX process was a tacit acknowledgment that compensation in some form was acceptable. Boy, were they wrong.

The owners' team included National League president Chub Feeney, attorneys Barry Rona and Lou Hoynes, and Grebey. The players were represented by Rangers pitcher Jon Matlack, Expos pitcher and National League pension rep Steve Rogers, Orioles shortstop and American League pension rep Mark Belanger, Angels pitcher Steve Renko, Fehr, and Miller. Miller and Grebey sat across from each other at the table. The only topic was compensation.

"You know why we're seeking it," began Grebey. "Not all free agents are of equal quality."

"We never said they were equal," replied Miller.

"Marv, we have a proposal on the table." Miller hated to be called Marv and Grebey knew it. "It forms a framework for negotiations. We think it is a good proposal, but the owners have no intention of doing nothing. It is a negotiable item. But they will not take it off the table as a settlement. If the Players Association has an alternative, we'd be glad to discuss it."

This contentious beginning was exacerbated by the players interjecting as they saw fit. Grebey had never seen anything like it in his corporate history.

"How has the present system failed to work?" asked Matlack.

Grebey grimaced, his displeasure clear. "I'll refer you to my November 1979 statement that free agency has worked," he answered with some formality, and though he must have known what he'd said in that statement, he pushed Matlack away. "I need time to respond to you."

Feeney joined in. "What about the trades of Lynn and Carew and Blue?" The owners believed that these three blockbuster trades—pitcher Vida Blue from the A's to the Giants in 1978, first baseman Rod Carew from the Twins to the Angels in 1979, and, only six days before, Red Sox outfielder Fred Lynn to the Angels—proved their point that compensation would not hinder salaries. In those deals, a marquee player was prepared to play out his option year and go on the free agent market. Instead, his club, rather than get nothing once he left, received bunches of players and the receiving team signed the superstar to a huge deal.

The union didn't buy it. If Blue, Carew, and Lynn commanded big-dollar deals in the context of a player swap, they would undoubtedly have garnered more money if the teams that signed them didn't have to give up any players in the deal.

"This is what it's all about? You want to strengthen Kansas City for losing Darrell Porter [signed by the Cardinals], Los Angeles for the loss of Don Sutton [signed by the Astros], and San Diego for the loss of Dave Winfield?" Miller asked. "All of this is only about these three?"

Grebey and Feeney both nodded. "Yes." They saw, or pretended to see, this in a limited way. The terms they pushed for would affect only a select few.

Miller saw it more broadly. Anything that hurt the salaries of the select few had repercussions on everyone's salary. "What about the effects on Fisk and Cerone once Porter signed?"

Yankee catcher Rick Cerone had a great year in 1980, taking

over the full-time job from Munson. For that he was paid $120,000. Heading into 1981, he asked for a huge raise up to $440,000. Steinbrenner offered his new star $350,000. Instead of agreeing with Steinbrenner, Cerone decided to take the club to arbitration for the first time since 1974. Steinbrenner was insulted and furious.

Salary arbitration was one in a series of huge Miller victories over management. When it began in 1973, it was the first time players could preach the merits of their cases to an unbiased arbiter. The owners would present their case as well. The decision was made, using comparative players and their salaries as a guide. The high price paid to free agents was crucial for non–free agents who hoped to score in arbitration. And they always scored. Look at the Cerone case — win or lose, he was bound to get a serious hike in pay. So when the Cardinals signed Porter to a five-year/$3.5 million deal in December 1980, it had repercussions beyond St. Louis and Kansas City.

Arbitration was often uncomfortable, management explaining why one of their own wasn't as good as he thought he was, and the player explaining why he was. Cerone had told Steinbrenner before the hearing he'd have no hard feelings either way. No hard feelings? Just business? George would have none of it. "That's like Brutus telling Julius Caesar that there were no hard feelings after he stabbed him."

As to Carlton Fisk, he was part of a horrid Red Sox winter. Fred Lynn, shortstop Rick Burleson, and Fisk were all working on contracts that had expired, contracts that began in the old days, pre–free agency. The ruling on free agency made it clear that the Red Sox could renew the deals for one year only, and they had to do so by December 20, 1980. In an added layer of confusion, the Red Sox had a right-of-first-refusal clause in each contract. The players' association took issue with these terms, claiming the player couldn't sign away his rights. Boston backed off and embarked on a new game. Knowing that if they sent contracts to Fisk and Lynn by the 20th, they would be subject to arbitration, General Manager Haywood Sullivan decided he didn't need to send out the papers.

Problem was, on December 10 Burleson was traded to California.

There, Angels GM Mike Port, with the same type of contract in hand, *did* send a contract by the 20th. Once Sullivan caught wind, he was screwed. With no choice, he mailed contracts to Fisk and Lynn, but it was too late. The postmark was December 22. Whether the BoSox would be able to keep Lynn and Fisk was still up in the air. They dumped Lynn (and, ironically, the same Steve Renko who was sitting at the table as Feeney cited the Lynn deal) for nearly nothing—an arm-weary Frank Tanana, an over-the-hill Joe Rudi, and a throw-in pitcher named Jim Dorsey.

The meeting ended unconstructively. The owners weren't budging and the players weren't buying their arguments. Two more meetings were tentatively put on the calendar for February 5 and 12.

For all the Chicken Littles in baseball claiming their financial skies were falling, the end of January/beginning of February proved that there was much gold in them baseball hills. Eighty percent of the miserable Seattle Mariners, a team that had averaged 100 losses in each of its first four years of existence, was sold to real estate developer George Argyros for $10.4 million. The Chicago White Sox were purchased from Bill Veeck for $20 million by a group led by another real estate man, Jerry Reinsdorf, and television executive Eddie Einhorn. Labor strife wasn't at all a factor for Reinsdorf. He checked around, wanting to know for sure if there'd be a strike. It didn't seem possible, he was told, because the only issue on the table was compensation, and no one saw that as worth a stop. No one he spoke with on the owners' side thought a strike would happen, and they extended their own opinion to the players' minds.

As the bargaining parties met in early February, Bowie Kuhn, observing from afar, in touch with Grebey and the PRC but never at the table himself, tried to spin no progress and the union's resistance to direct compensation into a positive framework, which few believed. To Joan Kroc, wife of the Padres' owner, Kuhn wrote, "I think the cooperation we are getting from Miller is encouraging." To Reds president Dick Wagner, Kuhn parroted the company line: "I don't think it will help the financial picture in any substantial way."

In truth, the sessions were pointless. The owners may have pretended at the table that they were seeking compromise, but behind the scenes their talk was different. Cashen relayed the hard fact to Dalton: "Grebey's position is our way or no way." The union, to their credit, said the same thing at the table and behind the scenes. As expected, on February 19, Miller was notified in a letter from Grebey that "since agreement has not been achieved through negotiations, the twenty-six Major League Clubs have chosen to exercise the rights provided and agreed upon in the May 23, 1980 Memorandum of Agreement effective this date, February 19, 1981." The owners were unilaterally adopting direct compensation.

It was a declaration of war. Though it didn't come as a surprise, Miller was still incensed at the plan, especially at the defining criteria that would cause a free agent to become one of top quality and deserving of compensation. Defining a ranking player by how many teams chose him in the free agent reentry draft was absurdly arbitrary, especially when people such as Joe Burke, both a member of the PRC and general manager of the Royals, was quoted in the papers as saying, "Clubs usually pick a lot of people just to put their names and talk with them, and they really aren't that sincere in signing them." And that was before insincere picks decided who would be worthy of compensation.

Allowing a team to only protect 15 players was out of the question. That might not hurt the salaries of a Dave Winfield, but what if a team wanted to sign someone who was not as good as one of their top 15 players? Why would anyone sign such a player if it meant giving up someone better? In those cases, the bargaining power of a marginal player was, as Elvis Costello sang, less than zero. And what made it worse was that less than a week ago Grebey had told Miller that "need was not necessarily the basis for change." It was all punishment, loud and clear, for the players and the teams that wanted to participate in the open market of free agency. The players wouldn't have it. Miller joked, "If George [Steinbrenner] is so concerned about compensation, let him sell one of his players to

San Diego for one dollar. He signed Dave Winfield. Let him volunteer. If his heart bleeds for the Padres, let him do something unilaterally. We won't object."

It didn't take long for the players to react to Grebey's letter. Six days later, on February 25, all 26 player representatives met with Miller in Tampa. In the weeks prior to the vote, teams were asked by a union representative, usually Fehr, to think about how they'd vote if it came down to a strike. The players were completely unified, though the owners believed otherwise. Under the 1980 agreement the players had until March 1 to notify ownership if they'd decided to strike, a strike that could commence no later than May 31. The players had no right to strike until the owners acted; they had, now it was up to the players. The players were asking for nothing. They were happy with the gains they'd achieved in the last few years. For almost three and a half hours they hashed over the issues and their options. Then they voted.

In a dark Izod shirt, deep bags under his eyes, Miller came out to announce the results of the vote to the gathered press, who shoved a multitude of microphones in his face. All 29 members of the players' executive board had voted for a strike. This was an issue of principle for them; there was a freedom to protect that affected each and every player today and those to come. A Resolution of the Executive Board was executed, proclaiming that the players "shall strike, beginning with all games scheduled to start on MAY 29, 1981." The date was handwritten in a blank space.

The owners were confused. How could there be a strike with superstar salaries now hitting the million-dollar-per-year mark? Checks that size were dispensed by willing owners to accepting players; it was going to be impossible for ownership to convince the players that the owners were in tough economic straits. Phillies owner Ruly Carpenter, whose family came by their money through investments in DuPont, saw the fault lay not in the superstars but in the owners themselves. "I do not blame him [Marvin Miller]. It's ownership. Marvin Miller does not hand out checks."

And hadn't Grebey told them last year that compensation was a done deal? The players couldn't walk out. Ray Kroc hoped the players wouldn't strike. "They'd better not," he threatened, thinking that owners could still impose their will. Owners' edicts to the players didn't have the power they used to. Said Miller, "If you think you're God, you act like God."

With the strike now called, the insurance money the owners counted on for a war chest was in jeopardy. The owners may have been convinced that the players would never strike and risk their soaring salaries on such a trifle as compensation. But just in case, a strike insurance policy was taken out for $50 million with Lloyd's of London. Confidence only goes so far.

Underwriters didn't realize that the owners could trigger a strike. They assumed this was a traditional labor issue, where the union makes demands. They were shocked to discover the players wanted nothing, that the only people who could cause the strike were the ones with insurance.

Did the owners' issues have merit? If compensation didn't hurt a free agent's ability to negotiate, then why were the owners so intent on it? If, however, it did hinder free movement of players, then the association was 100 percent right in fighting it for all they were worth. Teams had recouped their investment in players. Any development costs were more than covered in service in the minor leagues and the six years that had to be put in at the major league level before free agency was granted.

The owners had wanted to avoid a strike on this issue one year previous. Why seek it now? And as to competitive balance, 1980 saw no team repeat as divisional winner from the year before. The owners' position seemed devoid of logic, and that recurring strain had paved the way for each of Miller's past victories.

On the same day the baseball world was thrown into turmoil, Kuhn was at the White House, presenting Reagan with a season pass to all games. Kuhn had wanted to substantively brief Reagan on the labor situation, but had no opportunity to do so. The president accepted the pass and a baseball, which he gripped along the seams for a curve, no doubt channeling Grover Cleveland Alexander, who

Reagan had played in 1952's *The Winning Team*. They were both living in a world of make-believe.

American League president Lee MacPhail said, "The owners feel the players have everything. It's the whole philosophy of the thing." The owners' philosophy was to take, the players' was to preserve. It was going to be difficult to compromise.

Grebey selected his words quite carefully: "I didn't reopen the contract. The twenty-six clubs didn't reopen the contract." The conclusion to be drawn was that the players did something out of bounds, something so far beyond the pale over the owners' implementation, but reopening the Basic Agreement was what was agreed upon in May 1980 should the owners put their plan in place. On February 26, the union officially reopened collective bargaining. The next day, in a letter from Fehr to Grebey, the union requested from the PRC income and expense figures, cash flow and profit/loss, insurance expenses and sale data on all clubs. It was getting ugly.

For Marvin Miller, baseball was never front and center. As a young boy, Miller would make the journey from his Flatbush home in Brooklyn to lower Manhattan to visit his father at work. Alexander Miller worked in the garment business, the streets lined on both sides with women's clothing stores. It seemed to Marvin that his father worked every hour of every day. Marvin rarely saw him, and the annual trips to the big city were exciting and provided rare father-son meetings.

One such visit during the early 1930s would open young Miller's eyes. As he headed down Division Street, Miller saw a throng of men, unlike any other crowd he had previously witnessed during his trips to the hustle and bustle of the *shmatte* business. Getting nearer, he could see his father marching in the group. It was a pickct line. The elder Miller told his son he would have a lunch break in 10 minutes. When his break came, he explained that his weekly hours had been cut from 50, to 40, to 30, and now 20, due to the Depression, and that the department-store union of which he was a member was not being recognized by penny-pinching bosses who were cutting commissions. At that moment, Marvin Miller's interest in unions was born.

After college, Miller got a job in the New York City Welfare Department. It was April 1940, and while the country was emerging from the Depression, the welfare rolls in the city were on their way to new highs. No heavy manufacturing jobs were available and times were more than tough. As an investigator, Miller saw amazing solidarity among working-class people.

Approaching an apartment house where one tenant was a subject of his investigation, Miller saw a silent mob gathered outside on the rainy curb, arms folded as the sheriff and deputies brought pieces of furniture one by one out to the street to get soaked. It was an eviction.

"What's going on?" Miller asked and asked, getting no response.

Finally one man somberly answered, "Wait."

Once the sheriff and his men cleared out, the crowd picked up every bit of the stuff carried out and carried it right back in. Miller was overwhelmed by what these people could do simply by sticking together, acting as one, against an unfair and seemingly all-powerful force.

After jumping from job to job, Miller found a home in 1950 with the Steelworkers Union. By 1960 he was their chief economist and assistant to the president of the third-biggest union in the country.

While the Steelworkers had muscle, Major League Baseball players did not. They had a players' association in name only, an illegally run, in-house sham of a union that left them feeling powerless. These feelings of impotence resulted in fumbling attempts to strengthen their union throughout the 1940s, 1950s, and 1960s. Rather than forcefully arguing for work conditions that suited them, ballplayers, contrary to their boldness and strength as athletes on the field, meekly petitioned their owners like a nervous Oliver asking, "Please, sir, may I have some more?"

"May we have new showerheads?" they humbly asked.

"Sure."

"Perhaps a toilet door?"

"We'll think about it."

"Can you replace the leaky watercoolers?"

"Are you crazy?"

By the mid-1960s the players were desperate for change. They searched for a new leader, looking at ex-stars such as Bob Feller and Hank Greenberg and ex–vice presidents such as Richard Nixon. Through a tip from a labor management relations expert, Marvin Miller joined the finalists. He was hired in March 1966 and the owners screamed.

This Miller has "liberal tendencies," Phillies owner Bob Carpenter, Ruly's father, wrote his fellow owners. He is "strongly committed to principles of union representation and collective bargaining, a difficult negotiator, unyielding and inflexible, theoretical rather than practical." Carpenter relayed inside information he'd got from individual negotiators who found Miller "impossible to work with in a relationship of personal friendship and confidence." Of course a union leader would represent his side to the fullest, but it came as a revolting shock to baseball owners, and they made it clear they expected Miller to play ball the old-fashioned way.

Miller found himself on a flight with American League president and Hall of Fame shortstop Joe Cronin. Cronin, 11 years Miller's senior at 60, gave the kid some advice:

"Young man, players come and go, but the owners stay."

Miller was taken aback. "What are you saying, Joe, that to survive I need to play ball with the owners regardless of the interests of who I represent?"

"I'm not going to translate for you."

Bowie Kuhn dreamed of hobnobbing with Washington Senators ballplayers like Cronin. Kuhn, who, for the public, represented the stiff-shirted, stuffy persona of baseball management, was an incurable baseball romantic and had been since he found baseball at a young age. While most Senators fans were cursed by the team's perennial losing, Kuhn was fortunate that his baseball awakening coincided with rare success for the hometown nine. At six years old,

Kuhn was a firsthand witness to a World Series appearance by the Senators in 1933. While young Bowie's favorites went down to defeat, the excitement of that year never left him, and when he was a bit older, he garnered through high school connections the dream job of any rabid fan—scoreboard boy at Griffith Stadium. For one dollar per day, he sat inside the scoreboard on hot summer days, like stew in a pot, watching his favorite team.

Kuhn came from an immigrant background. Alice Waring Roberts's family arrived in 1634, sailing from England to Maryland. Her ancestors included senators, congressmen, and judges. Kuhn got his patrician bearing through his mother's pedigree. Bowie's father, Louis, had a vastly different experience from Alice. Bavarian by birth, Kuhn's father came to the United States in 1894 and, though unschooled, rose to become head of a Washington, DC, power company.

Kuhn grew up in the DC area and, following his lifetime passion, sought a life in baseball. Rising up the legal ranks after attending Princeton and the University of Virginia Law School, he found employment at the law firm headed by former FDR challenger Wendell Willkie. Kuhn was a big fan of the Republican Willkie, but was drawn to the firm with the hope he could work for one of their prized clients—the National League.

In the summer of 1966, his first as executive director of the Players Association, Miller was invited to a meeting with Commissioner "Spike" Eckert and his Executive Committee to discuss the players' pension agreement. At this meeting Miller met Kuhn for the first time. Kuhn, now National League attorney, announced that at the conclusion of the session Eckert would face the press to inform them of the terms of the new pension agreement. Miller was nonplussed. Announcing a settlement before negotiations began would be tantamount to admitting that baseball flagrantly violated labor law. These men were completely uninformed and unaware of common labor practices. Miller desperately tried to catch Kuhn's eye, figuring that as a lawyer Kuhn would realize how illegal the owners' actions were, but there was no semblance of comprehension there.

For the next 15 years the two would lock horns, battling fiercely over whose vision, the owners' or the players', would shape the future of baseball. The Kuhn-Miller relationship was at the core of player-owner clashes for over a decade. When Kuhn was preparing to become commissioner in time for the 1969 season, he hoped to sit face-to-face with Miller and clear the air before he assumed office. Kuhn called Miller, seeking a meeting.

At the players' association offices in the Seagram Building on Park Avenue, Kuhn and Miller had a pleasant enough first official meeting. Kuhn was in good humor as the two discussed his new job. It was Kuhn's last visit to the players' home turf.

Ever since the creation of the office in 1920, the year after the Chicago White Sox fixed the World Series, commissioners of Major League Baseball had always been seen as the impartial arbiter for all of baseball. Judge Kenesaw Mountain Landis, the first commissioner, wielded immense power over owners and players alike. Each successive commissioner saw himself in the same light and, on the whole, was allowed to perform that way. None of them had had to contend with a Marvin Miller, and it was Bowie Kuhn's bad luck to do so. Miller made clear this indisputable truth: the commissioner of baseball serves at the pleasure of the owners. The commissioner is hired by the owners and, as all of them had found out except for those who died in office, fired by them as well.

Kuhn's role confusion confounded Miller, who saw him as "a prisoner of his belief in the totality of the commissioner's power." Reality was not Kuhn's strong suit, and he was weary of the press portraying him as the leader of a consistently defeated troupe, the captain of the Generals always crushed by the Globetrotters. It was farcical. Player advances had come from sources outside the commissioner— the courts, arbitrators, collective bargaining. Not by fiat. Not anymore. It was not how Kuhn wanted it. He wanted to be Landis.

In the initial years of Kuhn's term in office, he weighed in on various player crises of the time—gambling scandals (Denny McLain), recalcitrant players (Ken "Hawk" Harrelson), and mental illness (Alex Johnson). The players were hopeful that the new commissioner's occasional pro-player actions regarding a few individuals during his first year would be a sign of good things to come. But 1970 would begin to show that Kuhn's actions were less player-leaning than arbitrary, based not on some standard of balancing player and owner interest, but on some inner code that had neither consistency nor guiding principles other than the vague "best interests of baseball" phrase Kuhn loved to use as a catchall explanation. It incensed Miller, to whom Kuhn's "best interests of baseball" meant the owners' interests, not the players'. From Miller's perspective, everything Kuhn contributed to bargaining was negative.

Foremost was that, to Miller, Kuhn would say whatever he felt he needed to say no matter how untrue it was. Miller, and the players he was grooming, never felt that the commissioner was in tune with what was truly good for the game. Except one time.

In 1977, Kuhn testified under oath in the Charlie Finley case. Seeing that he would lose three stars at the end of the 1976 season to this newfangled free agency, the mercurial A's owner sold Vida Blue to the Yankees and Joe Rudi and reliever Rollie Fingers to the Red Sox. Kuhn voided the sales, concerned that mere money payments to Finley would be an improper form of compensation, that the need to maintain competitive balance was in the "best interests of baseball."

"Your Honor, he [Finley] had already had these ballplayers for many years, and they had been players who had performed very well for the Oakland baseball club. So, I think it's fair to say he had recouped his investment." No better case for the players' current position on compensation was made than this one, clearheadedly represented on the stand, under oath, by none other than Kuhn himself.

With that kind of leadership, it was no wonder that ownership looked to hire a more experienced corporate man to lead them in their labor relations, and in 1978 they found one in Ray Grebey. Like Miller, the 49-year-old Grebey had spent years in the steel industry, starting out at Inland Steel. By the late 1950s, Grebey had moved on to General Electric, where he'd spend the next 21 years. GE had a well-deserved reputation for being antiunion, withstanding a 105-day strike by the International Union of Electrical, Radio and Machine Workers in 1969–70, and that appealed to the owners.

Grebey, who saw himself as "serious, sometimes somber, very intense, certainly partisan for the people I represent and tough," was a real pro and the owners needed that. The traits that won the owners over were eerily similar to those that, when attached to Marvin Miller, were so scorned.

Like Kuhn, Grebey was a baseball nostalgist, his love for his hometown Chicago Cubs beginning with his first game in 1932, when he and his mother would head to the ballpark. Rooting for the usually hapless Cubbies had a connection to the work he chose: "There's a similarity between rooting for the Chicago Cubs and being a professional in the labor relations field. In both situations, you suffer immensely."

After getting a sense of the baseball business by touring the teams and getting to know their problems, Grebey helped set up the Player Relations Committee in early 1980. The PRC, and only the PRC, would represent the owners at the table. It was a professional way to conduct negotiations, how it was done in the business world. Out in corporate America, the owners never sat at the table with the workers. They appointed a team that would negotiate within a framework set by the principals. To Grebey's shock, baseball wasn't like the outside world.

The owners were individuals each with his own agenda, not a cohesive group like the players. What was in the best interests of the Dodgers and the Yankees was not in the best interests of the Twins and the Royals. Famed Washington attorney Edward Bennett Williams, then owner of the Baltimore Orioles, was an outspoken critic of Grebey's. Finally, called on the carpet for his comments that undermined the PRC, Williams (who looked like the son of Karl Malden and Broderick Crawford) swore, "Grebey, I'll get you if it's the last thing I do before I die." And this from Grebey's own side!

This was not how Grebey recalled GE, where he saw that management and union were all part of the same team. There was a love of the company and negotiations were professional, structured, with both sides well prepared. There were clear objectives. Grebey began missing the company he recalled with affection, especially when, in baseball, the individual owners didn't know what the hell they wanted, and different ballplayers came in depending on who was in town.

As for the commissioner, Grebey saw quickly that Kuhn only listened to those owners he felt could help him stay in power, and his belief in the old ways of management superiority was taking the industry down the wrong path in labor relations. Coming from the orderly world of General Electric, Grebey was at sea in the waters of major league business. The owners paid no mind to proper labor relations, and that mind-set led to myriad problems that hurt Grebey's ability to negotiate properly.

The players' association cobbled together a report on Grebey and didn't like what they saw. The owners had hired a "hatchet man" who came from a company that was hard-line all the way on labor negotiations. Miller knew GE's reputation as virulently antiunion despite Grebey's take on the corporate "family" and was stunned that baseball, which suffered from the absence of institutional memory, would bring in an outsider to take on the delicate relationship between players and owners.

Unaware of the players' opposition research, Grebey thought he might get along with Miller. Bill Caples, president of Inland Steel, knew Marvin Miller when he was at the Steelworkers Union and had one bit of advice for Grebey: "Miller is a bright guy, a nice guy, and you should get to know him."

Miller, Kuhn, Grebey—the three key players off the field. On the field, spring training had begun, and for all the hope missing at the negotiating table, on the diamond it was, as it tends to be in spring, eternal.

Chapter 2

Before a gathering of reporters and visitors who'd descended on As-trotown in Cocoa, Florida, James Rodney Richard misplayed two ground balls and kicked away two more. His reflexes were poor and his depth perception weak. Until he could figure out what was com-ing back to him on the mound, until he could clearly see the ball and not a ghost, Richard would not be able to pitch. It was a sad spectacle to behold.

Less than a year before, J. R. Richard was one of the most fearsome figures on the pitcher's mound, a 6'8" behemoth with 100-mile-per-hour heat and a slider that was faster than most pitchers' fastballs. He was in the elite, winning National League ERA and strikeout titles and turning the Astros into pennant contenders.

So why did fans and reporters in Houston doubt him when he complained of a dead arm in 1980? Why did they call him a quitter, lazy, epithets that carried with them a healthy dose of racism? Against the Braves on July 14, Richard, peering in to home plate, could hardly see the signs from his catcher. It was impossible to focus and nobody believed him when he said something was seriously wrong. Two weeks later, everyone would know.

First came the ringing in his ears. Then his legs went out from under him and he fell to the ground. Through a fuzzy head, Richard could hear a siren, feel the cold towels on his face, sense being lifted in the air. What started with a normal enough pregame catch ended in a massive stroke that paralyzed the left side of his body. In the ambulance, on a stretcher, Richard could hardly move or speak.

It took a lifesaving operation to remove a clot from an artery above his right collarbone that was obstructing the path to his brain. It took a second operation, when surgeons worked for 18 hours to bypass a clotted artery in his pitching shoulder, taking two four-inch segments of artery from his lower abdomen to transplant and splice to his right shoulder, to even allow for an attempted comeback.

Two full weeks passed before Richard became aware of where he was. He had only vague recollections of what had occurred. When he returned home in mid-September, severe depression kicked in. He had nothing to do but sit for hours on end. Sometimes he'd go for a drive, cruising through the Houston streets, purposeless, alone.

Now that he was back where he felt he belonged, on the field with his team, Richard spoke well. It was remarkable; he had regained mobility on his left side and walked without a limp. Only when he was limbering up, doing calisthenics or pitching motions, was it clear that he was far from back.

Once he got loose, there was a glimpse of the old Richard, his left leg raised high, his speed respectably in the mid-80s, an occasional 90 miles per hour giving the thrill that he'd return to form. Ironically, the stroke-related surgeries made his arm feel great. It was everything else that was a problem.

"It's going to shock some people when I come back," Richard said bravely, but on the mound, trying to reclaim what he'd lost, his face was slack and his eyes betrayed his fear.

With or without Richard, the Astros came into 1981 as the defending champs of the National League West division. The Dodgers, still sore from the playoff massacre that put Houston in the League Championship Series and the Dodgers on winter vacation, had the usual cast back and ready. Steve Garvey, Davey Lopes, Bill Russell, and Ron Cey, an infield that had been together since 1973, were still productive. In the outfield Dusty Baker was hitting his prime, and the pitching staff, even with the loss of Sutton, was superb. Old standbys such as Jerry Reuss, Bob Welch, and Burt Hooton were joined by 1979 Rookie of the Year Rick Sutcliffe and 1980 Rookie of the Year Steve Howe. Then there was Fernando.

Fernando Valenzuela came into 1981 on the reputation he earned with his 1980 end-of-the-year call-up. He even made the back cover of the "Dodgers Media Guide," where he was listed as 5'11", 180 lbs. There was no way he was less than 200. When he pitched, his overhanging middle obscured his belt and nearly touched his right thigh as he strode toward home.

The kid with the physique of the Michelin Man was the story of Vero Beach, the Dodgers' spring headquarters. A true folk hero, Valenzuela hailed from Etchohuaquila, a Mexican town of 150. The seventh son in a family of 12 kids, Valenzuela grew up poor on the family farm 20 miles north of Navojoa, a farm that would fit inside the Dodger Stadium infield. The man who found him, Mike Brito, an ex–Washington Senators farmhand from Cuba, had been made a scout after he discovered Dodgers hurler Bobby Castillo, back when Brito was running an amateur team and driving an RC Cola truck for a living.

After one year in high school, the young lefty started playing professionally. Brito had got a tip on a hotshot shortstop playing for Silao, in the state of Guanajuato, and went to see for himself. He'd never forget the date: March 19, 1978. Brito hurried to Silao but hadn't thought that, since it was Holy Week, the only two hotels in town would be booked. He was not to be deterred, making his way to the dirty bus station, where he put two chairs together to make a bed. When morning came, he set out to find the ballpark, moaning from his achy night of fitful sleep.

The field was a typical Mexican diamond—baked dirt as hard as concrete and not a blade of grass to be seen. It was easy for a fancy-fielding shortstop to look bad in those conditions, and sure enough, he did. No matter; by then Brito had feasted his eyes on a 17-year-old southpaw with a strong fastball and an above-average curveball, striking out 12 batters with the skill of an older man. Brito moved in closer.

"Who is this pitcher?" he wondered aloud.

The scout went to talk to the kid, asking questions and getting one-word answers in return. Typical teenager.

"Could you play in the big leagues?" Brito asked in Spanish.

"*Seguro,*" replied the confident kid.

Brito was struck. He thought to himself that this could be what the Dodgers had been looking for and filed the information away.

The next year, team vice president Al Campanis went to Mexico to see for himself. What he saw was Valenzuela, now with Puebla of the Mexican League, strike out Earl Williams, who had been Rookie of the Year for the Braves eight years before. He was impressed and sought out the team owner, a Volkswagen dealer named Jaime Avella, who promised the Dodgers they would get first crack at the rising star.

It was a good thing, because the Yankees had caught wind of Valenzuela and offered $150,000 for his contract. Luckily for Los Angeles, Avella stayed true to his word, and, on July 6, 1979, he sold Valenzuela for $120,000, Fernando himself getting $20,000. After his debut at Lodi in the Class A California League, the club could see that Valenzuela needed another pitch in his arsenal and asked Castillo to teach him a screwball during the Arizona Instructional League over the winter. One Brito find helped the other, and Valenzuela was a different pitcher forever after. In a short time, he grasped the *lanzamiento de tornillo*. Mixing the newly mastered screwball with straight and sinking fastballs, a curve, a changeup, and a so-so slider set Valenzuela on a hot streak that got him up to the big league at the end of 1980, where he immediately proved his worth.

The Dodger crowd loved him at first sight, the cheers growing with each outing. Over the winter, he packed ballparks throughout the Mexican Pacific League. All of his announced starts were sellouts, and the masses saw some good stuff: Valenzuela went 12–5, with an ERA of 1.65 and 154 strikeouts in 147 innings pitched. Valenzuela came to spring training ready and caught the eye of Hall of Famer Sandy Koufax. While appearing as a special pitching instructor that spring, Koufax said, "It's very unusual for someone that young to have such control over so many pitches." Koufax knew of what he spoke. It had taken him years to get where this 20-year-old was already. Valenzuela was thankful but unimpressed; he had never heard of Koufax.

As long as they could keep the kid away from the Mexican beer he loved and the massive quantities of food he would devour, he might be able to help in 1981. It was all good enough for manager Tommy Lasorda to consider Valenzuela a candidate for the fourth starting spot behind Reuss, Hooton, and Welch.

Commissioner Kuhn dropped in on the Dodgers as he made his tour of all the spring-training facilities, speaking to players and projecting himself as a man of moderation, looking out for everyone's well-being. He told the team that the compensation plan was eminently reasonable and that, in fact, the players' association had allowed it to be implemented, signaling a willingness to discuss its merits. Marvin Miller and Donald Fehr were conducting their own tours during spring training, countering Kuhn's account. "That's bull," Miller bristled. "What's more, he knows it."

In Cincinnati, the Big Red Machine was aging, parts being swapped out, some tossed, others overhauled. Tony Perez, the "Big Dog," was first to go. Joe Morgan, the little second baseman with the quick legs and potent bat, a two-time MVP, was in San Francisco under new manager Frank Robinson. Those losses hurt, but they were flesh wounds compared to the deep pain of Pete Rose playing in Philadelphia. Rose had left the Reds, the only team he'd known in the city he'd grown up in, signing a multimillion-dollar deal after the 1978 season. Without him, the Reds weren't quite the same team; with him, the Phillies won the World Series.

While the Reds weren't the team that had been to the World Series four times in the previous decade, winning twice, they were still respectable, division winners in 1979, third-place finishers in 1980. They had power at the plate with George Foster, speed with

Ken Griffey. They had Tom Seaver on the mound, still giving it maximum effort, though the returns were diminishing. (For the first time in his career Seaver threw over the winter in hopes of avoiding tendinitis during the season.) And the Reds had Johnny Bench.

If Rose was Red number one, JB was a close number two. He was the catcher of his era, perhaps of all time. Bench behind the plate was a thing of beauty, fluidly snagging each pitch with one hand, springing up behind the plate, tossing his mask aside as he glided under a pop-up, straddling the plate and nabbing a runner with a swipe tag worthy of Manolete. At 33, it seemed as if he'd catch forever.

That's what the fans saw. What Bench saw was a never-ending series of hurts, pains, and broken bones that would lead to the premature end of his career. He didn't want that. The drugs it took to keep down the pain and inflammation were overwhelming. "I'd have been scratched if I was a racehorse." Enough was enough. In August of 1980, Bench informed the club that, starting in 1981, he would catch only twice a week.

Where would manager John McNamara play him? Bench offered some options—first, third, or right field. He brought a variety of gloves to spring training. McNamara tried him out. To see Bench at first base, awkwardly backhanding a ground ball, was an odd and funny sight. This was not future Hall of Fame catcher Johnny Bench at work. This was nervous Johnny Bench with a look of surprise as a hot smash snuck up on him. What shocked him more than a wicked bad hop was the reaction of his teammates, who were unhappy that Bench wanted their jobs. The scuttlebutt around camp was that the Reds might trade him. "If Johnny wants to come to the Phillies, I'll be happy to find another position," said Rose with a grin.

Rose had a lot to grin about. His switch-hitting, headfirst sliding, and contagious energy (everyone loved when he giddily spiked the baseball on the hard synthetic turf after a putout at first) was just the jolt the Phillies had needed to get over the hump. By adding Rose to a roster that included megastars Steve Carlton and Mike Schmidt, Philadelphia had captured its first title in history.

The off-season should have been trouble free, but it wasn't.

In January, Rose appeared on the stand in a court case. A group of five Phillies, including Carlton and Rose, as well as the wives of Greg Luzinski and Larry Bowa, were accused of procuring amphetamines and diet pills. Dr. Patrick Mazza, the writer of the prescriptions, was the doctor of the Phils' minor league team in Reading. Mazza and his son picked up the drugs for delivery and testified that they'd given pills to Carlton and fellow pitchers Randy Lerch and Larry Christenson in the locker room at Veterans Stadium. For Bowa, Luzinski, and Rose, drugs were handed to the clubhouse man.

Amphetamine use was rampant to enhance performance, adding a little extra kick to throws and a little more pop at bat. Rose, in his most innocent, boyish voice, said on the stand, "What's a greenie?" However, he'd already told *Playboy* in a recent interview that he'd take pills before a game to get a lift. Performance-enhancing drugs taken by stars such as Pete Rose? Unfathomable.

Despite the turmoil, the Phillies were formidable, even more so after they traded for Braves outfielder Gary Matthews, made expendable after the outrageous signing of Claudell Washington by Ted Turner. But many observers saw the Expos as the team to beat in the National League East. For two years running, Montreal had been knocked out of the postseason in the final games of the year, but they were a mightily talented club. Gary Carter coupled the enthusiasm of Rose with the ability of Bench, becoming the preeminent catcher in the NL. Andre Dawson, even hobbled by bad knees, was one of the best and brightest outfielders in all of baseball. He was expected to be joined in 1981 by a much-ballyhooed speedster from the minors, Tim Raines.

The pitching staff was excellent, led by the unchallenged ace of the team, Steve Rogers, who went by "Cy" (short for Cy Young). Rogers was an ornery guy, deeply involved in the players' association and constantly at odds with manager Dick Williams.

"I am an arrogant son of a bitch. My personality is basically horseshit. I don't want to be their friends," Williams declared, and Rogers agreed. Their butting of heads nearly resulted in Rogers's being traded. Ultimately Rogers was safe in Montreal, and the Expos went into the season with a younger team than the Phillies, equally talented, with their top pitcher still in the fold.

The NL East would likely come down to a battle between Philadelphia and Montreal, but the Mets, vanquished in the Winfield war, tried to make a splash with a return to their better past. Since mid-1977, when the Mets had cleared house by sending Seaver, the greatest pitcher in their history, to the Reds, and their top slugger, Dave Kingman, to the Padres, the team had been a perennial cellar dweller, save for a second-from-the-bottom finish in 1980. Desperate for attention, the Mets advertised "The Magic Is Back," but the only trick they could do well was the one that made fans disappear. Manager Joe Torre had a huge challenge and little help from the front office.

They signed 36-year-old Rusty Staub, a star in their World Series year of 1973, as a free agent. They also brought back Kingman, he of the overwhelming home run and underwhelming glove. No one had ever launched a baseball into orbit like "Kong." When he connected—and that was not always the case—the ball flew up in a near straight line, stretching high into the sky and finally crashing back into the stands. Or the street.

The last few years, after signing with the Cubs after 1977, Kingman knocked them onto Waveland Avenue, over the ivy-covered left-field stands, even, at times, sending the battered ball north on Kenmore. He had a typical year in 1978 and a breakout year in 1979, hitting 48 dingers to lead the league and even getting his batting average up to .288, but 1980 was a washout and he'd worn out his welcome. Clubhouse poison, Kingman was unloved by his teammates. Cubs pitcher Bill Caudill said, "Kingman was like a cavity that made your whole mouth sore." Trading for Kingman was the best the Mets could come up with to compete with the Yankees.

Realistically, there was nothing the Mets could do to compete with the Yankees. Since shipbuilder Steinbrenner had taken over the club in 1973, leading a group that purchased the once-intimidating, now-weak team for a bit more than $10 million, the Yankees had been the greatest show on earth, winning divisions and World Series with regularity. Despite his announced plans for absentee ownership—"We're not going to pretend we're something we aren't. I won't be active in day-to-day operations of the club at all"—Steinbrenner found the New York klieg lights shining on him and he liked it. Managers came and went, put out quicker than a 6-4-3 double play. With the advent of free agency, and the enormous press attention focused on high-profile players, Steinbrenner dove right in. Through free agency, Jackson and Winfield became Yankees.

Jackson loved New York, craved the attention that he never got to the same degree in Oakland and Baltimore. Some saw the focus he put on himself as shallow and selfish, and it was that, but it was also much more. By turning the cameras' glare and the reporters' tape recorders on himself, Jackson knew that pressure would come his way, relieving the suffering of his teammates. The cockiness belied massive insecurity. "I have to wonder if my ego is small enough, if my false pride is false enough. . . . I don't know whether I can handle my false pride at not being top banana. . . . I don't know if I'm secure enough not to have the biggest number next to my name. I don't know if I'm mature enough or secure enough not to make as much as Dave Winfield," he admitted in a moment of psychoanalysis.

Jackson was smart. He knew that the signing of Winfield was good for the team and maybe good for him with his contract expiring at season's end and a second chance at free agency around the corner. Reggie Jackson needed to be loved, and love had to come in the form of a multimillion-dollar contract offered by Steinbrenner.

Before the full team had to report for spring training, the two met on the patio near the pool at Galt Ocean Mile Hotel, the Yankees' spring headquarters. For 90 minutes they spoke, Jackson explaining that he'd prefer having a new deal locked up before spring training finished so he could focus on baseball. Though Steinbrenner had told Jackson after Winfield's press conference that there'd be no long-term deals, now he was telling Jackson he wanted him to be a Yankee for life. It was friendly, cordial, and Jackson left optimistic, pleased with Steinbrenner's change of heart. He figured that Steinbrenner knew how mutually beneficial their relationship had been, how they'd made scads of money for each other, and that, as an excellent businessman, Steinbrenner saw the wisdom of continuing their fruitful relationship.

There'd been no change of heart. Steinbrenner was intentionally deceiving Jackson. With Winfield locked up, Steinbrenner had decided that this was the year he'd get back at Reggie for all the troubles he'd caused, for all the times he sassed "the Boss." It was time to put Jackson in his place.

Trouble began immediately when Jackson asked if he could stay in California on personal business and report to camp late. It was a small request from a player of Jackson's stature. His request was denied, and worse, he was fined $5,000 for the two days he missed. Steinbrenner ordered new manager Gene "Stick" Michael to blast Jackson to the press. It was a tough spot for a skipper trying to project a strong image to a veteran team. Criticize Jackson or ignore Steinbrenner—either way Michael was bound to lose. Steinbrenner played the victim: "I'm very hurt that a man looking for a new big contract would pull something like this. You kind of hope that a guy known as Mr. October, who wasn't Mr. October in 1980, who didn't drive in a single run in the playoffs, would want to come back with the same dedication as the other guys."

On the field, Jackson and Winfield got along well. They weren't tight, but what could have been a strain was working out fine. But with no sign of progress on his new contract ("I believe in paying a man for what he will do in the future, not for what he has done in the past," announced Steinbrenner), Jackson, standing in the middle of the clubhouse, declared himself a "walking keg of dynamite," and Steinbrenner was not tiptoeing carefully around the explosives. Every opportunity he had, Steinbrenner poked and prodded, toying with Jackson as he commented on how good Winfield looked and how much Jackson seemed to be struggling. Steinbrenner did all he could to undermine Jackson's fragile psyche.

As the weeks went on, Jackson became eager to have it out with Steinbrenner, who, it seemed, was avoiding his volatile slugger. "I think Steinbrenner has a true dislike for me," Jackson said sadly.

Steinbrenner, living in an irony-free zone, said of Jackson, "He's acting like a young kid, going in a corner and crying and screaming. When a kid goes in the corner and wants a cookie, you don't necessarily give it to him."

Confused, unsure, bewildered, Jackson began openly musing on life after the Yankees, maybe a more contented existence with the Angels or the Mets. The Jackson-Steinbrenner feud would be enough to dominate one team's spring, but for the Yankees it was one story among many. Cerone and Steinbrenner were still going at it after the catcher's arbitration win, a win that still angered the Boss. Steinbrenner sent Cerone a package with a new uniform—*ET 2* was sewn on the back of the jersey.

Ron Guidry, the team's best starting pitcher since 1977, was due to become a free agent after the season, after posting win totals of 16, 25, 18, and 17. "Louisiana Lightning" was after $1 million per year, a nice lift from the less than $200,000 he'd averaged in his first four seasons. When Guidry lit the baseball world on fire in 1978, he made $47,000.

Always looking for more, the Yankees finalized a trade with the Pirates for Jason Thompson on April 1. In exchange for Thompson, whose left-handed power swing was perfectly suited for the short right field of Yankee Stadium, the Yankees sent first baseman Jim Spencer (and part of his salary), two minor leaguers, and $850,000 to Pittsburgh. But Kuhn had set a cash limit on all deals of $400,000 and blocked the trade.

Simple monetary compensation, mutually agreed upon by two consenting clubs, was not exactly what Kuhn was looking for. In exchange for Thompson, the Pirates were happy to accept $850,000, as well as a major league player, one who was conceivably the 16th best player on the Yankees and the type the owners' negotiators were looking to acquire for clubs through direct compensation.

The Thompson deal did more to show how disingenuous the owners' pursuit of compensation was. When the commissioner forced the two sides to repackage the trade, the whole deal collapsed. Steinbrenner was incensed, and the Pirates ended up with nothing. Kuhn, the big believer in "fair" compensation for a team losing a free agent, was unwilling to put his money where his mouth was. Or at least other people's money.

As spring training drew to a close, and Winfield closed out batting a weak .212, Jackson and Steinbrenner bumped into each other in the manager's office. It was friendly but stiff, the old romance all but gone. Jackson would enter the new season in emotional, and physical, pain. He'd torn a tendon in his right calf.

If the defending AL champs were entering the season in turmoil, the Milwaukee Brewers were not. With each recent year, the Brew Crew had improved in their attempt to catch up with the Yanks. For 1981, they were confident that the new guy with the old-timey handlebar mustache would lead them to first place.

In Wisconsin they were calling it the Trade. Like Cher or Charo, it was identifiable enough with one key word. After Kuhn refused to allow Finley to sell Rollie Fingers in the great closeout sale of 1976, Finley, thinking his brilliant reliever was washed up, let him leave. Fingers signed with the Padres, where he excelled, but when new St. Louis Cardinals manager and GM Whitey Herzog offered catching prospect Terry Kennedy and a passel of players for Fingers and a few others, he was shipped to the Midwest on December 8, 1980. The next day Herzog got Bruce Sutter from the Cubs.

Having signed Royals catcher Darrell Porter on the seventh, Herzog could afford to trade veteran Cards catcher Ted Simmons. Packaging Simmons with Fingers and starting pitcher Pete Vuckovich (the latter two in the final year of their contracts), Herzog turned to the Brewers. They had the need, and Fingers, even at 34, was at the top of his game. Milwaukee put together four players and the deal was done on the 12th. The Brewers were thrilled. There was one hitch. Simmons was a "ten and five" man. It was another player right that Miller had won over the years. Simmons, as one who had played a total of ten years in the majors and the last five with the same team, had control of the situation and he used it. "I had a certain leverage I wouldn't normally have. I didn't use money as a guillotine, but it was a considerable factor." A quick $750,000 bonus later and it was off to the city that *Happy Days, Laverne and Shirley,* and beer made famous.

Billy Martin made beer famous. The hard-drinking, harder-punching Martin had found a new home in Oakland. After his second firing from the Yankees, Martin took over an A's franchise that had fallen and couldn't get up. After three World Series wins and a 1975 American League West title, the A's had finished dead last in 1979, losing 108 games and drawing slightly over 300,000 fans, if you could call them that. For an April game against the Mariners, 653 showed. Some may have got lost heading someplace else. Divine intervention was needed.

"I believe if God had ever managed, He would have been very aggressive, the way I manage." So sayeth Martin, with an interesting view of self. After he turned the A's into an 83-game-winning runner-up in 1980, who was to argue? Behind "BillyBall," an exciting throwback style of squeeze plays, runners in motion, and steals of home, the A's won on the field and off, with attendance leaping to 842,000.

The A's marketed BillyBall in 1981. Martin wasn't out between the white lines, except for the occasional umpire run-in. The A's succeeded because they had the most thrilling young player in the game, Rickey Henderson. Out of Oakland's Technical High School, Henderson had debuted in 1979 at 20. He could hit hard and hit for average, and he covered a lot of ground in left field. And he could run. Man, how he could run. In his first full season of 1980, Henderson stole 100 bases, nearly breaking Lou Brock's single-season record of 118. Plus, he had style—crouching low from the right side of the plate, strutting around as if he owned the place, nabbing a fly ball in his glove, then bringing it to his side like a jai alai player snapping a pelota in his cesta. Martin loved the kid.

Martin, as he always did, brought in Art Fowler as his pitching coach. They'd been together for nearly every one of Martin's managerial years. Many looked at Fowler as simply comic relief, Billy's drinking buddy, and nothing more, but Fowler knew his pitchers, knew how to coach, and knew a few tricks to boot. Did his pitchers know that if they put Ivory soap on the inside of their pant legs, they could easily apply the slippery soap to their fingers when their throwing hands touched the wet, sweaty area? They did now.

Martin and Fowler had some other ideas, such as, with a weak bull pen you could, and had to, keep your starting pitchers in the game as long as humanly possible, sometimes longer. Rick Langford nearly hit 300 innings in 1980, and Mike Norris, Matt Keough, Steve McCatty, and Brian Kingman pitched more than they ever had before. Each responded well. Norris, winner of 22 games in 1980, felt gypped that he didn't win the Cy Young Award and came to camp gunning for it.

If Norris was bitter, Carlton Fisk was apoplectic. A native New Englander, Fisk was a Boston legend whose 1975 World Series home run over the Green Monster at Fenway Park had put him in the same class as Paul Revere and John F. Kennedy. Now, after the Red Sox had botched his contract, he was declared a free agent on February 12.

Instead of courting the hometown hero, Sox GM Sullivan blasted him, saying that Fisk's contract was more bothersome to the catcher than an arm injury he'd complained about. Still, Fisk wanted to stay in Massachusetts, and his agent alerted management that a decision would be rendered in March and the team should be represented on the West Coast as time drew close. Sullivan wouldn't send a soul.

Reinsdorf and Einhorn, the new White Sox owners, watched. They didn't jump in right away; they were afraid of offending the other owners. The pair expressed interest, but gave Boston as much time as they needed to re-sign Fisk. Oddly, for a player of Fisk's caliber, there wasn't a frenzy of competition for his services. Most clubs were holding back. Collusion? Reinsdorf suspected it, but he had no hard evidence.

When Fisk put pen to paper and signed with Chicago on March 18, it sent shock waves throughout baseball. Nobody had thought the White Sox would be able to sign him. Would they have behaved differently had the new compensation rules the owners had proposed been in effect? "We don't have sixteen good players to protect," said Reinsdorf, laughing.

The acquisition of Carlton Fisk set off a ticket-buying frenzy in Chicago, the team looking at a gate-busting possibility of 2 million in attendance. The attitude of the city toward the White Sox changed for the better. For the Red Sox, nothing could have hurt more.

How to keep track of all these players, all these stories and stats? In spring, millions turned to a time-honored system of information gathering—baseball cards. The turmoil in baseball, the interweaving of business and sport, of tradition and progress, was mirrored in the collectible world. Topps, the only card company that generations had grown up on, had competition for the first time in 25 years. Like free agency, the decision came from an outside arbiter.

Cards were big business, 500 million traded, collected, and clothespinned on bicycle spokes every year, generating $10 million in revenue. It was no wonder others wanted in. When Fleer first challenged Topps in 1959, Topps had nearly every player under an exclusive deal. In 1975, the same year the first free agent, "Catfish" Hunter, was pushed out into an open market, Fleer filed a $13.6 mil suit against the Topps monopoly.

It took almost six years to end. On June 30, 1980, Topps and the players' association were ruled to have violated the Sherman Antitrust Act, restraining trade in the card market. The players' association, much to Miller's shock, was sued as well because it had only licensed Topps. Miller disagreed with the Topps assertion of exclusivity, but by not granting other companies the same right, the union had helped Topps remain the only cardboard in town. The players' association was thrilled, for once, to lose. They saw more licensing money on the horizon.

For all of Fleer's work in the courts, it was a Memphis concern, Donruss, that jumped in first. Fleer, seeing the normal calendar compress, released its full set before the Super Bowl, rather than in mid-February as was customary. Statistical errors were numerous, with Bobby Bonds credited with 936 career home runs. The cards came out too early to picture the recent crop of free agents in fresh garb. Winfield as a Padre, and Fisk and Lynn as Red Sox, made the new cards outdated on arrival. Each company had a hard time completely covering the expected top rookies. Topps featured Tim Raines in a triptych of future Expos stars. Fernando Valenzuela got the same treatment. Donruss offered a full, more in focus, solo card of an incredibly young-looking Raines, his big Afro pushing his cap skyward, an empty Wrigley Field lower level in the background. Fleer had the only Valenzuela card, though he was labeled "Fernand" Valenzuela.

The flood of new product, giving every purchaser a free choice, would lead to an explosion of the hobby. By year end, three times the usual number of cards were collected. The union garnered an additional $600,000 in revenue. An open market was good for paper images of the players; why not for the real thing?

Grebey and Miller had met twice recently, on February 17 and, in Arizona, on March 26. Neither meeting went well. The players offered their own compensation proposal but not a direct line from signing team to losing team. Their idea was to have a money pool to pay teams losing a free agent. The players also put forth limiting the number of free agents whose signing would result in compensation and an enhanced system of trading potential free agents, thereby giving clubs on the verge of losing a player easier access to receive compensation via trade. In response, MacPhail said that so few players would be covered in the players' proposal as to render it meaningless, though the owners had said the same thing in support of their own plan.

Kuhn was on a ceremonial trip. In celebration of the season ahead, Kuhn and 32 Hall of Famers visited the White House on March 27. The president, who often fondly recalled his days as a Cubs broadcaster, re-creating the action on the field for WHO radio, swapped stories with the legends and looked forward to throwing out the first pitch in Cincinnati on April 8 versus Phillies. Three days later, the president, accompanied by Secretary of Labor Raymond Donovan, delivered a speech to the national conference of the AFL-CIO Building Construction Trades Department at the Washington Hilton Hotel. After the event, around 2:25 p.m., Reagan left the hotel via the T Street side entrance, passing a crowd standing behind the rope line. John Hinckley was waiting and unloaded six shots in less than two seconds. In a flurry, the president was whisked away, a bullet lodged in his lung. There'd be no first pitch for him in 1981.

With neither side having a worthy solution to give both owners and players what they wanted, negotiations on free agent compensation began in earnest with a 75-minute meeting in New York on April 7. It was an inauspicious beginning. Immediately after the meeting Miller requested that Kenneth Moffett, acting director of the Federal Mediation and Conciliation Service, join the negotiations. Grebey agreed. Moffett had been part of the 1980 talks, asked in then by Grebey, and had proven extremely helpful. He was already familiar with the issues, and if Miller and Grebey could at least agree on Moffett, maybe there was room to work.

Miller often quoted an old labor adage: "There is no status quo. You either move on or are shoved on your rear end." It was too early to know who would end up flat on their ass.

Thank the Lord tomorrow was Opening Day.

Chapter 3

Opening Day in Cincinnati was a holiday. It had been that way since the Reds joined the National League in 1876, the year of its birth. The franchise had a special place in baseball history—the 1869 Red Stockings were the first professional team. It was the beginning of soon-to-be-tired memes, repeated verbatim in each successive generation—players were only in it for the money, current players were morally inferior to those who came before them because in the "old days" the players loved the game more than their salaries, that owners were being driven to the poorhouse because avaricious ballplayers were taking their hard-earned cash. The troubles of 1981 weren't new.

There was no relief pitcher for the wounded president. Instead, the near-sellout crowd shared a somber moment of silence. Patriotism was given its due, as two former Iranian hostages, Col. Leland Holland and Bert C. Moore, were honored. They'd already been given lifetime passes by the commissioner. The crowd erupted; it was great to have them back home.

The matchup was classic, two veteran warriors, power pitchers who'd been doing battle since 1967—Steve Carlton and Tom Seaver. Carlton was at the top of his game, winning his third Cy Young in 1980, leading the circuit in wins and strikeouts. His devastating slider, the wickedest of its type, and a still-smoking fastball, baffled hitters even at his advanced age of 36. Silent Steve, "Lefty," who'd taken a vow never to speak with reporters, didn't need to say a word when he was on the mound. His pitches spoke for him just fine.

Seaver was Carlton's opposite, and not simply because he threw from the right side. Where Carlton was mute as a mummy, Seaver was one of the most eloquent spokesmen and students of the game. Not only was his analysis of pitching astute; Seaver was insightful on every issue he tackled. He was the modern athlete—college educated, thoughtful and serious about his art and the business that surrounded it.

Like Carlton, Seaver was 36. Like Carlton, Seaver had won three Cy Youngs, but none lately. He'd had solid seasons since 1975, his last award-winning year, but coming into 1981 he was worried. The year before, for the first time in his career, Seaver had arm trouble, a sharp pain tightening his shoulder, pulling his elbow downward. As a result, his still-potent fastball stayed up and, too often, ended up out of the park.

"I'm definitely concerned," Seaver said somberly. "At this age, I have to wonder just how many more pitches I still have in my arm."

For seven innings the two old foes battled, the Reds scoring a sole run in the bottom of the third, the Phillies unable to touch Seaver. Carlton left first, pinch-hit for in the top of the eighth, leading to the tying run before Seaver hunkered down and got out of a bases-loaded jam. The Reds would win on a bases-loaded walk from Tug McGraw in the bottom of the ninth, but the big news was Seaver. Outlasting Carlton by an inning, Seaver scattered 6 hits and struck out 4, allowing a single run. Tom Terrific was back.

The next day in New York, Seaver's former stomping grounds, the Yankees were ready to unveil their new toy to the packed park in the Bronx. Winfield arrived in full regalia: cowboy boots, jeans, leather jacket, and a 10-gallon hat, as suitable for a kid's birthday party as for the Yankee clubhouse.

Amid the chattering and joking of his teammates, Winfield sat down to change. Pulling off his sock, a wad of bills, $700 worth, flew out. He'd planned to stick it in the clubhouse safe-deposit box but forgot.

"Please don't write about this," Winfield begged the crowd of reporters, to no avail. It was good copy for the 250 members of the media at the stadium for his debut: the big-contract guy with money pouring out of his clothes.

Having ended spring training with a low average and zero home runs, Winfield was apprehensive about the fans' reaction to him and his contract, the largest in sports history. He'd heard that Hunter, Jackson, Cerone, and Gossage all got grief from the fans after starting slowly. And they all came out to see him, the biggest crowd since the reopening of the remodeled House That Ruth Built.

Being a Yankee was different, he could sense it. The Yankees might seem loose, ripping into each other, talking shit, but when it came down to the business at hand, they played hard, together, and won, crushing the Rangers 10–3 behind a solid outing by Tommy John. Starting in left field and batting third, Winfield had 2 singles (his second sparking a 5-run rally late in the game), 2 walks, and a run scored, but the way he slammed into the Rangers shortstop turned the light boos, mixed with moderate clapping, into real applause. A bit of violence always won over a New York City crowd.

The biggest story of the day was not back East, no matter how New York styled itself as the center of the baseball world. In Los Angeles, an earthquake was about to hit.

Frank Sinatra liked to stop by the manager's office when he came to Dodger Stadium. He and Tommy Lasorda had struck up a nice friendship, two paisans with a lust for life, enjoying their mutual good fortune. Lasorda couldn't believe his luck, managing the team he'd grown up with and loved, the team for which, he often told the press, he bled "Dodger blue." Lasorda's office had a wall fully devoted to pictures of Frank, another to Don Rickles, and the other two to baseball. It wasn't uncommon these days to have the real "Ol' Blue Eyes" sitting in his office in front of the photographic ones.

Lasorda may have been having a laugh, but he was worried.

His scheduled starting pitcher, Jerry Reuss, had strained his left calf muscle during batting practice. Unable to turn to his second starter, Burt Hooton, down with an uncomfortable ingrown toenail, Lasorda thought hard. Bob Welch was down with some aches and so was Dave Goltz. Lasorda really missed Sutton now. Might as well give the Opening Day slot to the kid.

The fans were stunned, the press skeptical, but the team was sanguine. Could the 20-year-old Fernando Valenzuela handle the pressure of taking the mound against the Astros before 50,000 Dodger rooters looking for revenge over the team that booted them out at the end of 1980? It was impossible to ask him; he was taking a pre-game nap in the trainer's room. "No problem," thought third baseman Ron Cey when he heard the news.

Valenzuela slowly walked to the mound, oddly erect, most of his body lagging behind his barrel chest and protruding stomach. He warmed up, started his motion, nice and fluid, his eyes pointing to the heavens and slightly closed, his right leg kicked high, the stretch, his glove hand pointing downward, and a last sudden lunge where belly met leg.

Terry Puhl strode into the batter's box to lead off. Valenzuela tilted his head, turned his pocked face to catcher Mike Scioscia, and threw his first pitch, a fabulous screwball that Puhl swung at and missed. With that pitch, which Valenzuela had mastered in less than two years' time, he befuddled the Astros, inning after inning, shutting them down with no runs and few hits. A proud Mike Brito, in a sharp panama hat, white with black bands, and a huge stogie below his droopy mustache, watched as his protégé buzzed his way through the lineup.

With two out in the visitors' half of the ninth inning, Fernando got two strikes on Houston first baseman Dave Roberts. The crowd was on their feet, clapping, with him all the way, sharing the moment. Another screwball, another feeble swing, and it was over; a shutout win on opening day, in 2:17. "A little child shall lead them," said announcer Vin Scully.

Valenzuela's parents had warned him, "It won't be easy. It'll be difficult." It wasn't. Scioscia ran out to congratulate the rookie, and each Dodger in turn offered a handshake and a smile as the crowd chanted his name. Over 50,000 that day saw the beginnings of Fernandomania.

In Boston, the story was the return of Fisk. It was strange for Fisk to dress in the visitors' clubhouse at Fenway Park. Bad feelings permeated the aged halls of the 79-year-old park, with General Manager Sullivan talking trash about Fisk to the Red Sox staff. As for the White Sox, the public relations coup that resulted from Reinsdorf and Einhorn's making the deal rankled Sullivan. Every article rubbed its nose in his mistake. "At my stupidest, I was never as stupid as the Boston Red Sox," ripped Ted Turner.

Some of Boston's bad feelings were assuaged by a 2–0 lead entering the eighth inning. Dennis Eckersley had been in command the whole game, but then a walk, a single, and a sacrifice bunt moving the runners into scoring position sent things south in a hurry. Eckersley was out and Bob Stanley in, ready to face Fisk, who slowly walked to bat. With his nine-year-old son watching, Fisk set his sights out to the mound. He'd caught Stanley for the last four seasons; he knew what to expect. When the sinker came, he was ready. By the time the ball landed in the screen above the left-field wall, the crowd had turned from Red Sox fans to Fisk fans. They'd booed him earlier, but now they were delirious. They couldn't help themselves.

Fisk's 3-run homer sealed the Red Sox's fate, but at least there was something to cheer about. The season ahead seemed so depressing, with Burleson, Lynn, and Fisk all gone, that fans were planning to stay away. Advance sales were down almost 10 percent from 1980. Even games against the Yankees weren't sold out. For one moment, though, their exiled hero had come through. It happened to be for the other team.

Though Opening Day excitement dominated sports talk, the strike still loomed. During the first Saturday *Game of the Week* on NBC, color man Tony Kubek announced with certainty that there'd be a strike and that it was entirely the owners' fault. Naïveté and condescension toward the players was the norm. Angels owner Gene

Autry said a player strike six or seven weeks into the season "doesn't hit me as very nice." Autry spent too much time on his horse Champion, thinking the world was entirely made up of good guys and bad guys. He and his ilk were not used to wearing the black hat.

On April 13, the day after *Columbia,* the first space shuttle, was launched, the players presented two proposals they hoped would fly. This time they put their thoughts on compensation in writing. Grebey had previously berated the players for coming up empty. In reality they had, verbally, put forth their idea of a money pool and the easier trading of potential free agents. Now the players added a new metric on how to define quality free agents and a willingness to use that for a three-year look at compensation, but first they wanted to see detailed financial information from the owners. The owners declined to provide it.

One week later, in a one-off meeting in Washington, Grebey told the press that he'd been reviewing a Miller proposal that would limit the number of premium free agents to the top 5 percent.

"A grand total of three players would have qualified for compensation over the last three years—Pete Rose, Elias Sosa, and Geoff Zahn," shot Grebey. "Marvin has offered exactly nothing." Dumbfounded as to how Grebey could be so opposed to an idea that hadn't even been fleshed out, that would involve exploring various statistical standards to arrive at a true measure of quality, Miller spoke out: "More and more, their stance seems to be, 'Our compensation plan is in place. You'll have to strike to get it out.'" Though he would protest otherwise, Kuhn felt he could force the PRC's hand and keep them negotiating, but as internal meeting notes had shown, the PRC was not interested.

Though baseball labor talks were in the news, the conversation returned to the game as spectators began noticing the phenom. With each start the press machine revved up a bit more about Valenzuela. On typical mid-April night at Candlestick Park in San Francisco, typical meaning cold, in the low 50s, with a blustery wind. Cold, maybe, but Fernando was on fire. Though he allowed his first run of the season, the Dodgers romped 7–1. "They're good hitters," Valenzuela told Jaime Jarrin, the Dodgers' Spanish-speaking broadcaster. "It's not as easy as you think." Valenzuela just made it seem that way, outpitching Vida Blue, a former left-handed phenom himself. Giants manager Frank Robinson was dismissive; he'd seen it all before. This was nothing special. Three days later, in San Diego, Valenzuela was back to his shutout form, striking out 10 and rapping 2 singles against the weak Padres. "When I go to the mound, I don't know what it is to be afraid," Valenzuela said.

The American League was afraid, very afraid, of Billy Martin's A's. BillyBall was in full swing from the first pitch of the season, the team supremely confident coming out of spring training. They had the pitching, they had the hitting, and they had the smarts. In the first week, second baseman Brian Doyle pulled the hidden-ball trick. Classic Billy Martin chicanery, and it worked. The team was aggressive on offense, made all the plays on defense; their pitchers threw strikes (oh, how Martin hated walks!), their hitting was timely and powerful. At the end of week one the A's were 4–0. After the second week they were 11–0, breaking the record shared by the 1955 Dodgers, 1962 Pirates, and 1966 Indians for opening-the-season success. After three weeks they were 17–1.

The starting pitchers—Mike Norris, Rick Langford, Steve McCatty, Brian Kingman, and Matt Keough—may not have had the name recognition of Seaver and Carlton, but they were pitching just as well. Martin worked the starters hard and long. In 1980, they set a team record of 94 complete games. Critics were concerned that he'd blow out the arms of his young staff. Martin would have none of it.

"It's not the innings pitched that's important. It's the number of pitches thrown," he snippily replied. The charges that Martin and pitching coach Fowler were burning out their starters angered them. Each hurler was limited to 70 pitches in the bull pen during warm-ups. During the game Langford usually threw around 90 pitches, Norris and Keough 110, McCatty and Kingman between 125 and 140. The relief crew could take a nap during the game; there was little else for them to do.

The quintet had a lunch-pail, workmanlike nature, but one stood out. "Michael Norris is without a doubt the finest pitcher in baseball," said Keough. Norris, a high school star with a tragic background (his father was knifed to death when Norris was only seven), was brought up to Oakland in 1975, when he was 20. He shone in his first start, a 3-hitter, but after his third start he suffered a devastating arm injury. With much grit, he struggled back to top form, exploding for 22 wins in 1980. Norris's screwball mystified batters. That's what he called his go-to pitch. Others had a different opinion.

"It's a known fact that Norris messes around with the ball," squawked Twins manager Johnny Goryl. It wasn't only Goryl; the entire league saw foul play dressed in green, gold, and white. Whether they admitted throwing illegal pitches or not, what was going on was obvious (see Fowler's Ivory-soap trick), and the pitchers made it clear that they loved Martin and Fowler and would follow them anywhere.

The A's respected Martin—he taught them to win, and when they won, Martin was happy, and when Martin was happy, the team was calm and everyone had fun. When Mariners manager Maury Wills, in a haze of drug taking and insane decision making, attempted to cheat Martin by ordering the Kingdome grounds crew to extend the batter's box, Martin caught the trick immediately. (Wills would be suspended, fined, and fired for the incident.) This was old-school hardball, with old-school humor. Hotfoots were prevalent, no one exempt. McCatty even lit up Martin, who retaliated by cutting the seat off his pitcher's pants.

While the national media made much of the pitching heroics, the A's were so much more. Rickey Henderson was off to a blazing start, hitting well over .300 and averaging more than a run scored per game. He tore around the bases in hyperspeed, and when the cameras replayed another stolen base in slow motion, he still seemed faster than most players. "Mr. Excitement" banners sprung up at the Coliseum. Tony Armas was off to a hot start (who wasn't on this team?), quickly belting 6 home runs and amassing 17 RBIs. But despite what was happening on the field, it was Martin who got the attention. From his office, the Old Gunslinger railed at the press.

"I'm getting pretty tired of this BillyBall stuff. 'BillyBall'? I'd rather have it called 'A's' ball." Martin wasn't doing anything he hadn't done at all of his other managerial stops. The team was the man—aggressive, watching everything in the game with precision, hating to lose, and not afraid to make mistakes no matter the cost.

It was a thrilling team to watch. At home the fans were returning, crafting do it yourself T-shirts proclaiming WE LOVE BILLY THE KID. On the road, the A's were the top draw. They were a team for the new decade, big Afros and porn mustaches, coming to town to whup your team. They were looking forward to tearing apart no team more than the Yankees, scheduled to be in Oakland on the first of May.

The season was off to a magnificent start. Chicago was falling in love with Fisk. On White Sox Opening Day at Comiskey Park, with the festivities off to a rocky start when one of two parachutists landed outside the stadium, Fisk blasted a grand slam in a 9–3 victory over the Brewers. When Boston came to town, Fisk did it to them again, this time his low-looping swing sending the ball over Jim Rice's head in left, all the ChiSox needed in a 2–1 win. Fisk in a navy-blue sox cap and funny pajama uniforms with big, floppy collars and Victorian lettering wasn't so hard to get used to.

Opening Day in Philadelphia meant the raising of the World Series flag and the handing out of the rings, as the Liberty Bell light high atop the stadium flickered and the Phillie Phanatic danced deliriously. Rose was on a mission in 1981. He had Stan Musial's National League hit record in his sights. Stan "the Man's" 3,630 was only a few months of games away. Rose, from his exaggerated crouch from both sides of the plate, got 3 hits in the opener, a strong start on his way to, and past, Musial. The next day Rose would turn 40, but his exuberance was unchanged since 1963, his rookie year. By the end of April, Rose was hitting .362, playing as if something were chasing him.

Highlights weren't reserved to the major leagues. The minor league Pawtucket Red Sox and Rochester Red Wings took the field on the night of April 18. Rochester third baseman Cal Ripken Jr. was the most talked about prospect in baseball, only a matter of time before he'd be in Baltimore, joining his third-base-coach father. PawSox third baseman Wade Boggs wasn't as heralded, but the guy could hit.

It was a normal game, becoming better than average when the Sox tied it at 1 in the bottom of the ninth. On they played—10, 11, 12 innings. The International League had a curfew, 12:50 a.m., but the copy of the rules that the home plate umpire had was missing this increasingly important piece of information. As Saturday turned into Easter Sunday the teams kept at it.

The players rose to superhuman status as the game advanced. After Rochester scored in the top of the 21st, Boggs tied the game with a double. His teammates wanted to kill him. Rochester's Jim Umbarger pitched shutout baseball starting in the 23rd inning. Red Wing catcher Dave Huppert caught 31 innings before he was replaced. The players were walking dead, nearly hallucinogenic from exhaustion. Hitters were sent up to the plate 10, 12, 14 times. The umpires needed to go to the bathroom.

After 3:00 a.m., a call was placed to league president Harold Cooper. He was mortified and ordered the game stopped after the completion of the next full inning. After eight hours and 32 innings, the game was halted, to be resumed at a later date with the score tied 2–2.

While fans came out in droves to the stadiums, in the sterile rooms on the 17th floor at the Doral Inn on Lexington Avenue, the players and owners were all tied up in negotiations with no end in sight. The players put forth some new ideas, proposals circling around different criteria to determine free agent quality, floating the idea that a club losing a player to free agency could get a preferential pick in the major league draft of minor league players (not of players on the major league roster). The owners put forth their 1980 position again, unchanged.

The owners were "insulted" by the players' proposals. Though Moffett had arrived on April 20, no headway was made. At the owners' intransigence, Miller said, "They are simply refusing to bargain." No new meeting dates were set.

Some looked to Kuhn's office at 75 Rockefeller Plaza for guidance; none was forthcoming. Unlike in the past, when Kuhn seemed eager to enter the fray, he had no plans to get involved this time around, except to reiterate through the press his support for direct compensation. Miller had to laugh. Kuhn on the owners' side? That was "as newsworthy as if President Reagan were to announce that he favors Republican Party politics" or "[Israeli prime minister] Begin were to state that he sided firmly with the Israelis." This kind of biting sarcasm drove the owners nutty. They weren't used to being ridiculed.

For now the talks were background noise compared to the deafening roar that was building around Valenzuela. Houston had a second chance against the rookie, this time at the Astrodome, and though ex-Dodger Sutton pitched well, he was no match for Valenzuela, an army of one, pitching a shutout, again, displaying fine fielding and nearly picking off an Astro who'd wandered off first base. He even drove in the only run with a fifth-inning single to left.

Like a Broadway hit, Valenzuela had taken his show on the road and received glowing reviews. He hadn't been in Los Angeles since the opener, and he returned on April 27 as a full-blown phenomenon. The game, versus the Giants, had been sold out for a full week before, and for the first time since the Dodgers came from Brooklyn, there would be a huge Latino turnout.

When the Dodgers arrived after the 1957 season had ended, a war broke out between Walter O'Malley's team and the residents of Chavez Ravine, an enclave of Mexican Americans living where O'Malley wanted to build a new stadium. Adding to the Dodgers owner's sinister reputation for taking "Dem Bums" out of Brooklyn was the destruction of another community in the interests of greed.

The reality was different. The city had, long before a Dodgers relocation was a possibility, purchased nearly all the homes and begun dismantling the neighborhood in preparation for a housing project that never came to be. By 1957, only 20 families still lived there. But when the morning of May 8, 1959, came, and the sheriff's deputies, in front of rolling TV news cameras, went door-to-door, removing people from their homes, some meekly acquiescent, others violent in their revolt, it was painful and ugly to watch. Terrorized residents screamed and struggled in the arms of the law, who dragged them away and put their belongings into vans. When the people were cleared out, a waiting bulldozer demolished home after home as former inhabitants watched in horror. Some pitched tents and stayed the night, joined by many more huddled around a campfire.

As reports spread throughout Los Angeles, a great anger was stirred, especially among Latinos, who saw their brothers and sisters treated like dogs. The myth took hold that the Dodgers had done it, and from that day onward, anti-Dodgers sentiment was very real, the perception trumping the reality. Despite team outreach, it was a tough hurdle to leap. Valenzuela was blissfully unaware of this sad history.

The Los Angeles Dodgers had been on the prowl for a Mexican star to heal the rift between the team and the Latino community. The 1980 census counted over 2 million people in L.A. County of Spanish origin, the main source of immigration being the Mexican state of Sonora, but the Dodgers drew poorly among Hispanics. As Brito thought back in 1978, Valenzuela could be the answer: the Mexican Sandy Koufax.

While Valenzuela had his pregame nap, fans filed past hawkers selling Valenzuela merchandise and into the picturesque ballpark sculpted into the hillside, palm trees soaring above the wavy outfield pavilion roof, orange-and-blue Union 76 gas station signs throughout the inside. They were ready to see the Dodgers, off to their fastest start in 26 years, square off against the Giants. And they were screaming for Fernando. Valenzuela took it all in, gazing around the packed ballpark, impishly grinning as they yelled his name and waved banners. Then it was time for the youngest pitcher in the league, a kid tough beyond his years, to take the mound.

The Giants never had a chance. The Giants tried—a walk here, a few singles there—but after the third inning Valenzuela had shut them down. When he went out to hit in the bottom of the inning, the crowd leaped to their feet at the sight of his satin jacket with the long last name arching on the back. When he knocked a base hit, they went crazier still. Standing at first base, it took a few words from coach Manny Mota to get Valenzuela to tip his cap to his adoring admirers. It was hard for him to process how special he was to this crowd. He knew for sure when, back on the mound, a pretty girl wearing a 34 jersey, his number, ran out to the field and kissed him smack on the lips.

The game itself was anticlimactic to the lovefest. Valenzuela made the hitters look sick as they flailed at balls uncoiling out of the strike zone, far beyond their reach. In the Giants dugout, manager Robinson, if now impressed, was not amused. Back in his hometown, Robby was off to a rough start as manager. The team was sloppy, making mental mistakes that drove Robinson into fits. He wasn't above making his own. The following week, obsessing over his club's troubles, Robinson left a pouch containing his credit cards, 1979 Orioles World Series ring (he was a coach), and a number 20 ring (his uniform number) made of 16 diamonds in a New York taxi.

The Dodgers won 5–0, another shutout for their shimmering jewel. The missing *o* from Valenzuela's Fleer baseball card was needed on a scoreboard running out of zeros. His ERA dropped to 0.20, and in going 3 for 4 at the plate, Valenzuela raised his batting average to .438. It was all like a dream. Even Koufax was transported: "I wouldn't presume to give him advice. Anyway, what could I—what could anyone—tell him?"

Reggie Jackson wasn't telling anyone anything. He wasn't talking. In his first game of the season after returning from the torn calf suffered in spring training, he'd clouted a double to the base of the left-center wall in Texas. In his first at bat at Yankee Stadium he hit one out, but overall Jackson's first month was a washout. He'd kneel in the on-deck circle, watching Winfield at the plate, and couldn't help himself from thinking about how much more Winfield was making than him.

It took Winfield almost a month to get his first home run, after which he put a sign over his locker in the visitors' clubhouse at Tiger Stadium: PRESS CONFERENCE HERE AFTER GAME. He thought it was funny. At least Winfield was hitting .300. Reggie was at .250 and sinking fast, wearing the pain of failure on his face, in his demeanor and in his swing. Still, with one key hitter flailing and the other powerless, the Yankees held second place in the American League East.

The A's were out of this world, at 18–3 tops in baseball. Martin's perfectionism was motivating, his desire to win contagious, and these new A's played old and no one could stop them. Winning the division seemed a foregone conclusion, though fantastic starts didn't guarantee pennant finishes. But first there was the matter of the Yankees, who were riding into Oakland on May 1. During the Yankees series the A's were set to pass, after 11 home dates, their entire 1979 season attendance.

Martin's history with the Yankees was well known—scrappy infielder, World Series star, Casey Stengel's pet, banished after Martin got into a brawl at the Copacabana. As manager he was twice fired by Steinbrenner despite getting the team back to the World Series in 1976 and winning in 1977. Martin had his issues—temper, alcohol, ego—and they all clashed with Steinbrenner's. Theirs was a love/hate relationship that was not for the squeamish. Martin so loved the Yankees that he would stand being publically abused by a sadistic Steinbrenner to get, and then keep, the job as Yankee skipper. Back in Oakland, managing the best team in the game, Martin was having a ball and loving every moment.

Not that he was above holding a grudge, praising the new A's owners while slamming Steinbrenner. Martin also took shots at the Yankees' big prize: "He couldn't make our outfield. He's the softest hitter I ever saw for a guy who's six-six." Martin planned on bringing in his outfielders to play shallow when Winfield was up.

Winfield took it in stride. "I'm not a marshmallow salesman."

The A's jumped out fast, winning the first two games of the series. In the opener, Oscar Gamble put the Yankees ahead with a 2-run home run in the third, but it was all A's after that. In the seventh inning, ex-Yankee Cliff Johnson, who looked like a giant walrus in cleats, hit a towering drive over the center-field wall. Henderson's bottom-of-the-eighth triple, the prototypical display of his power and speed, drove in a run, and when Henderson scored, it was the cushion Oakland needed. The Yankees didn't go down easily. Gamble hit a 3-run home run in the top of the ninth, but that was as close as the Yankees came, losing 8–6. Proving Martin's point, Winfield was good for two harmless singles.

Guidry was roughed up in the second game. First, Armas took one out to give the A's the first run of the game, then, one inning later, light-hitting shortstop Rob Picciolo hit a homer to left, and Henderson, the next batter, popped out of his stance for another round-tripper.

Martin was having fun, but he, more than anyone else, knew about Yankee pride. In the first game of the Sunday doubleheader, Martin suspected Yankee starter Rudy May of throwing a spitball. He'd had enough of his own pitchers being maligned all year and had the umpires check the ball. Out of the dugout came Yankee manager Michael, trying his best to keep the umps away from May.

The 2–2 nail-biter headed into extra innings. In a flash, center fielder Jerry Mumphrey hit a tie-breaking home run to lead off the top of the tenth inning, and behind the tall, lean Ron Davis, the Yankees owlish-looking reliever with the oversize aviator glasses, who struck out all five batters he faced, the Yankees triumphed. The Yankees were shaken out of their stupor and won game two behind Tommy John's eight scoreless innings.

Though the series was split, it showed that the A's were for real and the Yankees were not to be counted out, not yet. But a crisis was brewing for the Bronx Bombers. Jackson had gone 0 for his last 12 at bats, and the streak continued into the second game of the next series against California in Anaheim. As designated hitter, Jackson took another collar, no hits and only two weak ground balls. He was now hitless in his last 20 at bats and his average was at a horrifying .177.

Spotting Michael in the hotel coffee shop, Jackson burst in.

"Am I in there tonight or am I just a half player?" Jackson yelled. Though a strained hip flexor muscle had hampered his mobility—and he wasn't a good outfielder to begin with—Jackson hated the one-dimensional role of DHing. Michael put him in right field the night of May 6, and Jackson responded with a double. But all was not well.

In any other year, the baseball world would have been focused on Tim Raines. A rookie over or around .400 for most of April with 16 stolen bases was rare indeed. Raines, with the body of a fire-plug—5'8", 160 lbs., and less than 8 percent body fat—was Valenzuela's physical polar opposite, but as to importance to their teams, they were equals. But 1981 was no normal year; it was "the Year of Fernando," and Raines, playing in Montreal, out of the public eye, took a far backseat in the media.

To baseball experts he was not second-class. The 1980 Minor League Player of the Year, in Denver, Raines was much in demand during the off-season. GM McHale was inundated with requests, 18 clubs in all offering whatever was needed to pry "Rock" from Montreal. The Cubs dangled Bruce Sutter with no success. When Ron LeFlore left via free agency, Raines was brought up without hesitation.

"This kid can do more than LeFlore," said churlish manager Dick Williams, who'd had his problems with LeFlore and had no problems knocking him in the press. His rookie outfielder "fields better, hits better, runs intelligently instead of just stealing, has good instincts, and gets to the park on time." The Expos, who had lost the National League East division on the final weekends of both 1979 and 1980, were looking to change their luck, and with Raines they felt their position was more solid.

Behind Raines the Expos found themselves atop their division as April came to a close. The massive crowds turning out despite the antiseptic concrete surroundings of Olympic Stadium were rabid. Who said baseball couldn't succeed in Canada? With a team like the Expos the people couldn't be kept away.

Catcher Gary Carter played with the exuberance of a child, always smiling (sometimes too much for his teammates; one of their nicknames for him was Teeths), always hustling, and enjoying life as a major league ballplayer. He loved to play. Hell, "the Kid" still collected baseball cards. Starters Rogers and Scott Sanderson were strong and solid, Bill "Spaceman" Lee was strong and strange (eccentric enough to be the subject of a song on the previous year's album *Bad Luck Streak in Dancing School* by Warren Zevon). They had talent up and down the roster, but at the heart and soul was Andre Dawson.

Dawson was a wonder; tall and lithe in the white home uniforms with red and blue shoulder stripes, he was the picture of a baseball player circa 1981. Strong, but not massive, sleekly athletic, not bulgingly muscled, tightly packed into double knits with a thin strip of sanitary sock connecting shoes to pants, not baggy pajama pants with cuffs tucked under cleats. Starting with his Rookie of the Year season of 1977, Dawson was *the* Expo, the graceful outfielder with power, who excelled though his knees were shot from playing on the unmerciful hard surface of the Olympic Stadium outfield. The pain was terrible, but he persevered, and when the Expos rewarded him with $1 million per year, no one had a problem with it. It was much deserved.

The first-place Dodgers rolled into town to face the first-place Expos. Twice as many people came to see Valenzuela in the third game of the series as had attended the day before. Montreal was as susceptible to his charms as every other city in the league that had fallen madly in love. The Dodgers jumped out ahead with a run in the first and Valenzuela held the Expos until the eighth inning. The Expos were so good they did something that no other team had done in the last 36 innings against Valenzuela—they scored a run. Shortstop Chris Speier singled to tie the game. The crowd and Youppi!, the Expos' orange, Muppety mascot with an ! on his back, temporarily went wild; the Dodgers won in extra innings. On the field, surrounded by cameras and lights, tipping his hat, Valenzuela overshadowed them all. Back in Los Angeles, the Montreal game drew a 59 percent share of the television audience.

"A nationwide baseball strike is imminent," read the players' association position paper. Haggling over financial data had taken center stage. Various owners had spoken publicly about how free agency was causing financial ruin and that direct compensation would be the cure. No one said it more clearly than Kuhn in his Dallas speech. Though the players didn't believe these poorhouse claims, there was a big difference between doubt and fact. They saw the hordes of fans every night, the merchandise being sold with their images, and the passionate love people had for their hometown team. If indeed the game was suffering, the players needed to see the numbers in black and white. If it was true, then they might alter their position to address concrete problems. The players didn't want to ruin baseball; they just wanted to be treated fairly in a game they were starring in.

The owners were playing something of a shell game, having their principals speak out on impending bankruptcy while having their authorized bargainer, Grebey, say nothing across the bargaining table. Having Grebey keep mum at the table led the owners to think they were walking on the right side of the legal line. If financial difficulties were not officially spoken of during bargaining, then financial data did not need to be legally provided. Miller was willing to put that to the test and, on May 7, a case was filed in New York with the National Labor Relations Board. Let the government decide the validity of the union's position that the owners were refusing to bargain in good faith by refusing to open their books. The ante was officially upped.

Across the bridge, or tunnel, in Queens, the Mets were engaged in their own battle, for last place. Thank heavens for the Cubs. The Mets may have only had 7 wins so far, but Chicago had 4. If not for them, Joe Torre's team would have sunk to the bottom. And now the Dodgers were headed to town, with Valenzuela slated to pitch the first game of the series.

To get fans to Shea Stadium, Mets management pushed the arrival of the amazing rookie on Friday night, May 8. It's not as if they had anything at home to promote, and the fans had stayed away so far. The Mets themselves were miffed. "I get a little tired when I look up at our own scoreboard and see constant plugs for a visiting team and a visiting pitcher," lamented Torre. All feelings aside, this was business, not personal, and the Mets set up additional ticket booths at the Roosevelt Avenue subway exits. The Mets, averaging a meager 11,358 in attendance, expected a box-office windfall. If the press interest was any indication, the crowd was going to be huge.

The day before the game, on the night of the NLRB filing, 100 reporters hustled into the Diamond Club at the Queens ballpark to meet the man of the hour, who'd been limousined up from Philadelphia. Even sports artist LeRoy Neiman, there to take photos, was in the packed room. With Jarrin acting as interpreter, Valenzuela faced the media. The New York press corps loved the story of this innocent boy, and he was still a boy, delivered by a midwife into a house of whitewashed adobe and a roof of mud and sticks, with windows cut out of the walls, paneless, and dirt floors, how he dreamed of a big league career from the moment he was noticed at 12, his parents' tearful good-bye as he boarded the bus to a new life of horrendously long bus trips and awful hotel rooms.

They were charmed by his quietness, his fondness for movies, cartoons, soap operas both American and Mexican, baseball clowns Max Patkin and the San Diego Chicken, and, as was plain to see, food and beer. They couldn't have made this guy up if they'd tried.

"I understand most of the questions. I understand more than people think," Valenzuela said. He'd been listening to cassettes to improve his weak English, but for now his interpreters were there to make sure he wasn't misunderstood.

Valenzuela's infectious enthusiasm countered the increasing strike talk he seemed oblivious of, not even knowing of the coming May 29 deadline, and reminded fans, and players, what they loved about the game. His teammates couldn't keep away from him, playing with him in the dugout, lovingly smacking him around. He had a fine sense of humor, playing along whenever Lasorda would translate his words, going on much too long about how Valenzuela "loves the Dodgers, loves Lasorda." Fernando would catch on, leaning forward and giving a sweet grin before laughing. He was in on the joke.

Friday evening was clear and cool at Shea, perfect weather for late deciders to head out to the game. Advance sales were at 17,000, ahead of the usual pace, but by game time almost 40,000 turned out. The registers rang even more than expected. Twice as many credentialed press as usual showed up to cover the event, Fernando taking a bite of the Big Apple. In Los Angeles, home to many a transplanted New Yorker, nearly half the city tuned in to watch on KTTV. In Etchohuaquila, crowded into their tiny living room, Valenzuela's family heard their baby pitch for the first time, listening to the broadcast on a radio/cassette player.

Lasorda closed the clubhouse door to give Valenzuela a break from the demanding horde, but there was no need; he was ready. In the first inning, the Dodgers scratched out a run on an error and a single by Dusty Baker. The public address system blared "La Bamba" as Valenzuela took the mound. It was an easy song to program, a classic Hispanic raver, generating a quick laugh that teetered on stereotype. Mexican American and Spanish-speaking reporters were outraged at the tone in the coverage of Valenzuela, almost always carrying with it a dollop of caricature and worse. Some called him Pauncho, some gibed he'd overdose on burritos. There were the *Olés*, the taco jokes, the brief excursions into Spanish by announcers and reporters who, perhaps subconsciously, saw in Valenzuela a cartoon, Speedy Gonzales come to life. In the *LA Herald Examiner* contest to give him a nickname, the winner was El Toro (though that was already listed in the press guide). Some others: Senor Silent, El Nevera (the icebox, because of his build), Tortilla Fats, and Guacamole Grande. Very nice.

Valenzuela wasn't on his A game, giving up a single and two walks in the Mets' half of the first, but he squeaked out of the bases-loaded jam without a score when he induced Kingman to hit into a 5-4-3 double play. Valenzuela didn't have to be in top form. These were the Mets. Valenzuela walked slowly off the mound with a shrug and a smile.

For eight innings the Dodgers were held to a sole run, but the Mets were held to zero. Valenzuela scattered 7 hits and walked 5, but, after early struggles, gained power, whiffing 10, including Kingman three times (not an unusual day at work for "Kong"). Laboring into the bottom of the ninth, holding on to the slimmest of leads, Valenzuela went to the mound to finish what he'd started. Back home, his father, Avelino, listened nervously, sweating, as his son neared another complete game. After notching two quick outs, the game came down to Lee Mazzilli, the Mets pinup boy, the "Italian Stallion," who looked like an older version of Scott Baio. But 1981 provided few happy days for the Mets, and, on Valenzuela's 137th pitch, the most of his career, Maz popped to Steve Garvey at first base, who drifted into foul territory for the final out. There were claps and hugs all around for Valenzuela's seventh win of the year. Since Opening Day, now seemingly so long ago, Valenzuela was 7–0 with a 0.29 ERA, with 61 strikeouts and 16 walks in 63 innings of work, on his way to the cover of *Sports Illustrated*.

The owners hoped to shut down dissension as well as Valenzuela shut down National League hitters. They'd created a five-man disciplinary committee to establish a code of behavior for management, to ensure that their own side said nothing to the press that would undermine the story line that the players were greedy and selfish, putting their own interests before the health of the game itself. If anyone broke the gag order, fines of up to $500,000 could be levied. For the public, the committee didn't even exist until Harry Dalton, the Brewers general manager, spoke out. For his trouble Dalton was fined $50,000 for violating the self-imposed management gag order. After Dalton's indiscretion, Kuhn would not even confirm whether he was involved. When word leaked, Grebey dismissed all questions on the matter as an internal issue.

What horrible thing did Dalton dare say? "I hope management is really looking for a compromise and not a victory, but I'm not certain that's the case." Further, he prayed this wasn't a macho test, and that, from what he'd heard in front of and behind the scenes, and what he'd seen firsthand in dealing with Boone and Bando, the players were genuinely reasonable, looking for compromise and room to settle the issues. That was enough to have a sizable cash hammer fall heavy on his head. Perhaps it was because Dalton had sat for nine months on the joint study committee that his words stung the most. It made his remarks more pointed, more significant. He wasn't an outsider looking in. His statement was clearly dead on the mark. Punishment was in order.

Miller laughed at the owners' attack on Dalton. Often the owners would demand that the players vote on strike issues with a secret vote rather than a show of hands. They had no idea that the players' association had, at no time, dictated how the ballot process should be conducted, and further, Miller was rarely present during the votes. Even during discussion, Miller often left the room as the players discussed issues. Still, ownership was convinced that Miller despotically ruled, and that the players, without peer pressure, would show themselves to be lacking in unity, and left to their own thoughts, they'd see the merit of the owners' case. There was a whiff of hypocrisy from the "free speech" advocates. "They're the ones who are going to give us a lesson in democracy, but they suspended the Constitution," Miller said, pointing out the obvious double standard.

Owner/owner discord was every bit as problematic as owner/player strife. When Edward Bennett Williams proclaimed that he could not believe that a settlement was beyond being worked out, no fine was levied. Williams, a high-powered Washington trial lawyer, was not used to toeing anyone's company line. As owner of the Washington Redskins he had experienced firsthand a different and better way to strengthen league finances, but when Williams suggested revenue sharing like in the NFL, other owners screamed, "Communism!"

Williams spoke in support of extensive revenue sharing, an equal sharing of nascent cable TV fees and new local television and radio monies, as well as a new, and more even, split of gate receipts. As to the realities of present-day finances, Williams was sure that

the unwillingness of team owners to open their books to the players' association was simply a matter of protecting the wealthiest
owners.

Williams was right. The Expos were getting $6 million from lo-
cal cable, the Yankees and Phillies $4 million each. The Brewers and
the Mariners were close to $1 million, and the defending American
League champion Royals received a mere $500,000. The gap be-
tween rich and poor was fully expected to widen; only 15 million of
56 million homes were wired for cable. Nobody was listening and
Williams wasn't used to being ignored, but, as one of the newer
club owners, he'd have to get used to it. Or fight.

Continuing to speak out, Williams saw no point in provoking a
strike over such a minor issue. Not that the players shouldn't strike
over it, but that the owners shouldn't insist upon it. In daily calls and
typed messages, he begged Kuhn to find a solution. "Your strategy
stinks!" he wrote to the PRC and Kuhn. "Get a new crowd and do it
over?" he both questioned and demanded. In a 14-point laundry list
of questions and solid points, Williams tore apart the assumptions of
the owners and excoriated them for lack of foresight and planning,
for misreading the players and an inability to come up with a way to
settle matters. "Grebey's on an ego trip," he added. "Let some owners
sit down with Miller and his players and work it out."

Williams was doing just that. Two Orioles, Mark Belanger, as
AL pension rep, and Doug DeCinces, as AL rep, served on the four-
man players' bargaining committee. Williams had an in on how the
players were receiving the messages from the owners' side and got
clear information from his players, who had no reason to bullshit
him. Belanger and DeCinces respected Williams as the team owner.
That opinion wasn't shared by his colleagues. Grebey hated him,
and members of the PRC, knowing full well that he was conducting
ongoing negotiations with some players one-on-one, were furious.

He wasn't acting alone. Texas Rangers owner Eddie Chiles was
taking action too. A conservative political icon, Chiles, 70, was
chairman of Western Co., the largest oil-well-servicing company in

North America. Like Williams, Chiles was not used to sitting down and shutting up, especially when he saw a mess. Speaking out on a Dallas sports-radio show a few days before Dalton's fine was levied, Chiles said nearly the same words as the Brewers GM: "I'll do anything to avoid a strike. We have a worse problem with some of our owners than we do with Marvin Miller." Asked whether compensation was necessary, Chiles replied bluntly, "I don't think it is."

The PRC had no love for Chiles either. He was seen as "a buffoon," and they had a joke about Williams and Chiles—"Let's see what 'the loose cannons' have been saying." But these were still owners, and different rules applied. For "help" such as Dalton, the fine dropped a heavy curtain down on any management comments. No one was comfortable speaking out who wasn't an owner, and no owner was on the negotiating team. The fine of Dalton gave management a black eye, but some sensed that the wrath of Kuhn, working behind the scenes, was not to be incurred.

Miller ran things differently. His experience led players where they needed to go, though the players spoke for themselves. Miller always saw the big picture and could hone the arguments into clear points. On their own, the players would discuss for an hour or so, then Miller would come back in and listen. He could summarize the previous hour-long talk in seconds. "This is what I'm hearing," he'd state by way of confirmation, and everyone would nod in agreement.

Players were a team, they were *trained* to behave as a team. The owners were different, 26 organizations with 26 different agendas. Williams and Chiles were only part of the problem. The interests of Kansas City were very different from those of New York. It was why you couldn't bring owners in to negotiate.

Their behavior was another reason. No owner was more erratic than Ted Turner. His pronouncements were strange, immediately contradicted by his own actions, and entertaining enough to eat popcorn by. If the strike came to pass, Turner swore he'd bring up minor leaguers or even Little Leaguers to play in Atlanta. Speaking for, as he saw it, the little people, Turner complained, "Now that our new government is going to take away our food stamps and make us go back to work, people don't want to hear this stuff anymore." *Our* food stamps? No one thought Turner was in such dire straits.

Some owners were looking for a way out, an exit complete with huge payday. Carpenter, whose family had bought the Phillies in 1943 for $400,000, announced they were looking to sell—and expected $30–$40 million, a huge amount, despite Carpenter lamenting the spiraling costs of the game (at the same time, signing Matthews to a reported $700,000-per-year upon acquiring the outfielder from the Braves after his mediocre 1980 season) and expressing his horror at the state of the game. (Said the Phillies' Boone, member of the players' Executive Board as National League rep, "It's an odd way to sell a club, to tell prospective owners it's not financially feasible to own one.") Carpenter's colleagues bemoaned the potential loss of one of their own, one of the old school.

Like the season itself, the business of the game was starting to heat up. Grebey, announcing that nothing had been accomplished at the bargaining table, began looking at how the clubs would cover their losses when a strike hit. There was the $11 million financial assistance fund cobbled together through team contributions (to be distributed by the Mutual Assistance Committee) that would last through the first 12–14 games of a stoppage. Then came the big payout, the one that owners had paid a $2 million premium for—$50 million in strike insurance. You could almost hear the owners smack their lips in anticipation. With interest on the financial assistance fund (the prime rate had been between 17 and 21 percent since mid-December 1980), the grand total of the war chest approached $70 million. If the players went on strike, the owners would still have a huge payday.

The players had no money on reserve and were getting angrier. Rogers, from inside the negotiations as National League pension representative, was increasingly ticked off. "We know the real intent of the owners is not to gain compensation for a team that loses a free agent. They couldn't care less about strengthening that team."

True enough: When did major league teams seek to enhance the skills of a rival club? "They want to punish the team that signs the free agent."

The growing feeling was that the owners were ill informed and it was Grebey's doing. No owners were involved in the negotiating. In the real labor world, the head of a corporation didn't sit down to hash out the details of a contract with the rank and file; in baseball it seemed logical. After all, if the players were there, why weren't the owners, rather than their chosen negotiators? Worse yet, Grebey was telling owners either the players wouldn't strike or, if they did, it would be over in days. This reinforced the belief that the players weren't committed. They were.

An anonymous Kansas City Royal summed it up best: "Salaries are up, attendance is up, everything is going so good. It's just not worth it." The owners hoped that most players felt that way. They didn't, and as both sides awaited the NLRB's decision, nerves were tightening.

The cover of the tradition-leaning *The Sporting News* put the off-field actors on the field. With Miller's face on first base, Kuhn's on second, and Grebey's on third, the intertwining of negotiations and play were made clear. At home plate was a sad vision of a baseball cleaved in two by an ax. "Will They Kill Baseball . . . Or Save It?" asked *TSN*.

The inside analysis was fascinating, at times undeniably true (Kuhn was "sitting on his duff," destructively inactive)—at other times so pro-management as to be silly. Citing Miller's proposals on compensation, the paper deemed them "ludicrous," with no chance of serious discussion. Now whose fault was that? Each union effort was rebuffed.

The Sporting News saw the truth, pointing out that Grebey was not "remotely interested in achieving a settlement," and while the players' unity was questioned, a stubbornly common misjudgment, the owners' need to enforce cohesion through fines was mocked. Fans were urged to write the three principals.

As the strike date drew near, a general accounting took place.

The players stood to lose approximately $600,000 each day in salaries. The owners predicted that a few days of lost pay would cause the players to scurry back. Miller, who vowed to refuse his own $160,000 salary in a strike, pointed out that if the players lost all their salary for the final two-thirds of the season, they'd still make more from the first third of the year (an average of $56,600) than they averaged for the entire 1976 season ($51,501). The owners may have had no better example of skyrocketing pay.

Kuhn was busy defending himself, at least to *The Sporting News*. In response to their recent criticism, Kuhn penned a letter to the editor, published, with stunning lack of respect, next to last. That's how seriously *TSN* took a comment from the commissioner.

As if by rote, Kuhn reiterated that he supported the owners' compensation plan, not because he was pro-owner, but because it was fair. He'd proven himself, in his own estimation, as equally pro-player. Hadn't he forced the owners to open spring-training camps in 1976 after they locked out the players? Hadn't he pushed for a settlement in 1980?

Huffily, Kuhn did his own cover of Johnny Paycheck's 1977 hit, "Take This Job and Shove It," recently released in movie form. "Though I am honored to have been Commissioner the past 13 years, I have never needed the job; I could, I believe, do better financially elsewhere, and would quit in a minute if any general effort were made to restrict my independence of action." Which begged the question—what action?

Action from the outside, by the NLRB, was the only hope that a strike would be postponed. If the players won, assuming no appeal, then the strike would be delayed until 1982. Miller had no doubt the players would prevail. The owners had made no new proposals and the players were under no obligation to make any further suggestions, especially since the owners had declared that the players' ideas were an affront to their dignity.

The union's plea to the NLRB: the owners are not bargaining in good faith, and if they're claiming financial need, then they should prove it. Though the owners had their insurance lined up, if the

NLRB ruled for the players and decided the owners had induced the strike, that money was in jeopardy. That would send thunderbolts through their ranks. Without coverage the owners were looking at daily ticket-revenue losses of $1.25 million, depending on the team.

But if the owners won, they'd be flush when the strike hit. Then the insurance money would be parceled out. It was a win-win situation for them. Either they won in the negotiating room or they won at the insurance payout. Said Hal Middlesworth, the spokesman for the PRC, the owners never claimed an "inability to pay," though Miller reminded all listening that the commissioner and a vast array of owners had consistently spoken of their losses.

The fans, though worried, weren't staying home. They wanted baseball as long as it was still available. A strike seemed far off in the distance, the fans pacifying themselves with the belief that the two sides would come to their senses and settle. There was no way the season would come to a sudden halt, was there?

Through May 14, American League turnstiles had spun 520,943 times more than at the similar juncture in 1980. Martin's A's alone accounted for 341,682 of the increase. The National League was up a comparably meager 53,915, the Expos bringing in 131,016 of that. There was other good news: the New York cabbie returned Frank Robinson's credit cards and rings.

By mid-May, eight games into his rookie season, Major League Baseball was running 30-second TV spots of Valenzuela marching to the mound, Valenzuela scraping his cleats on the mound, Valenzuela throwing a strike as the sound track of deafening *Olé!*'s crescendoed into a bleat of trumpets. "Baseball Fever" had been caught, and the Dodger Stadium video screen mirrored the commercial, first a shot of the mound and shoes, then a pulling back to show the legs and bulk of Valenzuela. The fans watched the monitor and the man himself, erupting into *Olé!*'s of their own.

The Expos were hurting when they arrived in Los Angeles for three midweek games against the first-place Dodgers. Outfielder Ellis Valentine had pulled a hamstring, third baseman Larry Parrish had a sore wrist, infielder Jerry Manuel needed knee surgery, but worst of all was Raines's jammed pinkie. The loss or hobbling of the others could be dealt with. Not having full use of Raines was different. Still, the Expos were hanging tough in third place, a half game behind the lead. After two quick losses, they were further behind and facing Valenzuela.

It had been over two weeks since his last home appearance, and no one wanted to miss Valenzuela's return. The May 14 crowd of 53,906 pushed through vendors selling records ("The Saga of Fernando"), T-shirts, and toy bulls. Inside fans waved multicolored VIVA VALENZUELA banners and GO FERNIE signs.

Speier, who'd knotted up the game Valenzuela pitched in Montreal, was undistracted by the mass rally and put the Expos ahead with a third-inning home run. The Dodgers scored twice in the bottom half of the sixth to forge ahead. With Valenzuela hunkering down, the score stood at 2–1 entering the ninth. All looked good.

The first two batters, Jerry White and Rodney Scott, went down easily, the former on a ground ball, the latter on a fly out. One out to go for win number eight, but it was a tough out, the toughest in the Montreal lineup—Andre Dawson. He took his position on the right side of the plate, tapped the ground with his bat, then cocked it at a 45-degree angle toward Valenzuela and, after a few slow windmills, went perfectly still, arms away from his body, right elbow pointed straight back.

Dusty Baker saw Dawson's slight step forward and whipping of the bat and watched as a rocket skied high above him in left field. It tied the game, and after Carter flew out into Baker's glove, it was the Dodgers' turn to hit.

It was easy to see the magic in Valenzuela. Each game was a feat, another chapter in the adventure, but when Pedro Guerrero (known as an Anglicized "Pete") drilled reliever Steve Ratzer's pitch 370 feet away over a forlorn White in left center, it was pure fairy tale. From the booth, Vin Scully was exultant and, in a rare moment, personal. "It's gone, Fernando, it's gone," he proclaimed, happy to see Valenzuela win as much as any fan. Could it go on forever, asked Jarrin?

"Es muy difícil pero no imposible," said Valenzuela.

Difficult but not impossible? The optimism of youth.

The pressure of media attention and fame was growing. It was getting harder for Valenzuela to go out in public. Appearing at a clinic at Terrace Park in East LA, an event that would normally bring out 300 fans, 3,000 turned out for an up-close glimpse at their new hero. Valenzuela, arriving in a sheriff's van, made it, with protection, through the crowd and to the podium, where he was handed roses. Valenzuela, normally shy, was shocked at the outpouring of love.

Keeping calm and safe during the clinic was a challenge. When it was over, he couldn't see a way out, and as the crowd began grabbing at him, Valenzuela grew scared and ended up finding refuge in the ladies' room. There he was found and escorted safely out by the police. Fame had its dark side. John Lennon had found that out in December, Ronald Reagan in March. The day before the Montreal game, Pope John Paul II had been shot. It would be nice if the focus could be elsewhere for a little while.

Twenty-four hours after Valenzuela's dramatic victory, for one day the pitching hero of 1981 was in Cleveland, not Southern California.

It wasn't easy to be Cleveland in 1981. Unemployment was high, factories were closing, and there'd been a mass exodus out of the city. As if those troubles weren't enough, ever since the Cuyahoga River had burst into flames in 1969, Cleveland had been a national punch line.

The Indians hadn't been good in quite a while. That 1966 team that got off to the same 11–0 start that the A's tied earlier in the year? They ended up going 81–81, a .500 club smack-dab in the middle of the American League pack. There'd been few highlights since, but on Friday night, May 15, with mist blowing in from Lake Erie and temperatures struggling to hit the high 40s, everything was perfect.

Watching Len Barker warm up in the bull pen before the game, pitching coach Dave Duncan knew that something special was afoot. Barker's curveball had such a tight rotation and sharp break that it was nearly impossible to follow. Each curve zoomed in like a fastball, at 85 miles per hour, and broke so late that it vanished into the fog and rain. The few thousand fans that were filtering in to watch Barker face the Blue Jays that night were in for a treat.

Only Duncan knew Barker was totally in control. That was not always the case for "Large Lenny." In his younger days, as a flame-throwing prospect for the Texas Rangers, Barker was wild on, and off, the field. As a prospect, he once threw a pitch that soared over the backstop and hit a tower in the center of four connected diamonds at the Rangers' minor league facility. He also tossed a pitch into the press box in Sacramento.

Luckily for Barker, his first year in Cleveland was also Duncan's first as pitching coach. A weak-hitting catcher during his 11-year big league career, Duncan was a shrewd student of the game, and he saw in Len Barker a worthy project. Under Duncan's tutelage, Barker refined his changeup, and his newfound consistent control of his curve made all the difference.

Barker's beer drinking was also curtailed. In switching from beer to iced tea, Barker shed pounds and got down to a trim 215. His concentration noticeably improved. No longer did he stop what he was doing to stare at airplanes as they flew overhead, a formerly sure sign that he was finished for the night. No longer was he likely to heave a fastball halfway up the screen as he'd done at Fenway Park.

The payoff began in 1980, when Barker won 19 games and won the AL strikeout title. For 1981, the 25-year-old Barker's goal was to get to 20 victories and avoid late-season fatigue. He gave up pitching winter ball for workouts on a Nautilus machine and entered the year with good velocity, breaking pitches he could pinpoint for strikes, and a much-improved changeup. His right elbow pained him and swelled up due to a bone spur, but it never hurt during games, just before and after. As long as he stayed strong and healthy, there was no stopping him. Barker was on fire. A shutout against the Royals, a complete-game win against the White Sox, and an eight-inning no decision against the Twins. The Blue Jays, who had a hard enough time hitting the worst, were getting ready to face one of the best.

Leading off for the Jays was Alfredo Griffin, a former Rookie of the Year. Barker quickly got Griffin tied up, and the Jays shortstop hit a slow roller over the mound. Indians shortstop Tom Veryzer charged in, scooped up the dribbler, and barely nabbed Griffin at first. A solid play, sure, but one that would loom large as the game progressed.

Barker felt good after the opening frame, three up, three down, and watched from the bench as the Indians put up two runs in the bottom of the first. It was all he needed. Inning after inning, Barker delivered. His 91 mph fastball was sinking, and his curveball was breaking so sharply that Blue Jays hitters thought it was a slider. Barker's slow delivery and high leg kick, so high that his bushy mustache was blocked from the batter's view by his left knee, normally gave base runners a license to steal. On this night, Barker solved that problem by not letting anyone get on.

By the time Willie Upshaw, the Jays designated hitter, came up to bat in the fifth, 13 Jays had faced Barker. All had been retired. It was way too early to think no-hitter, certainly too early to think perfect game. A perfect game hadn't been thrown in over a decade, since "Catfish" Hunter threw a gem against the Minnesota Twins in 1968, thirteen years almost to the day. But funny things start to happen on the field that turn a fan's, and player's, thoughts to the idea that history is in the making.

Toby Harrah was already feeling it at third. When he saw Upshaw's pop fly head his way and drift toward the stands, he was determined to catch it; every out mattered. Streaking over to the railing, eyes heavenward tracking the high pop, Harrah dove into the stands, fully extended two rows deep into the box seats adjacent to the Jays dugout, spearing the ball and springing back onto his feet, his cap falling off after brushing against a fan to reveal his balding pate. The 7,290 fans scattered throughout the 78,000 seats of Municipal Stadium went wild.

It helped to have one of the finest fielders in the league at second base. In the sixth inning, Duane Kuiper sprinted toward the hole to backhand a grounder. In the seventh, Kuiper went the other way, going four strides to his left to nab another grounder. Both runners were out by a half step, and now things got real. No one had gotten on base.

In center field, Gold Glover Rick Manning started thinking about it. On the bench, manager Dave Garcia's heart began pumping. In the stands, Bonnie Barker, normally superstitious, was overcome by nerves. Len's brother Chuck, never a baseball fan, was oblivious to what was unfolding on the field.

John Mayberry struck out in the Blue Jays eighth. Upshaw grounded out. Damaso Garcia struck out. Twenty-four men had come up, 24 men had gone down. The Indians scored their third run on a leadoff homer by Jorge Orta in the bottom of the inning, but no one cared. They were waiting for the ninth.

So was Barker. He was well aware of what was going on, what was at stake. Baseball tradition has it that no one dare speak of a perfect game or no-hitter as it's happening for fear of an all-powerful jinx. Most of his teammates kept their distance, except for Harrah and Manning, and Manning was either unaware or so excited that he threw tradition to the wind.

"Go get it," he told his pitcher before he headed back out. "C'mon, go get 'em. You can do it."

Easier said than done. Slowly, hiking his pants, and nearly stumbling, Barker made his way to the mound. Once there, Barker was overcome. He felt his legs shaking. He heard the crowd chanting, "Lenn-nie! Lenn-nie!" Everyone in the big ballpark seemed to be behind home plate. The scoreboard flashed a trivia question: Which two teams have never been in a no-hitter? Answer: the most recent expansion teams, the Seattle Mariners and the very same Toronto Blue Jays that were up to bat. Barker's nerves got to him; he dropped the ball.

"Keep the ball down. Make sure. Make sure." Barker repeated those words to himself as he watched Rick Bosetti make his way to the plate. It was time to pitch.

When Barker uncorked, he knew he was in trouble. It was a curve, the same curve that had served him so well all night, but it didn't break down. It stayed high, right down the middle, the first bad pitch of a flawless night. Bosetti connected, but missed it, managing only to foul the ball back. It was a close call, and after Bosetti fouled to Harrah at third and Alvis Woods, pinch-hitting for Danny Ainge, struck out on three pitches, it all came down to one more batter.

Back in the Philadelphia suburb of Trevose, Barker's mother was listening on the radio. Or trying to. It was a long way to Cleveland and the signal was erratic, fading in and out during the game. In the ninth inning, with her son on the verge of making history, the game was replaced by static.

Picking from scraps, Blue Jays manager Bobby Mattick sent .198 hitter Ernie Whitt to pinch-hit. When Whitt lofted a lazy fly to center, Barker followed the ball intently, his head looking toward the sky, not a plane in sight. He knew it was headed to Manning, who caught everything hit his way. The crowd was in near hysterics. Manning wanted that last ball hit his way, and running in with his arms spread out, he watched the ball rise and descend, almost jumping up and down even before the ball landed safely in his mitt. Before long Manning was at the mound, joining his teammates in a mob around their pitcher, who had just completed only the 12th perfect game in major league history,* the first ever thrown in the near half century of baseball at Municipal Stadium.

Surrounded by press, employees, and police, a jacketed Barker tipped his cap to the delirious fans and faced the cameras. "Lucky I had everything going for me. That's the way it is. You have to have luck in this game. I had good control of everything. I was throwing mainly fastballs and curveballs, a lot of curveballs. After a while, they were swinging at everything." And so they did. Over his 103 pitches, Barker threw 74 strikes (though pitcher Wayne Garland,

---

* When the rules on what counted as a perfect game changed in 1991, requiring a minimum of nine innings pitched, Barker's game became the 10th in history.

one of the most infamous busts in the still-new history of free agent signings, told the press Barker threw 84), 60 curves, 41 fastballs, and 2 changeups. Not once did a batter go to a 3-ball count, and only 5 balls left the infield. Eleven hapless Blue Jays went down swinging, and of course, there was not a single walk.

Though it seemed the crowd would never let him leave, that they would cheer him forever, Barker finally exited to find a carpet of white towels laid down by the Indians equipment manager from the end of the dugout up the concrete runway to the locker room. Awaiting Barker were six beers forming a big 0 on his chair, three bottles of champagne on ice in his locker. Barker opened each one, took a quick slug, and passed it around.

The press swarmed around Mr. Perfect, including Blue Jays beat reporter Allison Gordon. Under club president Gabe Paul's strict order, women were not allowed in the clubhouse. Gordon had pleaded with the team vice president in charge of public relations, Bob DiBiasio, "Bobby, you can't keep me out tonight." DiBiasio led her in, at his peril. "It was the last bastion of male chauvinism in the league, and the roof did not cave in," said Gordon. (The next day, Paul angrily called DiBiasio to his office. To his credit, DiBiasio said the team needed to change their no-women policy. Paul replied, "Every time we pitch a perfect game, a woman can come in the clubhouse.")

Not until early morning did Barker return to his condominium. His neighbors had covered his garage door with congratulatory posters. After a little party with some of his teammates, Barker needed sleep, if only for an hour or so. The perfect game was big national news, and Bryant Gumbel wanted to talk with Barker on the *Today* show. Barker would need to drive to the Channel 3 studio in downtown Cleveland by 5:00 a.m. The Indians were going to send a limo at 4:30.

DiBiasio called Len, who told him that he didn't want to get up that early. He wasn't interested in having the spotlight, and after all, he had to report for a day game in hours. DiBiasio had the unenviable task of relaying the bad news to Gumbel.

"What kind of PR guy are you?" asked the incredulous Gumbel.

Barker took the phone off the hook, but he couldn't sleep. The night had been too thrilling, and he talked with Bonnie until 6:00 a.m. Finally he drifted off until seven, when it was time to wake up for another game. But it sure wasn't going to be a game like the one he just had. Few were.

By mid-May the A's were flailing, in the middle of an 8-game losing streak, their hot start a distant memory. When their woeful ways ended, the A's had gone from 17–1 to 25–16, but still held on to first over the surging White Sox and Fisk. Last year's champion Royals were dead in the water, mired in last with the league's worst win-loss record, terrible in the field, no power at the plate, last in runs scored, and George Brett on the bench after injuring his ankle on a slide into home against Texas.

Martin kept composed, for Billy Martin that is. He couldn't help the occasional jabbing of thumb and forefinger at umpires, in need every so often of restraint. Nothing out of the ordinary. He tried all he knew to maintain calm, taking players out for dinner and drinks, or, when in Boston, heading to St. Cecilia's for higher help. "Alexander the Great had a temper, but he kept his cool on the battlefield," the historically minded Martin said. "I do keep my cool on the battlefield. That's my strength. A temper is an asset. If you use it, then it doesn't use you. I'm *not* a short-fused person." Like Steinbrenner, Martin was unaware of irony.

He was totally alert to how his pitchers were given a hard time based on rumors of doctored baseballs. It was unjust, a joke. "We're going to put our uniforms in plastic bags and pick 'em up with pliers, untouched by human hands. They were going to send out police dogs to try to detect Vaseline."

Baseball's 162-game season has a way of knocking out the highs and the lows. A team as hot as the A's inevitably cools off. A team as crummy as the Royals eventually finds its footing. It happens all the time.

Fernandomania was still cresting like the waves at Redondo

Beach when the Phillies came to town on May 18. The groupie scene around him was growing. It wasn't uncommon to see young women waiting for him after a game. He was a big-time celebrity, entering the domain of Cheryl Tiegs and Erik Estrada, when he signed a poster deal for $50,000 over two years, not bad for a rookie making $42,000. Offers were pouring in from Coca-Cola and 7UP; the William Morris Agency called. The luxury life of a big leaguer was easy to get used to—the planes, the fancy hotels, the food. Oh, yes, the food. Strip steak was at the top of his list these days. He'd ring up room service for a meal as he watched cartoons. The *Pink Panther* was his favorite; it had no dialogue.

There was a lot of excited talk before the game. Rose had his picture taken with Valenzuela. "It's for my son," he made clear. Valenzuela's parents flew up to see win number nine. Expectations were high, but waves do crash. When Mike Schmidt homered in the first, his 12th, there was little cause for alarm. When the Dodgers found they couldn't touch Phillies starter Marty Bystrom, there was concern. When the Phils scored 3 in the top of the fourth inning, it was over. Valenzuela hadn't pitched badly, giving up only 3 hits in seven innings of work, but Philadelphia made the most of those hits and 2 walks to hand Valenzuela his first loss of the year.

His next start against the red-hot Reds, on an 8–1 tear, was worse. Wild on the mound with 6 walks, erratic in the field with 2 errors, the Riverfront Stadium crowd saw a Valenzuela no one had thus far seen. Calm, as usual, Valenzuela blew bubbles on the bench, but his had popped. The kid was human after all.

The Yankees were subhuman, at least if you listened to Steinbrenner after his team was crushed 12–5 by the Indians before a Yankee Stadium Jacket Day crowd of nearly 54,000 on the 24th. The night before, the Tribe had turned a quick triple play against the Yankees when, for the second and third outs, Nettles was forced at second *and* called for interference on a tough slide, resulting in the batter, Bucky Dent, being called out. Nettles went berserk. That's how things had been going lately.

"If they embarrass New York in Baltimore, there's going to be hell to pay," George said. He ripped into Guidry, who complained of a sore foot. To George it was all nonsense and whining, especially for a guy scheduled to become a free agent and wanting a million bucks. Rumor was that Gene Michael was on shaky ground.

There were reasons why the Yanks ended the night in third place at 23–16, behind Baltimore, winners of 20 of their last 27 games, and a surprising Cleveland club. Winfield had been in a yearlong power slump, with only 4 home runs. Jackson had one more, but was below .200 and miserable. "There are times when I'll play for peanuts," Jackson said in ads shilling Planters, but these were not those times, and mentally he was out of it, obsessed with his contract, distracted. "This isn't a slump. I'm scared to death," he said about his option-year performance.

Steinbrenner picked at Jackson's open sore, ratcheting up the Jackson-versus-Winfield game he was playing: "Dave Winfield has done all I could ask of him. Reggie has killed us." Laying it all on Jackson was cruel, but regardless, this high-paid team had better kick it into gear, and soon. It was almost Memorial Day.

Steinbrenner's rant backfired. The Yankees went to Baltimore and got obliterated. In a 3-game sweep, the bats of the O's were blazing, none more so than DeCinces's. The Oriole third baseman had had a tough April, spending most of the month mired in a slump. DeCinces was understandably preoccupied. The strain of the bargaining was difficult to get out of his mind when on the job. Guys would ask him for the skinny on what was happening at the table. Would they lose free agency? Were the owners for real? What was going on? He had to separate game time from the other times. He couldn't walk to the plate thinking about Grebey. Or maybe it was simply a matter of getting his chronic hurt back loose. After 2 home runs, his first and second of the year, and 4 RBIs against Detroit, he was feeling pretty good, unfortunately for New York. DeCinces had his stroke back, as did Eddie Murray, the offensive leader of the club, on the rebound after a weak April. The Yankees headed to Memorial Stadium to encounter huge crowds and a streaking flock of Orioles.

The Monday opener was over nearly before it began. The Yankees felt confident behind Guidry, but he was horrible. In the second inning, DeCinces came up and, with one long, slightly upward-sloping swing, plated 2 runs. When Belanger came up and knocked one out of the park deep to left field, it wasn't a case of his getting back to form and keeping labor thoughts off his mind. Belanger didn't hit, and he never hit home runs, not since 1977 anyway. The faithful went crazy, and the O's shortstop came out of the dugout to take a sheepish bow. DeCinces was not so shy when, after his second of the game, he emerged for a curtain call of his own.

Behind Jim Palmer, who'd been fighting arm trouble all year but managed to still pitch in between Jockey-underwear photo shoots, the Orioles romped 10–1 and won again the next night. In the final game of the series, DeCinces hit two home runs, again, and the Orioles beat Gossage in the bottom of the ninth to complete the 3-game trouncing. The next game DeCinces hit another round-tripper, his 7th home run and 15th RBI of the week. He was hitting as if something were gaining on him and maybe there was. Up in Rochester, third baseman Ripken was equally on fire.

A slight postponement of the strike deadline was agreed upon while the NLRB sought an injunction. In the interim, the parties met four times, with no progress. On Memorial Day, the 25th, there was nothing but shared pessimism, the only thing Grebey and Miller could agree upon.

The PRC made three proposals—a ranking free agent could negotiate with more than 13 clubs if selected by as many in a secret draft, an expanded number of statistical markers, and ranking free agents with 14 or more years in major league service would only cost an amateur draft choice. (The much-dismissed amateur draft choice had proven to be valuable for the Orioles; Ripken Jr. had been one.) Unchanged was the big item: the PRC still insisted that a signing club could only protect between 15 and 18 on their major league roster, the balance for the losing team to pick from, plus an amateur draft choice.

The owners sought to base free-agent compensation in part on the numbers of clubs that selected players behind closed doors. No club would be allowed to pass, ensuring that more clubs would draft. The result: a signing team would surely be penalized. It was a rigged game and, Miller made clear, not in the best interest of individual clubs. In fact, he said, this was not a club request but one straight from the PRC.

Grebey said it didn't come from him; it was, in fact, a players' request. The *players* were asking for a secret draft that would end up with more free-agent signings resulting in compensation? It was specifically what they were fighting against. Could it be so?

Not so, said Miller. In fact, the players announced that they did not want this and wanted it withdrawn. Did Grebey, upon hearing that the players wanted to pull an idea that he said was generated by them, let it go?

"We are not prepared to do that," said Grebey.

Moffett reported, after a 90-minute session on May 26, that productivity was at 1 on a scale of 1 to 10. After a seven-minute meeting the next day, they were below zero. "It's not two rams butting heads anymore. It's two rams standing off to the side making a plea to a rational third party. And I assume a federal judge would be rational," assessed Brewers catcher Simmons. With tensions mounting, there was a need for a laugh.

With the talk of a strike and NLRB hearings, and players, owners, and fans glumly facing the realization of a halted season, a burst of comedy blew in from the Northwest. The most memorable play of 1981 had its only showing in Seattle.

Lenny Randle had performed at Zanies, a local comedy club in Chicago, after his only season as a Cub, his three-week engagement peppered with what passed for baseball wit ("Why do you think they call Wrigley Field 'the Friendly Confines'? It's 'cause the ivy-covered walls are planted with weed!"). Granted free agency by the Cubs, Randle signed with the Mariners. In his ten years as a big leaguer, Randle had become a versatile player, and except for his belting his Texas Rangers manager, Frank Lucchesi, in the face in 1977, resulting in a broken cheekbone for the manager and a fine and suspension for the player, Randle was perceived as a pretty good guy to have around.

The Mariners hosted the Royals at the concrete mausoleum known as the Kingdome. The Royals were already up 7–4 in the top of the sixth when their center fielder, Amos Otis, stepped up to the plate with two out. Otis made feeble contact off a Larry Andersen slider, topping the ball slowly down the third-base line. Randle charged the ball and dropped down on all fours, following the roller like a crab as Andersen, standing in foul territory, watched the ball hang stubbornly in fair territory.

That was, until Randle started puffing away, finally edging the ball over the chalk line, where catcher Terry Bulling immediately snatched it before a breeze blew it back in the other direction. Home plate umpire Larry McCoy called the ball foul, and as the umpiring crew laughed, Royals manager Jim Frey ran out to argue.

"He can't do that!" yelled Frey, and he was right. A rule forbid a player from interfering with the course of the ball, though it didn't quite cover this situation.

"Fair ball," decided McCoy, blowing in the wind himself as he reversed his decision and awarded Otis first base.

Now Randle had a few words to say: "I didn't blow it. I yelled, 'Go foul, go foul.'"

McCoy's second try at the call was correct. Under rule 9:01c, each umpire had authority to rule on any point not specifically covered in these rules, and extreme exhaling was certainly not covered. After the game the American League office announced it was looking into the matter and might seek a rule change to clarify what was on the books.

For everyone who worried that the 1981 season might blow away, Lenny Randle provided the visuals.

The owners resented the players' seeking the help of the NLRB and were angry that the government would even consider taking up the cause of players making upward of $1 million per year. The Twins' Calvin Griffith was sure that government agencies were not there to protect "affluent artisans." They were there to protect the hourly-wage-earning working stiff. Back when the board was formed, people were making $14 a week, poor mugs, and needed help. In reality, the government was there to protect any group from the illegal and harmful practices of another. The dollars involved were irrelevant.

This Week in Baseball, the weekly highlight show brought to you by Major League Baseball Productions, presented management's case. After all, *TWIB* was a management tool. In a tweed jacket, striped shirt, and print tie, the salt-and-pepper-haired Grebey explained to the national audience that "all twenty-six clubs were satisfied with the compensation plan." Holding a pipe filled with Dunhill No. 1011 pipe mix in his right hand, the birdlike Grebey made it clear to the viewing audience where things stood: "We've left nothing on the table. There'll be no need for eleventh-hour dramatics." If alternatives were not accepted, Attachment IX was in full force and would remain so until the parties agreed to change it. There was no mention of the players' right to strike. The NLRB would undoubtedly be more thorough.

And they were: "The owners are the principals. Ray Grebey is their agent. When a principal makes a statement, it is questionable whether the agent can disavow it." NLRB general counsel William Luebbers issued an unfair labor practice complaint against the owners and sought injunctive relief; the players had won, and Luebbers would now become the prosecutor on their behalf. Seen in black and white, it was an amazing charge that the owners had failed to bargain in good faith, insisting publicly that heavier compensation was "essential to the economic survival of many major league clubs, while adamantly refusing to produce financial data to support that claim." Kuhn's claim of losses, echoed by a multitude of owners, was too much to ignore.

Grebey was steaming. There is "no merit to the complaint." He protested that absolutely no basis existed for an injunction and that the players were undermining the collective bargaining process by seeking such relief. Miller had argued all along that the owners were subverting the process by stonewalling. "We are the innocent party," he told the press. "We did not violate the law. We should not wind up worse than the guilty party." Whether Miller's verdict was correct was still to be decided.

The role reversal was deliciously ironic. Now the players were seeking a way to delay the strike. If the injunction was granted, a one-year postponement of the owners' compensation plan and the players' ability to strike (until February 20–25, 1982, and June 1, 1982, respectively) would follow. The owners, by fighting the injunction, were pushing for a strike. Kuhn's thoughts on the matter were unknown; he felt it inappropriate to comment.

The owners were almost certainly better off with a silent commissioner. His speech in Dallas had formed the basis of the players' argument. The NLRB citied Kuhn's strong statements on baseball's financial difficulties, and though the owners officially claimed no one was crying poverty, Kuhn had put it on the table.

That the NLRB took the players' part was enough to make some owners desirous of a settlement. This was the ideal time to avoid a strike, they thought, before they'd be forced to open their books. Why not open the books? Why fight? Newer owners such as Williams and Reinsdorf had no problem with it; from their point of view, there wasn't much money in the game. And, in reality, the books could be made to show anything. Even if opened, what did they, what could they, really mean?

This was a turf war. The older owners, still thinking—or hoping—they could regain complete authority, did not believe that the peons had a right to look at their private finances. Who were *the players* after all? According to one PRC member, players took rules and orders from their bosses. So what if labor law made it clear that cries of hardship needed to be proven, not taken at face value? They were the owners, they said it, and that was that.

If the injunction the NLRB sought was granted, the owners would be forced into the dreadful position, to most, of providing their financial data. A player win would cause a postponement of the strike date. With the books in hand, the union would need time to study the numbers. A delay pleased some in the owners' camp who sought their own relief from the negotiating style of Grebey and the PRC.

"To use an Abbott and Costello line, 'Who's on first?'" clowned Judge Henry F. Werker, as he opened the NLRB hearing on the afternoon of May 28 in Room 312 in the US Court Building at Foley Square. Werker fancied himself a comedian, a judge who saw a spotlight was on and, with the show about to begin, was ready for his star turn. There were a few polite chuckles; no reason not to humor the judge.

NLRB regional director Daniel Silverman asked for a quick start, but Werker let everyone know he was skipping town, off to Rochester on Monday for two weeks of criminal casework. The news was not well received. The judge didn't understand the time pressure. The parties adjourned to the robing room to discuss.

"Do you have any objection to going to Rochester?" Werker challenged.

Silverman was taken aback. The unexpected change in location would make it hard to produce his witnesses, and many beat reporters were coming from all over the country. Now they'd be needed in an upstate courtroom. Louis Hoynes, National League attorney (Kuhn's old job) and lead lawyer for the PRC, explained the tight timetable the owners were on, that after June 1 their position began to deteriorate quickly. Waiting two weeks until Werker returned to New York City was not a pleasant option for either side.

"Listen, there are millions of hot dogs and millions of beers that depend on what I decide in this case, right?" Werker was ill informed, as became apparent as each side attempted to explain why a delay would cause trouble. It was finally agree to begin in Rochester on the following Wednesday, June 3.

Looking ahead, Fehr and Hoynes debated about when the players could call a strike if need be. Would it be 48 hours after the close of the hearing? Or 48 hours after his decision? Fehr pointed out that if it was two full days after the hearing closed, the judge might take longer to render his decision.

"I don't keep anybody guessing for very long, so you may get a decision right from the bench the day the clearing closes," Werker quickly countered. Deliberation was not his strong suit; he shot first. Back in open court it was announced that the players could strike 48 hours after the ruling.

When 45,000 swarmed into Dodger Stadium on a non-Valenzuela night the day after Werker set the hearing, it was impossible to believe the owners weren't raking in the dough. American League attendance was now up nearly 750,000, fans cramming into ballparks before the rug (real grass or AstroTurf) was pulled out from under them.

It was May 29, the original strike date, and thankfully, baseball was still on. The Mets, a dozen games out and spluttering, sent young reliever Jeff Reardon to the Expos for outfielder Ellis Valentine. A rising star until his jaw was fractured by an errant pitch the year before, Valentine was now fearful at the plate, wearing a half-football face mask attached to the right side of his batting helmet.

Still, the Mets needed something. If he was managing across town, Torre would no doubt have been fired by Steinbrenner by now. Instead, Mets owners gave him a vote of confidence, scoring points for kindness if not for winning.

Fortunately, Billy Martin didn't manage the Yankees either. The A's record-breaking start was receding further when they rolled in to Toronto. He'd tried his best to stay calm, but this wasn't sitting well with Martin. Yes, they were in first place in the AL West, but with the White Sox now 2 games behind and the Rangers only a half game behind Chicago, the standings had tightened uncomfortably.

Matt Keough, like all the A's pitchers that year, was under constant scrutiny. It was well known that Martin and Fowler had taught their young staff some extralegal pitches. Martin wasn't pleased with these slurs, his "Who, me?" false outrage getting more press. It was increasingly difficult to keep up the innocent front. Jim Essian, who caught A's pitchers in 1980, said that while Keough didn't load the ball, he was the only starter who didn't. They all had their preferred methods; Brian Kingman had a storehouse of Vaseline on his glove to dip into.

That night, home plate umpire Terry Cooney's ball-and-strike calling was getting on Martin's nerves, and when the Jays' catcher asked Cooney to check a Keough offering for foreign substances, Martin erupted. Cooney urged him to stop yelling from the bench if he wanted to stick around for the game.

Martin stopped his mouth from running long enough to get his legs to take over. Feeling baited by Cooney's calls, Martin charged out of the visitors' dugout full steam into the larger Cooney and got in one chest bump before turning to traditional dirt-kicking. Five times Billy tried to kick some Exhibition Stadium soil on Cooney's shoes. Five times he failed, his foot never making contact with the dirt. There had to be a more effective way. Realizing his hands were easier to control than his feet, Martin picked up some dirt and threw two handfuls of it at Cooney's back. The soiled ump had reached his limit. Martin was given the heave-ho. So much for his Alexander the Great–style temper control.

The next day, with Martin locked down in his hotel room, Lee MacPhail suspended him indefinitely, and though Martin could appeal, he refused. On the 31st, Martin flew into O'Hare, where he proclaimed he would file a civil suit. As if suspension weren't bad enough, Billy had just found out that his 79-year-old father, Alfred Manuel Martin, had passed away.

Each subsequent day brought another incident. On June 1, MacPhail altered the punishment to a $1,000 fine and a seven-day suspension, which Martin decided he would appeal, putting him back on the bench after three days, pending the hearing. He thought he had a good case. Cooney was uptight, having been lambasted by Steinbrenner all the way from Tampa over a recent Yankees loss. "Why wasn't George punished?" asked Billy. And the incident itself was a farce. "I was already thrown out of the game before I came out. I understand he was a football player and I only weigh 155 pounds, so what is he afraid of?"

On the 2nd, White Sox fans went into trash throwing overdrive, tossing biscuits, beer cups, and a once-bitten apple at Rickey Henderson. Being a left fielder was becoming quite dangerous, so dangerous that Kuhn urged clubs and players to press charges against abusive fans; he had something to say after all.

On the 3rd Cooney filed a common assault suit in Toronto. He first sought to have criminal assault charges pressed by the Toronto police, but they refused. Cooney found success at a local courthouse, finding a justice of the peace willing to issue a summons ordering Martin to provincial court on September 21, the next time the A's visited Toronto. If guilty, Martin could face a maximum of six months in jail and a $500 fine.

The umpires' union was ready to follow with a case of their own. It was a dream come true—Billy Martin takes on every umpire in baseball! Through his lawyer, Martin asked MacPhail to keep Cooney away from any American League West Division games. "How's he supposed to be unbiased?" mused Billy. MacPhail, though against Billy on the bump, was with Martin on the suit; it was regrettable and unnecessary.

On the 4th the Comiskey Park switchboard received a death threat for Mr. Martin. Billy wore a bulletproof vest that night, and though he promised he wouldn't risk it, he came out of the dugout several times. After the game, he held court in a Chicago hotel lobby. Beneath a black cowboy hat, legs crossed to reveal pointed boots with a crisscross design, Martin tried to put on his tough-guy face, but he looked haggard. The combination of events made Billy-watchers wonder if he would unravel, as he had so many times before.

Cooney's suit was the least important legal action of June 3. In Rochester, there would be three witnesses—Miller, Grebey, and Kuhn. Miller was first to testify. Press descended on the Post Office Building, where court was held. When reporters and cameramen saw a gray-haired man wearing black-framed glasses enter the building, they pounced.

"Are you going to the hearing?"

"Yes," he answered in the middle of a swarm of television cameras.

"Can we talk with you?"

"Sure, I'm going to see the judge before the hearing starts."

This was a scoop—Miller in a prehearing confab with Werker.

"Why?"

"To set up a golf game."

The scribes and mikemen exchanged puzzled looks. Miller golfing with the judge? It didn't make sense. And it shouldn't have. The faux Miller was Iggy St. George, a 60-year-old probation officer for Monroe County, in the courthouse to set up a tee time with Werker. The judge had mentioned to Iggy's brother, a federal marshal, that, while he was in Rochester, he'd be up for an occasional 18 holes. Good to know that the fate of the season was resting in the hands of a man more interested in his putting than his caseload. The cameras scurried away.

Inside the courtroom, Mary Schuette, attorney for the NLRB and the only woman appearing before the bench, began her direct examination of Miller. Some history was laid out before the matter at hand. Recounting the 1980 talks and settlement, and the obvious agreement on procedure rather than on compensation, Miller went into the press reports of owner claims of poverty resulting from free agency and the need for stricter compensation rules to stave off the outflow of cash. "The most important one of these" was Kuhn's speech of December 1980, which "predicted catastrophe." Hoynes objected to this "mischaracterization of the speech."

"Players [are asked to] give up a right they now have. In other words, it is a take-back issue of the most obvious sort," Miller testified. When asked by Schuette why the union didn't ask for financial material earlier, Miller explained the calendar. It wasn't until February 19 that the union knew the owners were implementing direct compensation and what terms they were implementing. That was a fact. There was no reason to ask earlier since it was true, though far-fetched, that the owners could have backed off completely.

Under Hoynes's cross-examination, the commissioner's speech and role was a main focus. Miller noted that in past labor negotiations Kuhn would call him to find out what players wanted, that he most certainly seemed like an active participant in negotiations.

Schuette pointed out to a doubting judge that a key issue under contention was whether Kuhn was involved in negotiations, whether the commissioner's office had agency status or not.

Werker got curt and nasty. "It is not relevant. I will not permit you to go forward with this." Miller was appalled at Werker's rudeness and especially bad treatment of Schuette, bordering on sexist.

Werker turned on Miller too. "Even though there is a large segment of the press here, Mr. Miller, you are talking to me. I am the fellow who ultimately has to decide this. Let's keep it on a professional level."

Miller saw the pot and it was calling him black. "I agree," he replied.

After several hours, a lunch recess was called.

In Grebey's affidavit, he reiterated that compensation "was not, and is not, financial or economic in nature" and "not directed at salaries but at a method of providing a more certain and less time consuming manpower replacement plan" for a losing club. Though he preferred otherwise, Grebey stated that "in principle, free agency had been accepted." He referred back to May 18, when the PRC Board of Directors met with the entire bargaining team. When told of the players' charges, the board voted to release a statement that "the Major League clubs have never stated or suggested that their financial status is at issue." It was provably false. "Clubs will suffer irreparable and substantial harm if the court grants the injunction sought by Regional Director Silverman," affirmed Grebey.

Grebey was called by Hoynes and made it clear from the start that only he and his bargaining unit were authorized to speak in regard to labor matters. Any outside chatter was not relevant and he paid it no mind, so much so that he wasn't even aware of Kuhn's speech until Miller told him about it at a meeting. It was so insignificant, this "state of the game" speech by the highest officeholder in the entire sport, that Grebey only read it once, and that was when he knew he was going to court.

Under cross-examination by Schuette, Grebey was pressed about direct compensation, and he conceded that, certainly, under the owners' compensation plan, a signing team would lose more than they had before. In discussing the present compensation of an amateur draft choice, seen over and over as insignificant, Grebey said, "The loss of a first-round draft choice represents some risk." What was not enough was now too much! Though Grebey had testified that the new plan would affect a few players, he admitted that when the union proposed a hard limit, he rejected it. "We are willing, if necessary, to incur a strike." Earlier, when it came to the players being put in a position to strike, Grebey, based on his years in the labor business, made it clear that "strikes are never inevitable. They are voluntary." So, with the only issue on the table that of free agent compensation, the owners' lead negotiator declared that the owners were willing to let a stoppage occur, voluntarily, no doubt.

Fehr got a chance to grill Grebey. Pointing out clubs are the parties to the agreement and that the PRC is merely an agent, Fehr asked whether it was true the union had never been told that the PRC and the clubs it spoke for had a differing point of view from management representatives on the issue.

"In those precise terms, that is true." The owners and the PRC were one and the same side. Fehr also noted that had the clubs not implemented their compensation plan, there would have been no basis for a strike. Grebey agreed to that as well.

Kuhn flew out of LaGuardia the night before, arriving around 8:00 p.m. and heading to his room at the Americana Hotel, across the street from the Post Office Building. Werker was headquartered there as well. The next morning, though he was scheduled to be the last on the stand, Kuhn arrived to watch the day's events unfold. Inside, the owners sat in a group, as did the lawyers. The commissioner sat alone, a visual reinforcement of Grebey's statements of Kuhn's nonrole in the negotiations.

It ate him up to have to hear he had no status, that he was irrelevant. In 1977, when Finley sued Kuhn, a US district court judge in Chicago ruled that Kuhn had any and all powers he chose to have, but now Grebey said that the commissioner was without any status whatsoever in the labor negotiations. Legally, he had to claim his nothingness, but he simultaneously needed everyone to know he spoke for the best interests of the game.

To quash these inner struggles and revise history, much preparation was needed. In a memo provided to him the day before he departed, "Potential Problem Areas on Cross-Examination," Kuhn was reminded that his own statements, made over many years, "might lend credence to the Association's claim that the Commissioner does in fact speak for Baseball management in labor relations." All of his grandiloquent pronouncements were set to bite him. He had to be ready to address the conversation from the '21' Club, either to rebut or explain, Miller's being told that management needed a "winner." Last, Kuhn had to prepare for questions about compensation's keeping a lid on salaries, and why baseball as an industry did not take internal measures to insure financial stability. And he'd no doubt have to explain, if possible, how in his December speech he waxed at length about the cost of free agents, the need for compensation, and the coming fiscal apocalypse and how what he really meant was that compensation was about leveling the playing field. It was a lot to take in, and Kuhn drew a little diagram to give himself a picture of his instructions and, perhaps, convince himself.

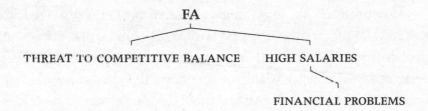

It also helped to have laid out his case in his affidavit. Of course he was aware that his speech had become an issue in the unfair labor practice charge, but he "did not intend to make either the connection or the claim that that Players Association contends." "A fair reading of my speech refutes" their argument. When he stated "a *companion problem* [Kuhn emphasis] brought about by free agency is the threat to competitive balance in baseball," it signified he had moved away from economic issues. Then he returned to his first topic and concluded his remarks on financial concerns. Clear enough?

Anyway it was no matter, those were his personal views. "I am not a spokesman for the PRC either publicly or in collective bargaining . . . [though] I try to remain informed and consider the merits of the positions of both sides."

After a few seconds of direct questioning from Hoynes, an introduction of sorts and enough time for Kuhn to state that compensation was a noneconomic policy that "in no way . . . would significantly impact" salaries, Schuette began her cross-examination.

No amount of notes and sketches could bring Kuhn to admit that he had no place in labor issues. Asked if he was made aware of management's proposals during negotiations, of course he was. "On one occasion you have been made aware of these proposals *prior* to the union having been made aware of them?" Of course he had. Schuette needed to make no further comment. Almost by definition that made him part of the team. Kuhn also admitted that he was often represented by management attorneys in various grievances, and in the biggest one of all, the Messersmith case, which decided for free agency and ended the bondage of the reserve clause, which made players property of one team as long as that team wanted them.

Honing in on the now-famous speech, Schuette dissected its contents, laying out that the first two pages of his Dallas statement were financial in nature, then on page four he referred to the reports on the financial health of the game that his office had requested. Was Kuhn really saying that "the single paragraph in the middle of page three has nothing whatsoever to do . . . with the financial problems of baseball?"

Well, Kuhn put forth, that speech "is not something intended to be a printed thing." If it were a book, he would've had "precise headings." This was a pretty weak showing.

Fehr's approach was a bit different than Schuette's. Terse, biting, and sarcastic, the contentious Fehr was brilliant, though dripping with the contempt that Miller and the players felt for Kuhn.

"What 'system' are you referring to in your speech," Fehr asked straight out, "that needs to be corrected to address the financial losses spreading? The free agent system?"

"Yes, but also individual negotiations," answered Kuhn.

"Free agency and salary arbitration are all collectively bargained. Individual contracts are within the framework of collective bargaining provisions," Fehr went on, trying to get Kuhn to admit the obvious, what he had already said in his speech—that free agency was causing a rise in salaries that was at the root of so-called financial problems.

After a frustrating series of questions and confusions, Kuhn said yes, that "unless the players begin to recognize that they are contributing to that escalation by the demands they are making," there'd be no solution. Demands are one thing, meeting them another, and only owners could meet them. They had the checkbooks.

At best obtuse, at worst tortuous, Kuhn tried desperately to walk the line that he had nothing to do with the owners and their negotiations while holding on to his time-honored belief that as commissioner he was powerful and spoke for the entire industry, owners and players alike. It had been a difficult afternoon.

The next morning at 10:00 a.m., both sides gathered for a shortened day. Miller was back on the stand to assert categorically that seeking this injunction, which would delay a strike to 1982, was not a ploy to avoid resolution.

"Demonstrably untrue," he stated. "We're only asking for the data and a thirty-day period to examine." This was the only relief the union sought.

Hoynes insisted that the only reason for the union to seek the injunction was to force owners to withdraw their position, the only thing they could do to avoid disclosing private information. There was no "inability to pay" when you had Wrigleys, Krocs, Carpenters, and Busches. Did these men seem to be in financial distress? These megawealthy men were simply showing an "unwillingness to pay, to refuse to be silly," not an inability, all evidence to the contrary.

Further, the clubs would suffer irreparable injury if the strike deadline or right to strike was moved back one year. They'd planned for a strike this year and conducted themselves accordingly. The insurance money and the $2 million premium paid would be lost with no assurance it could be obtained again.

Fehr tried, one last time, to clarify the issues, pointing out that the union was in a tough spot. Who were they to believe—Grebey, Kuhn, the owners? If Lee Iacocca, president of Chrysler Corporation, made public pleas on the demise of the car company, would it make sense that a Chrysler vice president in charge of labor relations could say, at the table, don't mind that guy, he's nothing? Of course not.

When it was all over, Miller said he wanted all the players to see the transcript. Hoynes objected, decrying the entire hearing as "a sham, a diversion." To Judge Werker the case was astonishing. He told the press it was "as extraordinary as throwing a manager out of a game." He certainly wasn't following the Billy Martin story. Werker, in every phrase and gesture during the previous two days, had acted as an unserious glory hound, ego driven and ill informed. That he'd turned down the three previous injunctions of the type that the NLRB had requested wasn't going to work in the union's favor.

After one and a half days in Rochester, negotiations continued on the 17th floor of the Doral Inn, the two sides in separate rooms. The players offered their pool proposal that a team losing a free agent would be entitled to an amateur draft choice or a selection from a pool created of major leaguers from all 26 teams' 40-man rosters. The players agreed on the concept of compensation, a huge move forward, and accepted that a team losing a player would need to fill that hole. It did not necessarily follow that the hole be filled by the signer. If the owners were truly sincere on helping the losing club, then a pool system worked just fine. The owners' direct compensation was a penalty, a tax, an additional cost to a signing team to give them second thoughts on whether pursuing a free agent was worthwhile.

Grebey sucked on his pipe and rolled his eyes.

The pool system, conceptually at odds with the owners' mind-set, was rejected by Grebey, after considerable study. Funny, that's how it worked when an expansion team entered the fold, but, of course, those teams were paying tens of millions in franchise fees. It was another nonmeeting, in the tradition of recent get-togethers. With nothing accomplished, Moffett thought the antagonists might meet again the following day. Or not. It didn't seem to matter much anymore.

Another player proposal, on defining what constituted a ranking free agent, a set of criteria that included selection by 10 or more teams in the reentry draft, at least 502 plate appearances in the previous season, and 502 averaged over the past three years, or, for pitchers, at least 162 innings pitched the previous year and averaged over three years, or 45 saves measured in the same way, was rebuffed.

"I guess we'll have to keep trying," said a frustrated Grebey. With the players seemingly the only side putting forth new ideas, who exactly was "we"?

In the NL East, "we" meant the Cardinals, Expos, and Phillies, all bunched at the top of the standings. The Expos swept the Cards at Olympic Stadium and, after a loss to Pittsburgh, came back to beat the Pirates behind Dawson's 12th home run of the year and Rogers's 6th victory against no defeats.

There was life at the bottom of the division too. The Mets were on a little hot streak, winning 8 of their last 13, capping with a 6–2 win over Philly. Phillies manager Dallas Green warned his team to stop thinking about the strike and start thinking about baseball.

Kingman was popping out enough gargantuan hits over the KINGMAN'S KORNER banner in left field to keep the apple rising from the Mets Magic hat past the outfield wall at Shea. The Queensmen may even have solved a franchise-long problem at third base. Rookie Hubie Brooks was making a splash, and with the call-up of Mookie Wilson, the future seemed a bit brighter.

Down two classes in the Carolina League, two Lynchburg Mets coaches came to blows over the number one overall draft choice of 1980. The languishing Mets were banking on a future around the skinny but powerful outfielder from Crenshaw High School in South Central Los Angeles. Now acclimated to Class A ball, the youngster was hitting well and feeling good. Coach Ivan Murrell, seeking to push the 19-year-old toward a more aggressive on-field demeanor, gave the fleet 6'6" prospect the green light to steal second, and then third, with the Mets up 9–3 in the fourth inning against Durham.

In the dressing room between innings, minor league instructor and former Mets great Cleon Jones, furious at Murrell, screamed at him for creating a situation where the franchise's best hope could get hurt unnecessarily. The two shouted and shoved until the manager broke it up. Coddle or push? What would be the future for Darryl Strawberry?

The present was looking better in the Bronx. As June began, the Yankees embarked on a 9-game winning streak, running through Cleveland, Baltimore, Chicago, and Kansas City. Winfield became the Winfield as advertised, hitting for average, driving in runs, hitting balls over the fence. "Winfield is the most valuable Yankee," a wistful Jackson remarked, remembering that not too long ago he was that man. Two 11-inning wins against the Orioles at Yankee Stadium, the second behind 8 innings of scoreless work by rookie Dave Righetti, brought the Yanks within a game of first.

Steinbrenner had wanted a phenom of his own to rival Valenzuela. The obvious choice was Dave Righetti, 22, a first-round draft choice of the Rangers in 1977 and the key to the trade after the 1978 season that sent Sparky Lyle to Texas. After going 5–0 in Columbus, "Rags" was called up on May 21 and hit the ground running, quickly getting two wins and tallying an impressive ERA of 1.17.

They needed him too. When the team took over first on June 6, Tommy John reached into his shaving kit, felt a pain, heard a rip, and pulled out his pitching hand, covered in blood. The cap had come off the razor, and his index finger was sliced. He was supposed to pitch that night against the White Sox. John relayed the bad news to his manager.

"Why didn't you tell me earlier?" Michael shouted. He was livid, annoyed at his pitcher and buckling under the increasing pressure from Steinbrenner, now calling the manager's office to give lineup suggestions Michael was expected to follow. It undermined his position with the team, especially the veterans, who assumed "Stick" could never be independent. Michael would cradle the phone, listening, frustrated that he wasn't allowed to do his job.

"I didn't cut it earlier. I cut it just now," John answered. There was no way to spread the news any quicker than he did. It was off to the disabled list, and John, wife Sally, and their kids headed to Indiana.

The Reds were surging even though Johnny Bench had gone down, fracturing his left ankle in a slide into second base against the Giants at the end of May. Four teammates and two trainers carried off their leader on a stretcher, Bench, arms across his chest, staring at the sky and seeing his hot start vanish. Still, Cincinnati charged up the standings, winning all but one of their June games. At day's end, June 9, the Reds had closed to $1\frac{1}{2}$ games behind the Dodgers and were gaining fast.

After a win to start the month, Los Angeles lost 4 straight. On June 6, Valenzuela seemed a cinch to get win number 10 at Wrigley Field. He'd pitched well in his last outing against the Braves, after Atlanta had handed him his second loss of the season four days earlier. The Dodgers were in first, the Cubs in last. The Dodgers had 34 wins, the Cubs 11. If any game had a foregone conclusion, this was one. It seemed that way through the first three innings, Los Angeles putting up a quick 4 runs, while Fernando only yielded a solo home run.

"In baseball there's no such thing as a small enemy," philosophized Valenzuela before the game. In the bottom of the fourth, the Cubs hit him hard. Triple, walk, single, fly out, single, and then infielder Mike Tyson, pinch-hitting for the pitcher, clouted a 3-run tater, and Valenzuela was done for the day after $3\frac{1}{3}$ innings, his shortest stint of the year. His record was now 9–3, and his ERA jumped to 2.45, the first time it was over 2 runs per game all season.

Still, Fernandomania was raging, reaching into the nation's capital.

"This is the White House calling for Mr. *Venezuela*." The Dodgers' press secretary relayed the message. Valenzuela was requested to join the president of the United States at a state luncheon in honor of Mexico's president, José López Portillo, on June 9. It was a nice, if superficial, way to put on a good face to the Latino community at the same time the administration stirred anti-Latino feeling by deporting illegal immigrants and replacing them with unemployed Americans. Unemployment had been 7.5 percent in January when the new president arrived. No better way to distract the workingman from his economic woes than finding a villain south of the border.

None of that was on Valenzuela's mind as he entered smiling, natty in his pin-striped suit and pocket handkerchief. To his left, John Gavin, the newly appointed ambassador to Mexico, smiled a movie-star smile. Like his boss, Gavin had done his years in Hollywood, most well known as the boyfriend in Hitchcock's *Psycho*.

The knife into the heart of the 1981 baseball season was plunged by Judge Werker on June 10. In a 23-page ruling, the judge denied the injunction as without "reasonable cause that the owners committed unfair labor practices." The request for data was a mere "tactic" employed by the union, and anyway, they had waited too long to ask. Werker stated the clock began early in 1980 and they should have asked for the information earlier, since compensation as an issue was known since then. Werker failed to realize that nothing was set into motion until February 19 and the owners' implementation. Had they forgone it, there would have been no need for data. On top of that, he ruled compensation was not economic, though if he had had a dictionary nearby, he would find that it was. The entire decision was delusional.

Kuhn was gleeful. Reading through the document, he made a joyful note on the right margin—"MM talks too much." He delighted in what he saw as an official declaration of Miller's insincerity. The PRC sent out word as fast as they could; Grebey was elated by the decision.

"PLAY BALL! SO ORDERED," Werker urged in his closing words. The owners had won a rare, though pyrrhic, victory. A strike was assured. Grebey alerted all chief executives and general managers of that fact. "Hopefully, there will be some scurrying around in the next forty-eight hours," said Boone. "Am I disappointed? Yeah, because I've felt all along that we're being forced into this strike action." "Everything's in gear," echoed DeCinces. "We're right back where we started from. His decision is going to create a strike in forty-eight hours."

Veterans Stadium in Philadelphia was one of several architectural monstrosities born in the 1970s, circular, concrete, multipurpose stadiums that landed like alien aircraft in major cities throughout the country. To call it nondescript would give it too much character. Unlike Connie Mack Stadium, the ballpark it replaced, the Vet was cavernous instead of cramped, antiseptic instead of warm.

It was not so on the night of June 10. That Wednesday evening over 57,000 Phillies fans crammed inside to witness history. Rose was on the verge of tying and, it would follow, breaking, Musial's all-time National League hit record of 3,630. "Charlie Hustle" and "the Man" had been intertwined since Rose's rookie year of 1963, Musial's last. The Cardinals faced off against the Reds in the last game of the season; Musial had 2 hits; Rose had 3. Musial had come to Philadelphia to present Rose a diamond ring with 3,631 on it, as soon as the inevitable occurred.

Leading off the game, hunched to create a strike zone the size of an Atari game cartridge, Rose peered from under his red helmet, overly long Buster Brown hair spilling out the back and sides, to see Nolan Ryan, all 6'2" of him, ready to kick his left leg high and unload 100 miles an hour of fastball his way. Ryan had surpassed Rose on the salary scale when he signed with the Astros after the 1979 season, becoming the first player to reach $1 million per year. With the addition of free agent Ryan, the Astros, who had come in no higher than third place since their 1962 inception, made the postseason for the first time in 1980 and seemed to be on their way there again in 1981.

Two pros, two top free agents who had turned their teams around, faced off with history on the line. Rose glared to the mound; Ryan returned the attempted intimidation with blank stoicism. On the fourth pitch, Rose cracked a single to center, and the crowd erupted both with the joy of witnessing the tying hit, number 3,630, and the knowledge, the absolute surety, that they were lucky to be there, in the flesh, to see history soon to come. It was only the first inning, Rose was guaranteed at least three more at bats, and all he needed was a solitary hit and the record was his.

In the bottom of the third, Ryan struck out Rose. In the bottom of the fifth, Ryan struck out Rose. In the bottom of the eighth, Ryan struck out Rose, and that was it. Though the Phillies won 5–4 after Ryan left with a stiff back, the crowd filed out with mixed feeling. They had the moment in their sights and it passed. One hit! Just one more hit!

Musial returned to St. Louis, ring in hand, jilted. The stadium emptied, the staff cleaned out the leftover peanut shells, soda cups, and hot dog wrappers. After midnight, the balloons, all 3,631 that had been brought to the Vet for the celebration, were released, lonely and sad as they climbed high above the stadium bowl. The lights went out on Pete Rose, on the Phillies, and on their season.

When would they come back on? Would they come back on at all?

Chapter 4

LIFE DURING STRIKETIME

JUNE

Six men, split into two rooms at the Waldorf Astoria, waited for word. Player Relations Committee members Dan Galbreath, John McHale, and Bob Howsam of the National League watched Seaver get his seventh win against the Mets. In another room, Clark Griffith (Calvin's son), Joe Burke, and Ed Fitzgerald, American League stalwarts, were tuned to the Yankees, the now first-place Yankees, winners of 9 of their last 10, against the White Sox. Jackson, the team rep, had told his teammates to expect an announcement in the morning.

Across Lexington Avenue at the Doral, 13 men and 1 woman sat on either side of two long tables stretching across two 17th-floor rooms. The negotiations that had begun in 1979 and, with compensation left to dangle, through 1980 to now were coming to a close.

"Are you really going to strike?" Grebey asked Miller. Had he not been at the meetings all these months? The players at the table couldn't believe their ears.

Now past midnight into June 12, the Astros' Joe Niekro, in white, button-down shirt, light jacket, and big belt buckle, and a freshly permed Sutton, in Western shirt, jeans, and Indian-looking belt, exited one of the two rooms and headed down the hall to room 1701. Sutton had been in the meetings all day. Direct compensation hit home for him; he knew the Astros would never have signed him to a four-year deal if they had to give the 16th best man on their team to their division rivals the Dodgers. Mediator Moffett stayed with the owners, then joined the players. It was 12:30 a.m. when they entered the pressroom. Their faces showed all.

"We have been meeting most of the day," said a dejected Miller, in a light-colored jacket over a dark sports shirt. "We have accomplished nothing.

"The strike is on."

At 1:45 a.m., Kuhn began a somber walk back to his office.

"Hey, Bowie, what's happening?" shouted a fan who recognized the tall figure in the dark.

"They're out, they're out," Kuhn yelled back, in no mood for chitchat.

It was a terrible miscalculation on Miller's part, thought Kuhn as he trod the New York streets. He was certain the owners weren't going to budge on the compensation plan. To Kuhn, Miller was the real problem, mired in a megalomaniacal pitched battle against Grebey and the owners.

But Kuhn was wrong. Miller and the players had tried everything to prevent the strike. And Miller had seen this day coming, telling a friend that the owners were going to blunder their way into a strike and had no idea how to get out of it. The first midseason strike in professional sports history was on, 650 major league players no longer playing. There'd been strikes before, but none like this one.

In 1972, the players struck on April 1, with 13 days, 86 games, lost, over a dispute on pension contributions. One year later, the early-bird camps of February were shut down and threats of a lockout emerged. By the time the resulting pact was ready to be renegotiated, free agency had been granted by an arbitrator's decision and led to early negotiations. The result: a 17-day spring-training lockout, which Kuhn ended by ordering the owners to open the camps on March 15. The owners were outraged by his action, a future member of the PRC declaring that, then and there, Kuhn should have been shot, but he was supported by the more influential owners. Others would never forgive him.

"We were like David without a slingshot," Steinbrenner sulked. "Marvin Miller took, took, took," as if any side can just take, as opposed to outsmart and outbargain. Steinbrenner vowed the owners would be tougher next time around. The owners had underestimated, again, the players' solidarity. Ultimately a four-year deal was agreed to right before the All-Star Game, ending in 1980, when the final eight days of spring training were shut down and a May strike was narrowly averted by leaving compensation on the table. That long, bumpy road led to the strike. Not the first, but shaping up to be the worst.

Though Grebey was flummoxed and owners such as Reinsdorf had thought that there'd be a game of chicken, talks going down to the end until everyone realized compensation wasn't worth a strike, the owners had planned for it. Internal memos were sent, instructing management to avoid helping members of the media contact striking players, urging teams not to arrange appearances by players for which they would be paid by others, and postponing clinics with players on strike or, at least, replacing them with managers and coaches. When the strike hit, no transportation allowances were to be allotted. "If players are on the road at the commencement of the strike, they should be left where they are."

Tossed out onto the street in Chicago after being told, "Make your own reservations, do what you want, you have nothing to do with the Yankees as of now," Bobby Murcer and Lou Piniella were stuck outside Comiskey Park, not a ride in sight. There was a Chicago cab strike. A friendly cop pulled up to ask what the matter was and gave the two a lift to the Continental Plaza Hotel. Other guys hitched rides. At the hotel bar, the players were on one end, executives on the other, not even willing to drink together, but willing to drink, hoping to dull the pain of a lost season.

The turnstiles were motionless. On blankets at Santa Monica Beach, tanning bodies that had tuned their radios to KABC to hear Scully melodically call Valenzuela's early-season heroics were now blaring Kim Carnes as she growled through "Bette Davis Eyes." In

bars throughout Chicago, Cub fans who'd watched their cursed
Cubbies start the season 15–37 sat through *The Afternoon Movie* on
WGN, laughing at *Road to Morocco*, crying to *Jane Eyre*. Sweating
riders crammed elbow to elbow on the D train reading their folded
*New York Post*s and *Times*es could no longer admire the all-around
athleticism of Winfield and the surging Yankees. Now they were
reading about a strange new cancer, Kaposi's sarcoma, which had
begun to mysteriously ravage the homosexual community.

Starting on June 12, radios went silent, TVs went blank, and
newspapers printed nothing of interest for millions of baseball fans
throughout the country. Baseball defined the American summer: fathers taking their children to the ballpark on a bright, sunny Saturday afternoon, sharing stories of their own youth and their own
father-son baseball moments; cabdrivers listening to the radio, curs-
ing at their home team as passengers cringed in terror at the sudden
outburst. The white noise of baseball—always in the background in
overheard conversations, in headlines hung from corner stands, and
on TVs in bars and electronics stores showing today's game to
passersby—was gone. That wasn't all that disappeared.

It was an old management refrain—my workers are good, simple
folk. They love their jobs, they love their bosses, and they'd never
strike if it weren't for troublemakers from the outside. It's agitators
like Marvin Miller who cause all the trouble. We swear, if only we
could talk directly to our boys in uniform, without that damned
Miller lurking about, they'd see we're right, that we mean no harm
to them, that they could trust us. Then they would flock back; it
was only because of that Svengali that they even walked out in the
first place.

So Miller left, allowing the owners the chance to test their hy-
pothesis.

It was a bombshell. Miller removing himself from the negotiations? Could it be? Were matters to be left to four players—Boone,
Rogers, DeCinces, and Belanger—with Fehr at their side? Miller
had told Fehr to say little. Let the players speak.

·   ·   ·

Doug DeCinces was from a factory town in Southern California—
Hollywood. His aunt Gloria Winters played Penny on the hit 1950s
children's show *Sky King*. His grandfather won an Oscar for sound
mixing on *West Side Story*. Lisa Loring, his cousin, was Wednesday
on *The Addams Family*. For all his movie pedigree, DeCinces was an
Orange County conservative, getting into arguments with Miller
over whether they had an association of professionals or a labor
union. DeCinces preferred the former. Miller laughed.

DeCinces had a long list of reasons to distrust management.
When he was starting out in 1974, the heir apparent to Brooks Robinson at third base, DeCinces was promised by the Orioles he would
get a major league contract if he played well in spring training. He
was one of the top hitters in camp, holding up his end of the bargain. Not so for management, who cut him instead. He'd never believe them again.

Orioles fans never let DeCinces forget that he wasn't Brooks, but
in time he became a fixture at third and a key part of the lineup. In
1980, he was elected to be the American League alternate representative for the union. With Belanger's endorsement, he was voted
in during the winter meetings and soon after rose to the top. From
that point forward, DeCinces felt a moral obligation to the players
to do everything he could to represent them. The more nonsense
he saw happening before his eyes, the harder he worked. He knew
the facts and could talk in great detail with Grebey and the PRC.
The OC conservative had learned to become a labor negotiator.

Mark Belanger came to it much easier. His family background
could not have more perfectly prepared him. Growing up in working-
class Pittsfield, Massachusetts, Belanger watched his mother work
at the local General Electric plant, Belanger's company town being
slightly different from DeCinces's. Mark's mother took a great interest
in union politics, fighting GE's antiunion efforts for years.

Growing up with a strong sense of right and wrong, Belanger
was a smart kid who grew up to be a smart ballplayer. With a sharp
mind for the game and an amazing glove, Belanger more than made
up for his notoriously weak bat. "The Blade," 6'1", 170 lbs., roamed

the infield like few others, winning eight Gold Glove Awards for his fielding excellence, the symbol of defensive prowess that the Orioles employed on their way to five World Series.

Coming up to Baltimore in 1965, Belanger predated Miller and saw firsthand the remarkable transformation of the game and its players. As Miller gained more rights for the formerly put-upon players and encouraged the men themselves to gain a voice they'd never had, Belanger followed in his mom's footsteps. First, he was the Orioles' alternate player rep behind Brooks Robinson, and when the pension plan caught his interest, he made his way up the ranks to American League pension rep.

That Belanger's mother's workplace struggles would intersect with baseball's labor strife was a long shot, but that's what happened. Belanger was the hardest hard-liner when it came to the players' cause. Knowing full well Ray Grebey's General Electric background, he hated the lead negotiator. Belanger wasn't happy that Miller excused himself, but his passion for the issue trumped his concern.

Bob Boone's family business *was* baseball. His father Ray was an All-Star infielder and a World Series winner in his rookie year of 1948 with the Indians. The younger Boone grew up around major league baseball, no doubt hearing from his father what it was like, good and bad, at the big league level.

Three years after graduating from Stanford with a psychology degree, Boone made his Phillies debut. In his first full year he placed third in the Rookie of the Year balloting. In his second year he became the team player rep, a man in his mid-20s carrying the interests of his older teammates.

He did it well, displaying the intelligence that quickly made him one of the top catchers in the league and, in time, the National League player rep. Boone balanced the needs of the union with play, serving on the joint study committee while engaged in the 1980 pennant race. Calm on the outside, aggressive behind the scenes, Boone was a leader both on the field and off.

Steve Rogers was aggressive everywhere. He couldn't help it.

Drafted in the first round by the Expos out of the University of Tulsa in 1971, Rogers battled management right away, refusing to pitch in winter ball. His arm hurt and he wasn't going to risk his career on a short-term front-office decision. His reputation as a malcontent with a bad attitude began before he even reached Montreal.

By 1973 he was in the major leagues, the next year he was an All-Star, firmly entrenched and the team's assistant player rep. He knew his engineering degree tricked people into thinking he was smart. Eventually he became the team rep.

At the 1976 Executive Board meeting of the players' association in Hawaii, a coin toss put Rogers in the position of NL pension rep. From then on, the education he received from Miller was deep and passionate. Rogers took much pride in his responsibility to all of the players who thought they'd play forever, not realizing how short their time actually was.

Miller and Fehr thought the union needed a core of four players, serious, smart, thoughtful, tough, and unafraid. They couldn't have had a better quartet than DeCinces, Belanger, Boone, and Rogers.

In the first week, Moffett called three meetings. The first was a two-hour review of how the two sides got to this point. The second wasn't really a meeting at all, the camps gathered in separate rooms on the same floor, Moffett shuttling back and forth, but never bringing them together. The third, all of ten minutes after a full hour apart, ended in a complete collapse. Labor practice required parties to meet and bargain, but it didn't say for how long. There was no point locking the two groups together, a grimacing Moffett told the press.

Grebey had a hard time with the players. Miller felt Grebey grew nervous around them, though the PRC chair dismissed that as baloney. In addition to the four main player-negotiators, a revolving door of players attended, creating a scene far outside Grebey's experience. Phil Garner, Jon Matlack, Rusty Staub, Reggie Jackson—any player who was in New York and wanted to participate in the negotiations was invited in, and when these players showed up, it threw Grebey into a paroxysm.

Grebey's tweedy outfits and Moffett's blue blazer and button-down shirt and gray slacks were mismatched with the players' jeans and sweat suits straight from the gym, with towels wrapped around their necks. Peering over his half-glasses, Grebey clucked his tongue condescendingly at the motley crew that was supposed to be serious. The flux of players, different guys at different times, took Grebey off his game. He wanted to control as much as he could, and with a continually changing other side, it was impossible. His frustrations came out in sarcasm and disdain that the players found irritating.

For a week, the news was that if Miller was out of the way, a deal could be made. It wasn't to be so easy. Boone emerged quickly as de facto leader. His composure at the table was soothing, and Grebey assumed Boone wasn't like the others. He was, but during the talks he let the other three play bad cops to his good.

When Grebey looked over his lenses and said, "This is not about breaking the union; we are trying to protect lesser organizations from free agency and the richer organizations. *You have to trust me*," Rogers blew his top.

"That is bullshit. You've pushed us by trying to break the union. You just don't know what you're talking about," he blasted.

Chub Feeney turned red-faced, his neck bulging, puffing on his cigar like a house afire. League presidents weren't spoken to that way. He nearly swallowed his stogie. "We're not trying to punish you guys," he blurted.

Afterward, the players told Moffett that if the owners said "trust me" one more time, they were going to upend the table and storm out of the room. Moffett kept the two sides apart. Grebey realized all of a sudden what he was up against. He may have believed before that Miller was a puppeteer, that the players were merely brainwashed, but that fiction was increasingly hard to maintain.

The players weren't smooth or eloquent, but the owners confused that with being unintelligent. They never quite realized how well thought out the players' ideas were. Miller's great strength had been in education. He didn't lead them around by the nose and would never have gone against what they wanted, even if he thought it was wrong. Miller wore blinders: his sole purpose was what was best for players and creating in them a principled group.

Miller knew when he left the negotiations that those remaining were terrifically competent people, a far cry from the players he had first encountered in 1966. That group, contrary to the common belief that all pro athletes were arrogant, profligate, and garish, in truth suffered from low self-esteem. Players realized they were powerless in those days, especially when the media and courts cooperated with owners to form an impregnable force. "When you feel powerless, and events show you to be right, self-esteem goes down," Miller said.

Not anymore. Without Miller at the table, the players were more outspoken, more able to act appropriately on their own behalf. It only furthered a bond that became extremely strong as they watched each other in action, informed, thoughtful, easily comprehending what was happening. It wasn't what Grebey wanted. Two, three times a week, Grebey would call Miller beseeching him to get back to the table. Miller may have been tough to deal with, but he had more in common with Grebey than the players did. Miller was seasoned and professional, sharp, organized, and devoted to his cause. Athletes might say, "Fuck you! You're just dead wrong," but Miller could calm a situation without giving in, keeping negotiations more unemotional.

When the phone rang at Joey Amalfitano's house on the morning of June 16, when he heard Cub owner William Wrigley's voice, he could never have expected the news.

"Joey," Wrigley told his manager, "I'm selling the team. Tell your coaches."

It was shocking news. After more than sixty years of Wrigley ownership of the terrible but beloved Cubbies, the family had sold the team to the Tribune Company for $20.5 million. For Wrigley, who cited club losses of $1.8 million in 1980, more to come in 1981, and estate and inheritance taxes of $40 million, it was a sad necessity.

In the *Trib* newsroom, word came around noon. Few knew in advance; most were completely surprised. Among the Cubs pennants, hats, and jerseys, reporters stood by their desks and computer monitors, some thinking it was a joke, others wondering if the White Sox fans, about three-quarters of them, would be fired. The deal seemed to have been struck overnight, not even leaving enough time to take down the Comiskey Park posters in some carrels, but negotiations had begun long before the strike had begun. The quick assurances that the newspaper would cover the Cubs fairly was followed by a quick donning of the team's blue caps.

General Manager Herman Franks gave Wrigley credit for being less interested in money than in keeping the team in the city, as if there were any danger of their leaving. Kuhn issued a statement praising the Wrigleys for their long commitment to baseball. President Reagan, hearkening back to his time as a young man broadcasting Cub games, was quoted by an aide as saying, "It's the end of an era, but hopefully the beginning of another era."

True enough. The Tribune saw future gold in a forlorn franchise. Owning a baseball team had an intrinsic value, and corporations were beginning to see it. A media company could obviously get great value from having a baseball team in the fold. The Tribune Company, through instant programming on their WGN radio and television stations, could turn the team into a national phenomenon. Major league franchises had so much untapped revenue potential once they were freed from old-time family ownership, which ran teams as a rich man's hobby. New blood wouldn't stand for the old ways.

A few hours before the Cubs news broke, Williams, Chiles, and Steinbrenner converged on Kuhn's office to warn him that his job was in jeopardy if he didn't get Grebey to find a solution to the strike. Chiles had set up the meeting and asked the other two to join him.

"Pretty fancy digs," Chiles said, grinning, looking around. "Here you are, sitting in your fancy office doing nothing. If you were my employee, I would have fired you last year." That was for starters. Kuhn sat and took the berating, for a while at least. Chiles couldn't tell if Kuhn was angry or not; he was usually flushed.

"Are you through?" asked Kuhn. "You're a lamebrained old fool." The commissioner was prone to antiquated adjectives. "I'm embarrassed for you." Kuhn believed, and told Chiles, that the commissioner tells the owners what to do, not the other way around. MacPhail watched quietly from the couch.

After the three irate owners vented their displeasure, and Kuhn put Chiles in his place, MacPhail entered the conversation, saying any changes in the PRC would come after the strike was settled. Williams had some suggestions on compensation, which Kuhn and MacPhail said they would deliver to the PRC. Contrary to his statements at the NLRB hearing, Kuhn boasted that, though he couldn't direct the PRC, he had considerable influence over them and could block them if he saw fit. Kuhn, for not being involved in the negotiations, seemed pretty involved.

The meeting that started with a bang ended with a whimper. Steinbrenner, in a complete reversal, pledged his support for the work of the PRC and Kuhn. Williams didn't appreciate the Boss's double cross. "I like George, but if I had to describe him in one quick sentence, it would be 'If something is wrong, it has to be someone else's fault.'"

Back in his office, Kuhn penciled down his thoughts. "I don't have to take any baloney from anybody in this biz." The threats leveled at him were "ineffective, [I] don't need [the] job." As he thought further on what actions he could take, under the heading "BIOB" he pondered that "BK can move," citing "1976." (Five years earlier Kuhn had ordered the owners to end their spring lockout and open the camps.) In the "best interest of baseball," he jotted down, "→ break union."

The effect of the trio's assault on the commissioner was a meeting of Kuhn and the Executive Council, his advisory body. The result—a complete vote of confidence for the PRC, Grebey, and Kuhn. It was curious that Kuhn was given a vote if he had no part in the proceedings. Miller scoffed. "They looked in the mirror and said, 'You're a fine boy, I endorse you.'" The splinter group of Steinbrenner, Williams, and Chiles, of which Grebey claimed he was unaware, waited for their real chance to voice their concerns to the entire ownership group at a previously scheduled meeting in Kansas City on June 24. Scared that the dissidents' heresy would infect a roomful of owners, the commissioner's office hastily canceled the meeting. It was getting increasingly difficult to keep the owners together, and while fines were threatened for public opposition, no penalties could be levied for comments in private. The solution: don't give the objecting owners the opportunity to speak. Let Grebey handle the next meeting.

"Do you have any questions for us?" DeCinces asked on June 19 at the Doral, assuming that the players' pool proposal would result in at least some back-and-forth. The core four were joined by Staub, Seaver, Fehr, and attorney Peter Rose.

"No," said Grebey.

"When you're ready to talk, let us know." DeCinces, and the others, stood up, collecting their papers and closing their briefcases.

Grebey was dumbfounded. "You're calling off the negotiations?"

"Have you got anything new?" snapped DeCinces. The owners had nothing, and the players had gone through all their ideas with no intention of making further proposals. With nothing to talk about, the meeting was over. With talks in ruins, Boone announced that no meetings would be scheduled until the owners' side came up with something fresh. It was hard to keep hope alive. In every meeting, the players entered the room with optimism, only to have it crushed and tossed back at them. It was impossible to believe the owners' team was interested in seeking an agreement, that the strike was not what they wanted, when they seemed to be doing nothing to bridge the gap between themselves and their players.

Seaver, seen as a moderating force, told reporters, "The owners are taking a very destructive position; it's very disturbing. If they are trying to alienate the players, they are doing a good job. But," he warned, "they are working with competitive individuals." Belanger, Rogers, Boone, and DeCinces shared a look of stunned sadness and downward glances as they spoke to the press. It became their strike mask.

Moffett, before heading back to DC, declared there was no need to call the parties together for a meeting until he saw a glimmer of something positive. What was the point until then? The players, always open with Moffett, vented their anger. Moffett wisely saw that bringing the parties together could do more harm than good. These negotiations were knottier than a Rubik's Cube. It was bizarre. The issues were resolvable, but there was no negotiating. He'd never seen anything like it in his 22 years as a mediator. Some owners were getting the sense that the season was a washout. "This thing is going over the cliff," said one involved in the negotiations. "This is a next-year situation." The 1980 delay to save one year was on course to kill two.

"Harmful, even ridiculous," protested Steinbrenner about Miller's absence. He was needed back if there was to be progress. Miller, in return, praised the Yankees owner's business skill and wished he would appear at the table. The absence of owners directly involved in the negotiations rankled the players, especially as they saw Grebey as an obstacle getting harder to hurdle with each passing day.

Though the strike kept the players and owners consumed and busy, outside of the clubhouse and negotiation table the world struggled to find something to fill the hole left by the strike.

On June 12, as if it were an ordinary game day, the Cubs' organist showed up and began playing. After 30 minutes, someone finally told him to stop. He hadn't been told of the strike. With no one to play for, he went home.

The media wasn't so fortunate. They still had to entertain their readers, viewers, and listeners. An audience still existed, hungry for baseball. The major networks did a quick scramble. On the first Saturday after the strike was called, NBC aired highlights of Game 6 of the 1975 World Series, Reds vs. Red Sox, when Rose was still a

Red and Fisk was hitting homers at Fenway Park. Red Sox fans would rather have seen a rerun of that game than the ho-hum squad they'd been subjected to lately. For the foreseeable future, a sports anthology show would fill in for the *Game of the Week*.

ABC followed on Monday, not a bit scared to rerun *Halloween* director John Carpenter's 1979 *Elvis* biopic. The TV movie smash, starring Kurt Russell as "the King," was the first pairing of director and star. The second was coming in July—*Escape from New York*. No, it was not the Reggie Jackson story.

Locally, newspapers simply made stuff up. *The San Francisco Examiner* ran a fantasy, free-agent bust Rennie Stennett finding inner peace by giving up his $600,000 salary to live in solitude on the beach eating abalone. In Philadelphia, *The Daily Bulletin* ran an extensive interview with the famously silent Steve Carlton. The *Los Angeles Examiner* had a whole series of fake stories under the heading "Strikeball," games created from computer stats provided by pioneering numbers man Alan Roth.

From Lexington to Bellevue, Minneapolis to St. Louis, papers resorted to printing accounts of board and electronic games. The *Philadelphia Journal* had Rose get his 3,631th hit against the Braves. The game was halted and the dice were mailed to Rose. The *Post-Dispatch* got Cardinals manager Herzog to lead his team over the Padres 4–1. "The guys played well considering they're on strike," he said.

Some outlets chose to make good of the strike by presenting baseball history. Astros followers got a double dose when KENR radio played re-creations of past games and *The Houston Post* reprinted their original stories. It helped to have a good time, to give the unpleasant reality a backseat.

In San Diego, they made the most of it. At first the Padres wanted everyone in the front office to take a vacation. What was the point of having a full staff and no business? KFMB radio had a better idea. What if we threw a party?

With the promise of free drinks, hot dogs, peanuts, and popcorn, 3,200 fans came to the Jack Murphy Stadium parking lot on

June 18 for "Fantasy Baseball." Milling around or resting in beach chairs under a typically sunny San Diego sky, fans listened as Padres announcers Jerry Coleman and Dave "Soup" Campbell, both wearing 76 KFMB T-shirts commemorating the day, picked the woeful Padres out of the second division and into a 10-game winning streak. The first three victories were real, the Pads having been on a mini-streak before the curtain fell. The next were fiction, games made up by the announcers. CBS was there to film for the *Morning News,* NBC for the *Nightly News with John Chancellor.* ESPN cameras were on hand as well. That's how bad it was—national media filming fans watch two guys create a fake game.

The fans had a great time, the parking lot teeming in front of an empty stadium. The organist played, the Tuba Man Band and the Trumpet Man joined in, and people smiled as they were handed free T-shirts and MARVIN MILLER STRIKE MUGS. It was easy to target Miller; his players had called the strike. It was much harder to fit the details of differing compensation plans on a coffee cup.

There may have been a baseball strike, but in San Diego they found a way to enjoy themselves without the game itself. That may have been the scariest thing of all for baseball brass to hear.

Actual baseball was still going on in the minor leagues. Attendance was expected to increase for the only live action around, especially with players such as Cal Ripken Jr. to watch. How long would Rochesterians have him? Rumors swirled that the major leagues might employ replacement players. Ripken had benefited from not being called up already. Had he been brought to the Orioles, he would have sat on the bench and then become totally inactive with the strike. What if he was called up now?

Belanger wanted to know and called. "Cal, you'd be the obvious choice to be called up as a replacement player," Belanger said, making that clear to the prospect already carrying a big name. "What would you do?"

"Don't worry Mark, I'm not going anywhere. I'd never be a replacement player." Belanger liked that the kid replied without hesitation.

. . .

While Fernando Valenzuela pitched in a couple of semipro games in Mexico, in violation of his major league contract prohibiting play for another team (Kuhn was investigating the matter), Miller appeared with Steinbrenner on CBS's *Face the Nation*. Miller may have been away from the table, but he wasn't far from the issue. He knew that collective bargaining took place on multiple levels, including the press. Grebey burned as Miller commented from afar, saying the PRC chief was in a three-front campaign to fool fans, owners, and insurance companies.

"When Mr. Miller has enough courage to return to the bargaining table, he can make comments," spat Grebey.

With no serious debate on TV or, for that matter, at the Doral, perhaps a higher authority could break the logjam?

Ten days into the strike, Williams told Kuhn that he was absolutely certain that the Reagan administration would intervene if the commissioner requested that the compensation issue be sent to an impartial arbitrator. Publicly, a White House spokesman said Reagan had "no intention of getting involved in the dispute." There was no reason to think he would. Reagan, president of the Screen Actors Guild when he was a B-movie actor, stood idly by during the Writers Guild of America strike that had started in mid-April. He wouldn't do anything for the writers and he wouldn't do anything for the players.

"Fascist. A modern Father Coughlin." These were among the nicer things Miller had to say about Reagan. "Worst of labor spies" was the nastiest, but Miller knew his history. Reagan, while president of SAG, had been an informant for the FBI, providing the Bureau with information on pro-Communist influences in Hollywood, while seeming active in the guild. It would have been a relief to Miller to find out that Kuhn never asked Reagan to intercede. The owners had no reason to seek a settlement with the insurance money on its way.

Lloyd's of London made their name insuring the oddest things—Betty Grable's legs, Jimmy Durante's "schnozzola." The high-profile policy became their signature. Lately they'd been on a losing streak—paying out $5 million to NBC when the United States boycotted the

1980 Summer Olympics in Moscow, $1.25 million to the San Diego Clippers when center Bill Walton was sidelined with foot problems, $14 million to cover lost butter when a Dutch warehouse burned down, flattening the town of Elst. Lloyd's had had no idea the amount of damage a large amount of butter in one place, like an unsuspected artery, could do. And they weren't up to speed on baseball either.

The $50 million in insurance that the owners had paid a $2 million premium for was to begin distribution on June 25th. Of the three different pieces of the insurance pie, Lloyd's was directly liable for $20 million, the rest spread among underwriters. The money would last until August 8, if the owners received it all. Late in the game, Lloyd's realized that the owners had precipitated the strike by implementing their compensation plan and might end up being found to have violated labor law. It was a matter of waiting for the NLRB decision. The hearing, originally set for June 15, was bumped to the 22nd, then the 29th. If the owners were found guilty, the insurance companies would have to sue for the money already paid.

Miller had sought insurance for the players, but found it difficult to obtain. It was not by accident. The owners had made it hard for the players to get insurance, claimed an industry insider. With the regular channels closed, Miller was anxious to get something to cover the bills of his players, who were receiving no pay while on strike. One night, he received an odd call from someone who wanted to talk about offering the money the players needed. Despite his wife Terry's fears, Miller agreed to meet this mystery man. He arrived at the meeting place, in a basement apartment, and heard the offer.

"No thanks," Miller answered quickly, anxious to leave. Who were these guys? Miller never found out, but suspected the mob.

Though the insurance money was of the utmost importance to management, their fast-held belief was still that the strike wouldn't last. It couldn't. General managers *knew* that when the mid-June payday came, and went, without a paycheck, the players would stop horsing around and come back to work. One to four weeks tops, said a New York labor lawyer. An insurance consultant thought it would last a week. It was nearly two when the sides sat back down.

On the day the owners began collecting their insurance money, they offered three new proposals. They dropped the number of those who would qualify as ranking free agents. Teams that signed free agents ranked in the top 25 percent, so-called Type A players, could protect only 15 players, but teams who signed those in the 25–40 percent range, Type B, could protect 20. Of the Type A, there would be no limit. A team losing a Type B would get two amateur draft choices as compensation. Boone saw it as movement, but of the smallest and most insignificant variety, not at all fundamentally different from what had been pushed before.

Grebey's struggles with the players continued. Dropping his head, shaking it in dismay, Grebey asked the players to leave. Joe Niekro swore Grebey winked at him as if he were a little boy. He and fellow Astro starter Bob Knepper adjourned to their room, where they watched *Blackbeard and the Pirates* on TV, shocked by Grebey's clear disdain for the "simple players."

When he wasn't shooing them out, Grebey was showing his disgust. Hearing Sutton whisper something to Staub, who laughed, Grebey tore into the Mets redhead, who always had a newspaper in hand.

"Rusty, if you think it's so funny, why don't you find a crossword puzzle to work."

The next session, Staub brought in fifteen copies of the *New York Times* puzzle and handed them out, lambasting Grebey. "If we're going to continue with these word games, let's at least do something that's constructive."

The talks crashed. Moffett said no meetings would be called unless either side had a proposal or they remained idle for too long. Emotions were hot. Miller slammed Grebey for consistently announcing progress when there was none, offering a sop to restless owners and nervous insurance companies, using the players to appease his constituencies. With the NLRB hearing now postponed until July 6, and the players signaling the need for one day of training for each strike week missed, the outlook for getting back on the field in the near term looked dim.

The PawSox and Red Wings returned to the field on June 23, finishing up the game they'd left off at 4:00 a.m. two months earlier. This time, a sellout crowd and over 100 reporters from around the globe came to witness the end. All it took was one inning. Pawtucket, behind Bob Ojeda, won in the bottom of the 33rd inning. Boggs finished 4 for 12, Ripken Jr. 2 for 13. A Hall of Fame exhibit was to be prepared in Cooperstown to showcase the scorecard and the records set: the longest time (8 hours and 25 minutes) and the most innings.

Fenway Park had been offered as the setting for the finale of the never-ending game, but the players declined to break the strike by playing at a major league stadium. Two days later, the Class AAA players of the Charleston Charlies and the Mets farmhands of the Tidewater Tides declined to play on cable TV. MacPhail sent a telex to all franchises, explaining that the Charlies refused to play because of the number of optioned players on their roster, players who could easily be recalled to the major leagues. "It would not appear there would be a problem at the Class A level," the AL president noted. If the strike went on, this information would be useful.

Kuhn thought more information from his office might be helpful as well. Once again he tried to explain himself to *The Sporting News*, and once again his letter was buried. Though he was not involved in the negotiations, Kuhn wrote, he was receiving telex messages from clubs on labor matters. Kuhn still saw himself as overseer of the game and could not allow himself to be thought of as a cipher.

His argument wouldn't wash. In a snideness unusual for the staid *TSN*, the editor's note appended to the commissioner's letter said, "We're sorry if we gave the impression that Commissioner Kuhn was doing anything in regard to labor relations. It was quite clear that he was doing nothing."

In fact Kuhn had ramped up his contact with the PRC. He spoke with them in groups and separately, he telephoned and met, working all night and all day. "At a time like this, I am busier, more involved, than at any other time—and properly so," Kuhn told CNN. Still pressing the notion of impartiality, "I am nobody's agent but my own," Kuhn compared his role to that of a federal judge. The judge's salary is paid by the government, but no one thinks a judge would bend over backward to be for the government. Alas, "the labor laws of the United States have placed limits on those [his] powers" to rule without question.

"I'm a great believer in liberty. Obviously the players want maximum freedom. Obviously the clubs would like to minimize or reduce mobility," he pontificated. Though he'd preach that reduced mobility via direct compensation had little to no effect on salaries, nothing hindered pay more than the absence of movement.

Reaffirming that Grebey had been brought in to bring a new level of competence to the owners' bargaining, Kuhn made it clear that he didn't hire him.

"Will Grebey step back from the table?"

"I wouldn't think so." Grebey wasn't going anywhere, for now.

As to his own role, Kuhn felt he could get involved but wouldn't. His assessment was that Miller thought the owners wouldn't hold out, but the commissioner saw that clubs needed to hold firm, that "it was important that the clubs retain control of the game." As a lifelong fan, he felt he had a superior feel for the health of the game than Miller, who, Kuhn claimed, was no fan at all. Kuhn firmly believed that Miller was pushing for player rights that would ultimately ruin the game and was certain that if the players could understand the overall picture, they would see that things would be better in the future if they learned there was a price to be paid now.

While Miller was gone from the negotiating table, the owners lost the currency of the "without Miller we'll get this sorted out" line. They'd had their chance to sort it out while he was gone and failed miserably. Miller returned on July 1, the 20th day of the strike. His point had been made, though Kuhn didn't grasp it. The players turned out to be no different from Miller himself! Instead of concluding that the players and Miller shared the same principled belief in their cause, the owners determined that Miller was too powerful a hypnotist. Without Miller the owners thought they had a chance, but without Miller the players were too brainwashed, they concluded. Grebey and the negotiating team seemed relieved to have Miller back. He was less prone to anger than the players.

DeCinces marveled at Miller's ability to keep his integrity, to listen and stay on task. It was much harder for DeCinces, a competitor by nature, to keep his cool.

"How do you not blast these guys?" he asked.

"There's always a time for that," Miller answered. He knew when and where anger could be most effective. Until then, he'd stick with his plan, stay diplomatic, keep his integrity, use occasional choice words, change tone as required, and focus on the goal. Miller played a long game; the owners didn't. It's why they always lost. It's why the players had such enormous respect for Miller. Now he was back, somewhat rested and spitting fire.

A settlement was impossible without Miller's stamp of approval, and the owners, who had said Miller stood in the way of an agreement, now realized they could make no headway with the players, that Miller alone wasn't the matter.

Miller didn't come back by himself. For the first time Reggie Jackson, after two weeks of kicking back at his Carmel home, came to the talks. Jackson proved the owners', and Grebey's, point that the players were out of touch with reality and asked for things they didn't understand.

In one instance, Grebey was reading back Miller's proposal aloud, and Jackson came bolting in. When he heard Grebey speaking, he yelled, "Grebey, we aren't taking any of your crap anymore."

Grebey replied, "Reggie, this is one of your proposals."

Jackson stood in stunned silence. Suddenly, he raised his hand, shouted, "Recess!"—and ran out.

The story has been told again and again and it's perfect—the scrupulously thorough Grebey carefully repeating a union proposal, an ill-informed player coming through the door at the last moment, not knowing what was going on, making a scene, and leaving sheepishly. And it was Reggie Jackson to boot, the most egocentric of them all.

It's too perfect, feeding every stereotype. The truth about Jackson was that he was smart, opinionated, and overwhelmingly self-interested. The union sought to exploit those traits. DeCinces and Belanger had been teammates of Jackson's when Finley sent him to Baltimore in 1976. If they could show him that the issues being discussed affected him directly, Jackson would be a passionate and intelligent spokesman. He was very much aware how much Miller had done for him, creating the world where he could sign for big bucks in New York and become a media star. Plus, he loved being the hero who rode in on a white horse to save the day. His teammates understood him well.

Miller brought him up to speed. Jackson admired Miller's honor and sincerity and his seeming inability to make a mistake. After two hours, Jackson realized how the issues mattered to him. It had been a rough year already, and he was glad to get away from the Yankees tumult. What he was hearing made his situation that much worse. He cared about other players as well, just not as much.

"You're kidding, they don't want to do that!"

"Why don't you come in and see for yourself?" asked Miller.

Jackson was flattered that his opinion was valued.

"You're a part of the players' association as much as I am," reinforced DeCinces. There was a deadlock, the players were being accused of stonewalling, and the frustration was building. "You should come in and hear for yourself."

He did.

After a few minutes, Jackson thought they should adjourn. The two sides were too far apart. He listened, and his concerns for older players, second-time free agents, in other words himself, caused dismay.

After 30 minutes, Jackson was nudged to take the floor. No wallflower, he was ready to speak. He didn't like what he'd seen and heard, didn't appreciate the gamesmanship.

"I know why I got here," he said with sincerity, looking at Miller. Jackson preached the players' case, adding, "No one is here to come see you." The biggest box-office draw this side of Valenzuela knew of what he spoke.

Speaking to the press afterward, Jackson wished that some owners were at the meetings, and, to Miller's dismay, said that perhaps a break until July 4 would be worthwhile. (Miller disagreed.) There'd be no settlement if service time was taken away. How could Jackson possibly tell teammates Jerry Mumphrey and Ron Guidry, and another 90 players, that they might not be getting credit for time during the strike, time that was needed to qualify for free agency after the 1981 season? It was a stronger issue than compensation. "My contract is up but I may not be a free agent," Jackson said in shock.

As if compensation hadn't been stomach-churning enough, the owners had tossed service time into the stew. Any days spent on the major league roster during the season counted, and the season hadn't been canceled, yet. Accumulated days were crucial to players. The number of days was how arbitration and free agency were granted, trade rights were reached, and, more important, because it affected everyone, determined the level of pension money.

Guidry, the biggest free agent on the post-1981 docket, entered the season with five years and four days of major league time. He needed almost all of 1981, 168 days' worth, to qualify for the big moneys. And the loss of credit for 1981 would affect other stars, such as Jackson. The players were absolutely certain that any strike days would count toward their major league time. Not so fast, said the owners, knowing that credit for service time had the very real potential of leaving compensation in the dust. In the near term, Guidry was supporting the strike, at least for as long as it was still duck season in Louisiana.

"The gap between us is so wide it defies my vocabulary to describe it," Miller announced after his first day back.

"We had the same results today as we did in the weeks without him," added Grebey. "He's always been part of their negotiating team whether he was sitting at the table or not."

The next day's meeting was equally hostile. Miller called Grebey out for telling some owners that the players were going to drop the pool idea. Those among ownership who were growing impatient would hopefully back down in the face of "new developments."

"Ray, it's a lie. The players have never considered dropping the pool idea."

"All I can tell you is that information did not come from my office."

"Where else would it have come from?" countered Miller. Grebey's strategy worked. Hard-liners were told nothing was happening; impatient moderates were told there'd been a change. Top executives told the press that they had received a call detailing this cave-in by the players. One owner said that without the false report that the players were backing down, he would have insisted on an owners' meeting.

These little things about Grebey drove Miller crazy, the offhand comment, the false denial. The players were conditioned to be skeptical, and two words set them off.

"Trust us, we're not here to punish anyone," said Grebey, exasperated.

If Grebey and his crew had said "trust me" once, they'd said it 1,000 times. The players didn't trust them, not at all, and for good reason. They'd all been burned, in various ways, by owners and management.

"We don't trust you," challenged DeCinces. "Show us your facts."

"I speak for the owners," Grebey would often remind his opponents. Why didn't Miller speak for the players? "Marv, we've gone over this before. You know why we need compensation." Grebey, still hoping he could control the conversation, talked past the reps and straight to Miller.

"These guys can speak for themselves," Miller answered.

Grebey's face contorted, his pipe dangling. He was prone to making faces when he was upset. DeCinces could always get his goat, but Grebey thought the world of Boone.

Judicious and low-key, Boone won over Grebey, who thought him "a fantastic guy, well-spoken, bright. He conducted himself properly at the bargaining table." Grebey's belief in Boone's reasonableness was a misread; it was style, not substance. Behind the scenes, Boone was as aggressive as the others, but he listened politely, considering. Grebey noticed that Boone, an inveterate tobacco chewer, would sit and place two empty cups on the table. When the second cup was filled with juice, Boone was done. Or maybe he'd simply had enough of the owners' intransigence.

As had the press. When it came to media relations, Miller always got the best of Grebey, and Grebey knew it. Miller's constant attacks and attempts to embarrass Grebey were effective: publicly discrediting the man in the opposite chair was potent. At first, the press was fairly split on who was to blame, more pro-management than pro-union, but as the weeks went on, more sportswriters saw that the strike was the owners' fault. The newsstands featured a *Sports Illustrated* cover in bold red type: "Strike!" Above a close-up of a glove cradling a clean white baseball in its pocket, with a noticeably empty stadium in the background, the subtitle summarized matters succinctly: "The Walkout the Owners Provoked." It really was that simple, and Kuhn could do nothing to stem the tide.

From his office in Rockefeller Plaza, Kuhn attempted to push back. He did not "foment" the strike with Grebey. The upcoming NLRB hearing was "fiddle-faddle." It's "paranoid to think I'd want to break the union," he averred, despite his personal scribbles. Compensation was "necessary for baseball and good for the fans," he offered without proof. "[There was] no one brilliant stroke or coup that the commissioner could make to settle it."

No one was accusing Kuhn of brilliance. When asked for his reaction to an owner who said Kuhn was calling all the shots and if Grebey were replaced, it wouldn't matter, Kuhn said, "It's ridiculous." He made it clear that Grebey didn't work for the commissioner and the commissioner didn't work for Grebey. With no owners on the negotiating team, who exactly did Grebey work for?

If the commissioner was coming across as incompetent at best, a self-parodying buffoon at worst, Grebey was cast as the real villain. Militant, hard-line, tough—he didn't mind the characterization. But when "they call me 'liar' and 'a snake' and cast aspersions on my integrity, I am offended. I boil inside. I can't describe how much it hurts. . . . And my whole family suffers with me."

During the negotiations, the Grebey family's privacy suffered mightily. Often video cameras would be on their lawn or a network truck in their driveway. His wife found protection at the local golf club, where she would camp out all day long. Their oldest daughter, living on 44th Street, was constantly harassed and phoned by members of the press.

But Grebey wouldn't, or couldn't, help his cause. When *The New York Times* wanted a profile of him, Murray Chass, the best reporter covering the business of baseball, told his editors that it wouldn't be flattering. Though civil, Grebey hadn't made any friends among the owners, the players, or the fans.

MacPhail asked Chass, "Why won't you write about the owners?"

"Because Ray Grebey won't talk to me," answered Chass. After that MacPhail became a source.

It wasn't only the liberal, pro-player *Times* that was shut out by the owners' negotiator. NBC had told Kuhn that they were trying desperately to be fair in their coverage, but they got nothing from Grebey. Kuhn was exasperated by Grebey's personality, better suited to the behind-the-scenes, nonpublic business world. Baseball was a public concern and needed an appealing front man. Kuhn sent a letter of advice:

"Please try to accommodate them as much as reasonably possible."

If Kuhn had issues with Grebey, it was more than mutual. Grebey saw Kuhn as an imperial commissioner, chauffeured and surrounded by bodyguards, cottoning only to powerful owners.

To Miller the two were one and the same: Grebey smacked of Kuhn, and Miller despised the commissioner's performance. Miller noted, "For some time now, it's been obvious that Ray Grebey and Bowie Kuhn have been intent on provoking a strike. Both of them have told the owners, 'We got compensation last year.' Now they've got to settle and get egg on their faces or bull it out, hoping to starve out the players and get compensation."

Grebey seemed to have as much internal trouble as external.

Word got out that Steinbrenner had secretly met with Miller at the Hyatt Regency Hotel. Williams, facing 20 percent interest rates on his Orioles financing, was in the lead, pushing aggressive action to settle. A core of owners still believed the players would be back soon, most likely in time for the July 14 All-Star Game in Cleveland. It was inconceivable the players would sacrifice over $2 million in pension contributions tied to the game. Fehr pointed out the players were set to lose more in salaries to the strike, $4 million per week. What would be the point of coming back for a little over half that? The players acted contrary to everything the owners believed. Kuhn believed it though. He sent a copy of a *New York Post* article, "Players Will Sit Out Past All-Star Game," to Feeney, MacPhail, and Grebey. "HYSTERICAL," Kuhn commented.

The All-Star Game? What about the season? Paul Molitor of the Brewers thought that unless the strike was resolved by the July 13 break, the whole season would be over. Some put the cutoff at the first week of August. A's president Roy Eisenhardt thought it would be worth playing even one month of regular-season ball in order to get to the playoffs and the World Series. Without the postseason how could any team generate next-season sales? Canceling fall baseball would be disastrous. For teams out of contention such as the Mariners and the Padres, low late-season attendance was almost assured. There'd be little reason for those clubs to push for more games, unless, maybe, the slate could be wiped clean and the second half would serve as a new start. A split season?

"I kind of look at this as a long rainout," said Jim Palmer. If he'd asked his teammate Scott MacGregor, he could have gotten a better forecast. Looking particularly unathletic, arms stiffly dangling at his sides, tie hanging as high above his belt line as his baffling slow curveball, MacGregor, a mainstay of the Orioles pitching rotation, stiffly delivered the latest on temperatures, tides, sunrises, and sunsets for WBAL-TV. Baseball's loss was weather's gain.

As the strike stretched on, players adjusted to a summer without baseball. For most, who'd been playing since they were kids, it was their first. Rickey Henderson had never had a summer free, and it was beautiful. He may not have fully understood what was going on in New York, but even without pay, he was having a fine time, relaxed, no worries. His A's teammates in the Bay Area spent their time fishing and golfing. Some even tried to stay in playing shape, joining Reggie Jackson at a local high school, major leaguers hitting, throwing, and fielding on the scattershot grass-and-dirt infield, batting-practice pitches shaking the chain-link backstop, back where they all began before contracts got in the way.

Some players didn't need to do anything, top-dollar guys such as the Royals' Hal McRae, who just kept it light, frequenting happy hours, boogalooing, and barbecuing. Some players fit the worst rich-player stereotypes—Giant Jack Clark, despite recently putting his name to a five-year, seven-figure deal, complained that, with Rolls-Royce *and* Jaguar payments to make, it wasn't easy to get by. The lower-salaried players faced different realities—Twins outfielder Rick Sofield was adjusting to peanut-butter-and-jelly sandwiches instead of steak, Pabst Blue Ribbon instead of Moosehead. Dan Duran, making the 1981 minimum salary of $32,500, began working as a heavy-equipment operator for his brother's construction company in Sunnyvale, California. Duran's wife was seven months pregnant, due on July 2 and on a leave of absence from her job. Dodgers reliever Dave Stewart was sorting nuts and bolts for $75 a day at Smith Fastener Co. These two didn't have the luxury of Clark's struggling to pay for his Rolls and Jag.

Bill Lee couldn't have cared less. He didn't want a strike, didn't believe in free agency, and told Miller he'd be happier barnstorming. Lee hopped on his bicycle and set out from Montreal to Toronto, before making his way to the Shakespeare Festival on Prince Edward Island. Without any phones or newspapers, Lee was oblivious of what was going on. He'd never been happier.

With unexpected time on their hands, ballplayers became full-time fathers and husbands for the first time during June and July. Tommy John enjoyed Father's Day with his family, watching TV, swimming, picnicking. Royals second baseman Frank White drew babysitting duty when his wife went to exercise class. More kid time, more family crises. While playing with his slot-car set, one vehicle set afire to re-create an Evel Knievel stunt, 11-year-old Ken Griffey Jr. had an accident. The boy was only slightly burned, much to the relief of his father. On the lawn of their Lakeland, Florida, home, Joe Niekro had time for a father-son catch with his boy Lance, like Griffey Jr. a future major leaguer. These striking players, fighting for the future of the game, never for a moment realized their own children would be beneficiaries.

Baseball players had a long history of community involvement and catering to the fans. In what other sport do so many in uniform sign autographs before, and sometimes during, a game? Even in the heat of negotiations, Boone spent two hours at the Concord Mall, penning his name and kissing fans. With suddenly open schedules, appearances, unaided by the front office, continued.

In Atlanta, Dale Murphy appeared at a shopping mall to meet fans, vowing to the faithful that baseball would return. In a benefit for the victims of the rash of child murders terrorizing Atlanta, the Mariner Comedy and Variety Act, put together by Lenny Randle, sang, danced, and joked for a good cause. It wasn't Richard Pryor level; a grab bag of "Kingdome" dances, booger jokes, and Randle's Mr. Rogers impersonations. Phillies Larry Bowa and Garry Maddox took their 1980-championship film on the road to the prison in Honesdale, Pennsylvania, watching with the inmates, chatting, and signing. The players were out in public. Where were the owners?

The players felt a kinship with the fans and were hurt by the lack of fan support for their cause. An NBC poll showed 53 percent of those asked supported the owners, 47 percent the players. It was strange. Why would the fans, the vast majority no doubt working for some boss who treated them like crap, be on the owners' side? Bando seemed to speak for the common man when he was seen sporting a cap promoting the movie *Take This Job and Shove It*. It was misinterpreted as strike commentary, but it spoke for most workers.

Baseball, unlike other sports, creates the illusion that, with a break here or there, the average Joe could be that guy on the field.

"I coulda hit that," the guy at home screamed when Schmidt struck out. "I can't believe he dropped it!" said the irate Yankee fan when Jackson flubbed an easy fly. Baseball at the major league level is played with great speed and intensity, but spectators believe it's the same game they played in Little League. It's easy for them to see themselves roaming the outfield. It's less possible to watch Julius Erving, "Dr. J," fly through the air for a slam dunk and think, "Yeah, that could've been me." As a result, baseball players were seen as spoiled brats, ungrateful for the fluke that got them millions and the average American $13,000 a year for his nine-to-five job.

Speaking for many, Ted Turner railed against the players and Miller. Picture all 650 players and Miller on a ship that crashed head-on with another ship, causing both to sink, Turner imagined. We would "get along without all of them. It [the world] got along without John F. Kennedy, didn't it?" While owners and fans were upset, only Turner was wishing aloud for the players' deaths. And who was on the other ship, the owners?

The press would've killed for a high-seas catastrophe. Instead they were left to their own fancy. In Los Angeles, the *Times* ran stories from the past, starting with the first Dodger game at the Coliseum. The *Long Beach Press-Telegram* resorted to staff members and readers recalling their favorite games. One Atlanta paper took to covering Little League games; another, top prospects in the Braves organization.

In St. Louis, KMOX radio re-created Cardinals World Series triumphs—the Game 7s of 1946, 1964, and 1967. Announcers Jack Buck and Mike Shannon provided the commentary, including analysis of a certain Cards third baseman.

"Boy, what a hothead he is," Buck ribbed old Shannon about his younger self.

With the media in need of filler and the players in need of something to do, a synergy emerged. The ranks of weathermen swelled; Palmer (also in talks to appear on *The Love Boat* and *Dynasty*) and Ken Singleton put in local-TV time. Tigers outfielder and DH Champ Summers wrote a six-part strike diary for *The Detroit News*. Billy

Sample, Rangers outfielder, turned his minute-long postgame radio commentary for an easy-listening radio station into a disc jockey job, quickly becoming as obnoxious as any other disc jockey who talked through the music. In Hollywood, Ron Cey took a little time to film a cameo in *Q: The Winged Serpent,* a throwback to 1950s horror flicks. Cey, "the Penguin," squared off against the mythical Aztec flying-lizard god Quetzalcoatl.

Johnny Carson was having a field day. It was a made-to-order joke—what would famous players do without baseball? In the *Tonight Show* monologue, Billy Martin was found buying inflatable umpires to kick, and Jackson hired Valenzuela for gardening work. Carson's network colleague Tom Brokaw, anchor of NBC's *Today* show and soon to be a free agent, was in the midst of contract negotiations. While NBC had got ample return for grooming Brokaw as he rose through the ranks, what would happen if they didn't reach an agreement with one of their signature stars? If Brokaw joined the reporters of CBS' *60 Minutes,* would Morley Safer have to be shipped off to sit beside Jane Pauley and Gene Shalit? The baseball owners' plan for direct compensation was ridiculous when applied to other situations.

Fans weren't finding humor in any of this (except in Los Angeles, where a group of 24 fans protested outside Dodger Stadium, holding signs that said A SUMMER WITHOUT BASEBALL IS LIKE LIFE WITHOUT SEX). Across the country, a rash of hunger strikes began. A Baltimore DJ announced that he was sticking to water until there was an agreement or until he got too weak to spin records. His last meal: hot dogs, peanuts, and beer. An Indians fan in Las Vegas said, "People might say there are more important things in the world, but I say this is a national tragedy." In St. Paul, four graduates/roommates at Macalester College were giving up ballpark food—hot dogs, peanuts, and frosty malts—though only one was giving up beer. After all, when it came to brew, "you can't carry your ideals to a ridiculous extreme." In Ireland, real hunger strikes took place in Maze Prison, starting in March when Bobby Sands starved to death. National tragedies are a relative thing.

At Memorial Stadium, with not an Oriole in sight, überfan

"Wild Bill" Hagy held an antistrike rally. The big, bearded, straw-cowboy-hat-wearing Hagy, a local legend for stirring up the crowd from his section of the upper deck with "the Roar from 34," complete with body spelling of O-R-I-O-L-E-S, was pro-player. And pro-beer. After a moment of silence, it was off to the bar. They needed the customers.

In Boston, business around Fenway was getting killed. The Batter's Box cafeteria across the street from the ballpark had done a $300,000 renovation before the season. They should've known better after 1980s near stoppage. Rico Picardi, head of Harry M. Stevens concessions at Fenway, felt bad for the vendors.

Some maintained a sense of humor. Urban Goeke, owner of Urban Suburban Tavern in Dayton, posted a help wanted ad: "Bus Boys Wanted, Must Be Unemployed Cincinnati Reds Baseball Players. Do not bring your agent." He should have contacted Rick Cerone, whose answering machine greeted callers, "Hi, this is Rick. I'm not home right now. I'm on strike. I'm on my way down to the unemployment office. I need a job. I can dance, sign, tell jokes, even play baseball once in a while. If you have anything, let me know."

Though fans in Houston and St. Louis were buying tickets for hoped-for future games, neither teams or cities could make light of the increasingly dramatic financial losses. The Dodgers had reportedly lost $5 million with the cancellation of a 10-game home stand. The Phillies were crushed now that Rose might break the hit record on the road whenever games returned, depriving the team of gate receipts that would total $750,000 for a normal weekend series.

Cleveland worried about the All-Star Game and the potential $4.5 million hit to the local economy if the game, and the 80,000 and more expected to descend on the city, vanished. Downstate Cincinnati stood to lose $10 million with the Reds on strike. In Milwaukee County, the loss of 500,000 in Brewers attendance was taking its toll, and, in Detroit, the city was losing 90 cents in tax revenue for every unsold ticket.

Even charities were starting to feel the pinch. The annual Pearson Cup, named for Canadian prime minister Lester B. Pearson, a big fan of baseball, started in 1978, with proceeds split between amateur baseball in Quebec and Ontario and the Canadian Federation of Amateur Baseball. The three games had raised $133,000. The July 6 game between the Blue Jays and Expos was canceled. Everyone was starting to suffer as the strike ended its third week.

Andy Strasberg, promotions director for the Padres, already had a challenge heading into 1981—how to sell tickets to a last-place baseball team. How could he keep baseball visible in San Diego during the strike?

Strasberg hatched up the idea to have a two-game California League series, one at Anaheim Stadium and one at Jack Murphy, on July 4 weekend. The parent clubs split the $18,000 cost for transportation and housing, while reimbursing Reno for lost home-game revenues. The players' association usually objected to minor league games of this sort, but Class A ball was of no matter to them.

For the first time in the century, no major league baseball was part of the Independence Day celebrations. At the Angels' home field on July 3, 9,556 turned out for the Reno Padres–Redwood Pioneers matchup. Gene Mauch, the Angels' new manager after the firing of Jim Fregosi, was there. So was Dodgers outfielder Rick Monday, covering the game for a local Los Angeles TV station.

The next day, July 4, when the imaginary Padres climbed into first place on the heels of a 23-game winning streak in Fantasy Baseball, the parking lot at Jack Murphy was packed, a party going on to celebrate the real thing, or as close as could be found. Seven tons of watermelon and free Coke from 196 five-gallon tanks were provided, and the Padres handed out cushions and coupons for free spaghetti dinners at Square Pan Pizza restaurants. While the Angels charged full price, between $2.50 and $5.50 per ticket, the Padres charged a buck, and 37,655 baseball-hungry Southern Californians turned out.

That night Strasberg did a turn as public address announcer, looking out at the huge crowd that was enjoying baseball the way they were supposed to on a summer night, feeling blessed to have come up with a way to give it to them. Fans, back in the stadium where they belonged, appreciated the hustling minor leaguers and slammed the big-headed, greedy major leaguers. Not knowing the issues, they'd cast the players as villains.

Historically, only the owners had access to reporters. The beat guys who covered the games depended on the team for everything— food, drinks, travel. No wonder they slammed the players. Dick Young, a pioneer in clubhouse coverage for the *Daily News,* had been a liberal in his younger days. A 1960s newspaper strike prevented him from writing his column, and he changed his tune, becoming antiunion in general. His pro-management stance (Young's son-in-law worked for the Mets) had been instrumental in chasing Seaver out of New York, when Young wrote nasty columns about Seaver's wife.

Young chastised the players for being sheep led by the menacing Miller. These poor dumb jocks should sit down with Grebey to understand, and agree to, the owners' very rational ideas. All the players needed to do was play ball, and without Miller they would see that. What was more important to Rose—money or the hit record? With the strike on, Rose could die, like Roberto Clemente, and his career would be over. "We can never be sure, can we?"

Over time, the Youngs of the world ceased to control the narrative, and more thoughtful writers such as Chass found their voice. Chass and Miller first met in Pittsburgh at the end of the 1961 steel strike. Then with the Associated Press, Chass was sent to get the story on the settlement and was honestly and thoroughly briefed by Miller.

Because he presented both sides of the issue, and because he would talk to the union and would point out the owners' inconsistencies that they didn't recognize themselves, Chass was damned as pro-union. "How much did the union pay you this week?" asked White Sox owner Reinsdorf.

Chass found that union officials never lied to him; the owners, Grebey, and Kuhn did. His evenhanded portrayal of the merits enraged the owners. During the sessions themselves the two parties would argue over Chass's latest piece. Young carried the owner flag against writers such as Chass, writers Young thought were so far to the left that he thought they should be writing for Tass, the Soviet news agency.

Most sports-page readers weren't getting the work of Chass or Leonard Koppett, who wrote detailed accounts on how competitive balance had been bettered with free agency and how roster turnover was nearly the same from 1979 to 1981 as it had been in the mid-1960s. Instead these readers got scribes such as Furman Bisher lamenting, "What kind of business is this when the hired hands take charge of the corporation? When the inmates take over the asylum?"

And with Kuhn spouting vapid platitudes—"For the fan, there is a replacement for whom he can cheer. . . . So fan compensation is indeed the issue"—it was no wonder most fans didn't get the real story. Neither did the owners.

Phil Garner, the second baseman for the Pirates, was the oddest member of the players' group of negotiators. A strict Randian with a business degree from the University of Tennessee, Garner hated the reserve clause because it closed opportunity. He was pro–player freedom, but antiunion from the time he was a young kid. Though not a constant presence at the negotiations, he was involved enough to be fully informed. It made sense for Pirates owner and PRC member Galbreath and General Manager Pete Peterson to ask Garner if he could get the players together for a face-to-face.

Garner did the best he could, corralling ten of his teammates to gather at a local Holiday Inn. The meeting started amicably. Galbreath gave the owners' point of view—the need for compensation, how few players would be affected, that the owners were offering reasonable proposals—and beseeched the players to compromise, citing some specific ideas. Garner couldn't believe what they were offering as new.

"You better look at what's on the table," Garner interrupted harshly, "because that's precisely where we are. That's our proposal."

Peterson and Galbreath exchanged looks of confusion and astonishment. The two left humiliated and furious at how they had been made to look foolish by Grebey for their lack of information and embarrassed by the way Garner had set them straight.

Owner confusion and hypocrisy were constant. At the same time Phillies owner Carpenter, a recent hard-liner on compensation, bemoaned the high cost of doing business, he renegotiated Steve Carlton's contract, though he was signed through 1983 at $400,000 per year.

Angels owner Autry claimed no animosity toward the players; he simply couldn't understand why they'd strike midseason, when it would hurt him the most. His vice president, "Buzzie" Bavasi, was equally at sea. He didn't mind a strike—"In a short strike, we'll lose money. But if the rest of the season is out, what with insurance and no costs, we'd break even, maybe even make a few bucks"—but he was upset at the players' betrayal. After all, he'd always been on the players' side. "Ask Koufax, ask Drysdale."

Yes, by all means, ask Sandy Koufax and Don Drysdale, whose joint holdout after the 1965 season, the first of its kind, occurred when Bavasi was general manager of the Dodgers. Bavasi thought that asking his former stars how he'd handled them would make him look good. It was pure fantasy that he treated players fairly before the union. Management's arbitrariness had made players rally behind a strong players' association and, over time, led to a strike.

Some players were doing fine financially during the strike. Nine of them put in claims for their salaries, default notices filed by the players' association. Clubs had ten days to correct the situation. If not, the players would become free agents. Some were on the disabled list, some had guaranteed contracts that made no exceptions for a strike. Rose, Rod Carew, and the Brewers' Larry Hisle specifically had clauses, which their teams accepted, that kept their pay flowing even during a strike. Hisle was shocked when Milwaukee caved on the clause. The owners had no choice but to pay; they didn't want to lose the players and could later file a grievance for recovery.

Steve Rogers, one of those lucky nine, got a bill for $18,000 instead of his June 15 check. Expos vice president and secretary-treasurer Henry Renaud sent a bill and an explanation. Rogers got his first check on February 1 and two more before the season started, with one to come. Though 35.7 percent of the season had been completed, he was paid for 41.7 percent. Rogers owed the team money.

Paying for not playing may have made some owners believe they could keep their players, but a situation was afoot that might cause them to lose *all* their players.

If this work stoppage lasted into 1982, the players might attempt to go out on their own. Miller believed no court would prevent a player from jumping to a new league if their contracts were canceled. "If the owners are foolish enough to end this season without a settlement, they'd spark a big fire among the players. It would take time to have a fully viable league, but you could start with four or six teams and build from there. It could be done," declared Miller.

It had been done before, though unsuccessfully. The Brotherhood of Ball Players, an early union, had started the Players' League in 1890 after owners had imposed severe salary limits. John Montgomery Ward, star shortstop of the New York Giants, college boy and lawyer, tried to settle, and though a strike was mulled over, a new circuit was formed instead.

In their manifesto proclaiming the new league, the Brotherhood stated, "There was a time when the League stood for integrity and fair dealing. Today it stands for dollars and cents. Once it looked to the elevation of the game and an honest exhibition of the sport; today its eyes are on the turnstile. Men have come into the business for no other motive than to exploit it for every dollar in sight." The Players' League failed after one year, and maybe history showed that the owners could prevail over a tenuously held-together group of players. Or maybe not? Would the owners be willing to risk it this time?

The Baltimore Orioles were trying to remain a family, albeit a dysfunctional one. The team provided airline tickets to the players after the strike was announced, unwilling to let them hitch rides with the police like the Yankees. Management knew the strike would end someday and they'd all be back together. Ownership and players stayed close.

Williams had a pipeline directly to Belanger and DeCinces. Belanger would make sure the owner knew the players were standing strong and not going to give in. DeCinces and Williams talked on the phone nearly every day, the player having to often set the story straight. Flown to Baltimore by the owner, the two would meet for dinner and discuss the day's events.

At one sit-down, at the luxurious Jefferson Hotel (which Williams owned), near the White House, DeCinces could tell that the Orioles' owner was steaming.

"You've been lying to me!" yelled Williams menacingly. "I got a telex update from Grebey, and you guys are being unreasonable!" Williams went into detail.

"That's not what happened," answered DeCinces calmly.

"What makes you think I should believe you and not them?"

"Because I'm still playing third base for your team when this is over. What do I have to gain from lying to you?"

"You may be one hundred percent right," Williams admitted sheepishly. As with Garner and the Pirates, another owner had been embarrassed by his own side, and he wouldn't forget the humiliation.

DeCinces continually delivered the facts. Williams had, until the recent episode, always trusted him, and for good reason. DeCinces had always been totally honest, telling Williams straight out what he thought could get player approval and what wouldn't, emphasizing that the players' interest came first. The two had a constant back-and-forth on the telephone.

The PRC was well aware of this too-cozy relationship and fed Williams incorrect information. If the false reports came back to them from DeCinces at the table, Grebey and others would know it came straight from one of their own.

At another dinner, Williams backed off. "I found out that the guys I speak to were told the same things I was told." The anti-Kuhn group was growing beyond Williams and Chiles.

Three weeks into the strike, Grebey asserted that, except for Chiles and Williams, all of the owners were supportive of his efforts. "I think his poll is about a month old," Chiles said, knowing there were more cracks, that others were becoming worried about Grebey's performance.

There was no trust between Grebey and owners, owners and Kuhn, players and owners, players and Kuhn, and among the owners themselves. Only the players and Marvin Miller were as one. And, after initially staying out of it, the government was now ready to get involved.

Chapter 5

"IT'S GETTING VERY NASTY IN THERE"
JULY

Melvin J. Weiles, the administrative law judge presiding over the NLRB hearing, was a baseball fan in general, a Yankee fan in particular. When he saw the matter of Major League Baseball Player Relations Committee, Inc. and Its Constituent Member Clubs and Major League Baseball Players Association, he assigned himself the case. With more than 200 labor hearings under his belt, Weiles had one that interested him immensely.

The NLRB general counsel declined to appeal Werker's decision on the injunction. It wasn't worth the time; Werker's decision was not binding on the new judge. The initial finding was on the injunction alone, not on whether the owners had bargained in good faith. That would be decided by a different judge, a judge who liked baseball.

The hearing began a little after 11:00 a.m. on Monday, July 6, on the fourth floor of the pyramidal former home of the Paramount Theater at 1501 Broadway. If the judge ruled for the players, the NLRB would take the decision to the federal Court of Appeals to obtain a writ of enforcement. The owners could appeal to the Circuit Court of Appeals and/or the Supreme Court. So could the players, if the ruling went against them.

After the petitioner's opening statement recapped the owners' unilateral implementation of their compensation plan (which was their right) without engaging in good-faith bargaining (which was not), a cease-and-desist order was requested to stop them from this unlawful conduct, and, further, a reestablishment of the status quo that existed before the illegal act began.

From the start Weiles was different than Werker—calm, subtle, with a classic judicial temperament and the willingness to allow much broader questioning than had been permitted in Rochester. Undoubtedly that would work in the union's favor. George Cohen, counsel on behalf of the players' association, said "at the bargaining table the chief negotiator has been falsely denying that financial hardship" applies to this single issue, direct compensation. The June 12 strike, he offered, came about principally as a result of the denial of important information to back Grebey's claim. Cohen mocked the very idea that $50 million in insurance would be obtained for a noneconomic issue and ripped Werker's conclusion that Kuhn and the owners were unauthorized representatives. "So the minion speaking on behalf of the committee, he is who we should listen to?"

Minion? This was going to be a full-out assault on Grebey, who along with Kuhn and some owners, was set to testify. This group wasn't used to being treated with disrespect, and they were bound not to like it. Would they be able to stand up under pressure? Would they be able to present their positions so they made sense? Owners and management were never so brazenly questioned, never had their actual words thrown back at them, in a court of law, under oath. It would be uncomfortable and force many admissions they'd otherwise choose not to make. As to Werker's ruling that dismissed the players' claim as a "tactic," a word that Kuhn rejoiced in reading, Weiles said that might be the case if the union was wrong. "Unless they're correct," he added. "Then it's not a tactic."

Weiles posed a question: What if the majority of owners made statements of financial peril and Grebey kept them from the table?

Would the owners still claim that such chatter could only be important if it came in a negotiating session? To take it to the extreme, what if *every* owner said to the papers that free agency without compensation was ruining them? Could Grebey alone ignore that?

"It would be inconceivable that the bargaining team would take a different position at the bargaining table," Hoynes, back as the owners' attorney, answered, "because the bargaining team is the servant of the board of directors." That was the union's point, that Grebey served the owners! After a recess for lunch, all parties returned at 2:20.

Miller took the stand, laying out how free agent salaries had a spreading effect. Since free agency began, the dollars commanded by the top players had impacted the entire salary structure. The owners' proposal to create a group of ranking free agents out of the top 50 percent of players based on appearances was a ruse. Under these criteria it was impossible to determine whether a player was truly top class or merely playing regularly. The lesser the player, the more compensation hurt him.

The new draft process would determine who was a quality free agent based on how many teams drafted them (and didn't allow teams to skip a turn). Obviously, said Miller, more teams will draft a player, which will then make them eligible for compensation. After all, utility man Dave Roberts was picked by more clubs than Winfield in the most recent draft, and most people could spot the difference.

If there were real, provable financial distress, Miller testified under oath, the players might very well think about this issue differently. Until then, the union had been put into a position to strike when it mattered, not, as the owners had initially proposed, before Opening Day.

"Would the union have agreed to a strike date, let's say, in November?"

"No, because this is a seasonal industry." There'd be no point and no leverage.

Kuhn had clipped an article from the new *BusinessWeek*—

"Reagan's NLRB Tips Toward Management." The author hadn't watched Weiles work. After the first day of the proceedings, when Weiles asked Belanger and Boone for their autographs (for his grandson, he claimed), the owners wished they hadn't either. Making matters worse, their unified front was crumbling.

As Chiles predicted, resistance to Grebey and Kuhn was growing, the splinter group becoming a two-by-four. Eight owners sent a telegram to Kuhn and the league presidents on the very day he was monitoring the opening to the hearing he called "fiddle-faddle." Williams, Steinbrenner, Paul, Chiles, and Reinsdorf/Einhorn of the American League were joined by Nelson Doubleday of the Mets, John McMullen of the Astros, and Ballard Smith of the Padres in requesting the commissioner call a meeting of all 26 teams during the week. Cancellation of the June 24 meeting in Kansas City had temporarily prevented a revolt.

Steinbrenner was both of and apart from the movement. He'd appeared with Staub on *Face the Nation* at the CBS Broadcast Center in Manhattan the Sunday before.

"I have been a big user of free agency, and I'm speaking against myself in some sense," Steinbrenner argued with himself as he pontificated on the need for compensation. Though never having been to the table himself, Steinbrenner expressed his dislike that so many people came in and out of negotiations.

The resistance made for strange bedfellows. The conservative Chiles and the liberal Williams had developed a mutual admiration resulting from their outrage that no one on the owners' side was seeking resolution, as well as their shared contempt for Kuhn. They couldn't believe the lack of concern the commissioner showed them in regard to the losses incurred. We "shouldn't be leaving the decision-making process to the staff," Chiles lashed. "He's supposed to work for us. If he can't take criticism, he should get out of the job."

The morning after, on the day the judicial world was pushed into modern times with Reagan's appointment of Sandra Day O'Connor to the Supreme Court, the NLRB hearing picked up before 10:00 a.m. A lineup of owners—the notoriously penurious and aggressively antagonistic Griffith of the Twins; the well-respected, old-money Carpenter of the Phillies; the modern businessman Reinsdorf of the White Sox—took the stand and were grilled, to the dismay of Hoynes.

The prosecutors can't "bring in people like Ruly Carpenter, people like Mr. Griffith, and others to badger them on the witness stand," Hoynes objected.

"People like"? Only in the closed loop of baseball were "people like" Carpenter and Griffith passed off as nobility, deserving of a special layer of respect. They were not to be subjected to harsh questioning. In the real world these emperors were clothesless, and Weiles saw that, disagreeing that the witnesses were being badgered. On it went.

During recess, Miller held court. "It has now come out that Mr. Grebey had considerably more room than he gave our committee on Saturday. He was authorized to make a more liberal proposal and didn't do it." Miller wouldn't say how he knew that Grebey had held back the potential for progress at that session.

Referring to the Saturday talks that had resulted in another breaking off of discussion, Reinsdorf said the players didn't counter and were stalling.

"Utterly false," countered Miller. "I would say Mr. Reinsdorf knows that. You still freeze fifteen players after eighteen months, and Mr. Reinsdorf has the nerve to say we're stonewalling."

"The primary area of responsibility is protection of the game, the public confidence in the game. Integrity is a broad concept," Kuhn proclaimed on the stand. "The commissioner," he said, lapsing into third person, "is a separate and distinct force quite independent."

Asked if a requested financial report from his "independent" office could be shared with the union, Kuhn didn't know; they'd never asked.

"Are you suggesting that if the union made a request to you for this financial data that you would be willing to turn it over to them?"

Kuhn put it off, simply saying the union had never asked, but no thinking person would believe that they could or, if they did, that their request would be granted. After all, they were all here in court because they couldn't get access to financial data. Their requests had repeatedly been denied.

Explaining his role, or nonrole, in the negotiations, Kuhn said he spoke with the PRC during bargaining about their proposals and his views on them. Certainly he knew those proposals before the union was presented with them, and he was advised by the PRC on negotiations.

But was he consulted?

"*Consulted*, I think, is the wrong word. I am kept abreast."

Reminded that he testified voluntarily in Rochester for the clubs and that he was represented by club lawyers, Kuhn didn't see it that way.

Had he ever been represented by union lawyers?

"No, I have not."

Has he ever testified on the union's behalf?

"Well, I'm not so sure about that." He was, as he saw it, the voice of the industry. When asked if the players favored compensation, Kuhn answered that he wasn't sure. "I'm not sure your question is correct."

"I think my question is correct. I'm asking what your answer is."

"Well, they may well be." A strike was going on right now outside the courtroom, and it was over compensation, but for Kuhn the players might, in their hearts, like compensation.

Fehr took over the direct questioning, asking Kuhn if he had ever testified for the players before Congress.

"No, but I represent the industry, not the clubs, not the players, but all."

"I'll tell you what's puzzling me, Mr. Kuhn, and I'll give you a specific example." Fehr read from Kuhn's 1979 testimony: " 'I am Bowie K. Kuhn, Commissioner of Baseball, and I am here today representing the twenty-six major league clubs of professional baseball.' "

Turning back to the 1980 speech, Fehr inquired, "Isn't it accurate, Mr. Kuhn, that your remarks were directed as much at the players as anyone else?"

"No. No, that would not be accurate."

"I'm puzzled by that, because on page four of the transcript of your speech that you make the following comments: 'Everyone in the game, both clubs and players, is going to have to recognize that there is a problem.'" Fehr left Kuhn twisting in his words, contradictory at best, nonsensical at worst. They adjourned for the day at 5:03, with Grebey the featured player for the following day.

Two hours later, Kuhn said he was invited to and would attend the owners' meeting called by the growing number of dissenters. The commissioner would also be much pleased to attend the players' meeting that night if he was invited. Miller laughed at the very idea before heading up to 52nd Street. The 30-man Executive Board of the MLBPA met for four hours at the New York Sheraton Hotel. Miller updated the group on where the negotiations stood.

"The owners have rejected our latest proposal and continue to seek compensation for free agent signings," Miller summarized. "The outlook for a settlement remains bleak." The players reaffirmed their support for Miller amid rumors they were prepared to take all their proposals off the table and tell the owners straight off that compensation was not needed. Neither the owners' direct plan nor the players' pool plan would be considered.

July 8 was C. Raymond Grebey Day in court, but the only giveaway was tough questions. The morning was Hoynes's time for direct questioning. Grebey, soft-spoken and barely audible through a cold, was repeatedly interrupted by union attorneys with demands that he speak up. Increasingly irritated, Grebey pressed on. Outside owner talk was no more relevant than player talk, he said, but his frustration for the whole process was evident. Most businesses "don't bring their entire membership to the bargaining table and have a free-for-all to see which side has the most strength."

After his hiring in 1978, Grebey recounted, he went on a tour of teams to get informed and never encountered any financial problems. Compensation, or "manpower replacement" as he rebranded it, was not intended to destroy free agency. The owners recognized it was here to stay, but skyrocketing salary levels had to be addressed.

Marvin Miller, Executive Director of the Players Association, reshaped the union into a smart, independent, and principled force.

(Howard/AP/Corbis)

Ray Grebey, lead negotiator for the owners' Player Relations Committee. Grebey had been brought in from the business world to add some professionalism to the owners' side. He and Miller butted heads constantly.

(Bettmann/CORBIS)

In 1981, Yankees' owner George Steinbrenner was at war with Reggie Jackson, with or against his fellow owners in the strike depending on his mood and, possibly, in a fistfight with Dodger fans in a hotel elevator during the World Series.
(Walter McBride/Retna Ltd./Corbis)

Fernandomania! Twenty-year-old Fernando Valenzuela was the feel good story of 1981, winning both the Rookie of the Year and the Cy Young Awards and putting in a gutsy performance in Game 3 of the World Series, turning the series around and leading the Dodgers to victory over the Yankees.
(National Baseball Hall of Fame Library, Cooperstown, NY)

In 1980, arm trouble gave Tom Seaver concern, but he surged back to a 14-2 record, leading the Reds to the best record in baseball. Due to the split-season format, Cincinnati was left out of the playoffs. *(National Baseball Hall of Fame Library, Cooperstown, NY)*

"Rickey is a once-in a-lifetime player. You see very few Rickey Hendersons. You might not see another one for fifty years," said Billy Martin. At 22, Henderson was the best player in the American League. *(National Baseball Hall of Fame Library, Cooperstown, NY)*

Behind "BillyBall," an exciting throwback style of squeeze plays, runners in motion, and steals of home, the Oakland A's stormed out of the gates to a 17-1 record. Billy Martin had much to smile about. *(National Baseball Hall of Fame Library, Cooperstown, NY)*

After Red Sox management botched Carlton Fisk's contract, the catcher was declared a free agent and signed by the White Sox. The signing set off a ticket buying frenzy in Chicago. *(National Baseball Hall of Fame Library, Cooperstown, NY)*

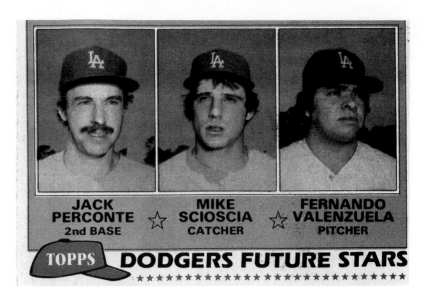

JACK PERCONTE — 2nd BASE ☆ MIKE SCIOSCIA — CATCHER ☆ FERNANDO VALENZUELA — PITCHER

TOPPS DODGERS FUTURE STARS

The Topps baseball card monopoly ended and collectors happily bought new offerings from Donruss and Fleer. Topps and Fleer were the only two companies to think highly enough of a young Dodger pitcher to include him in their sets.

(Topps trading card used courtesy of The Topps Company, Inc.)

The Astros made their first playoff appearance in 1980 after signing free agent Nolan Ryan. In 1981, Ryan led them again to the post-season, hurling his record breaking fifth no-hitter on September 26 against the Dodgers.

(National Baseball Hall of Fame Library, Cooperstown, NY)

Cleveland Indians' pitcher Len Barker tossed a perfect game on May 15 against the Blue Jays. It was almost thirteen years to the day since "Catfish" Hunter had thrown the last one. *(MAD/AP/Corbis)*

It had been a rough year for Commissioner Bowie Kuhn (light suit on left), a main instigator of the strike (according to the players) or uninvolved (according to the owners' negotiators). He was happy for the return of baseball, starting with the All-Star Game in Cleveland on August 9. (Vice President George W. Bush throws the first pitch under a bulletproof canopy requested by the Secret Service). *(Bettmann/CORBIS)*

Left needing one hit to break Stan Musial's all-time National League hit record when the strike hit, Pete Rose set the record in his first game of the second half on August 10 against St. Louis in front of 60,561 screaming fans in Philadelphia's Veterans Stadium.

(George Tiedemann/Corbis)

Reggie Jackson, under pressure all year from George Steinbrenner, finally exploded on September 23, tussling with Indians' pitcher John Denny after blasting a home run.

(Bettmann/CORBIS)

The shot that killed the Expos. Rick Monday powers the Dodgers to the World Series with a ninth inning home run off Montreal ace Steve Rogers, who was brought for relief during Game 5 of the National League Championship Series. *(Rusty Kennedy/AP/AP/Corbis)*

Dave Winfield was the prize free-agent signing of 1981 and had a fine year, but a post-season slump rattled him. When he got his first World Series hit, he mocked his own futility by asking for the ball. The players laughed; Steinbrenner did not. *(Bettmann/CORBIS)*

Was it a problem? "Read the *Times*, it's a delight; read the *News*, it's a concern." The Chass/Young war made a presence in court.

Cohen was ready to conduct his cross-examination after lunch. It all began pleasantly enough, Grebey recalling a chat with the league presidents on the salary situation. They mentioned that salaries were going up as a result of free agency, and Grebey concluded the same, though not just from their comments.

"If the escalation of salaries continues, baseball will be in severe economic difficulty. Some clubs are already in a serious financial position," Cohen read from an article quoting Ray Grebey, written by Jerome Holtzman of the *Chicago Sun-Times* on October 29, 1978.

As to escalation of salaries—"If you ask me if some clubs are going to have a hard time surviving, my answer is an unqualified yes," Cohen read from an article quoting Ray Grebey, written by Ross Newhan of the *Los Angeles Times* on January 31, 1979.

"I found most of the clubs I talk to have financial troubles," Cohen read from an article quoting Ray Grebey, written by Bill Liston of the *Boston Herald American* on March 18, 1979.

"We haven't produced any milk [profits] for six years. Sixteen clubs lost money last year," Cohen read from an article quoting Ray Grebey, written by Harry Bernstein, of the *Los Angeles Times* on August 4, 1979.

Grebey's busy next day began bright and early, back in the witness chair. Continuing from where they'd left off, another quote of Grebey's was introduced. Calling baseball's financial picture a "sick cow," Grebey confided to Holtzman, "I'm not free to tell you how much we lost, but we have not been making a profit in the industry."

After testifying, Grebey headed to the office of the administrative judge, where Moffett was waiting. Miller grabbed a chair, while Grebey plopped down on a short file cabinet. Behind glass doors, Moffett stood before the two adversaries, manila envelopes in hand. The envelopes contained a plan to spark discussion. Upon handing out the new proposals, Moffett said his good-byes, as he needed to return to DC. All this back-and-forth by the arbitrator was costing the government serious money. Moffett's suite at the Doral cost

$500 per night. (His bill for the entire strike to the Federal Mediation and Conciliation Service was $22,000.)

At the same time, MacPhail was testifying, holding the company line with distinction, then, after a break, Miller was recalled. When the witnesses were excused, the lawyers wrapped up. The union lawyers summarized why they believed that direct compensation would negatively affect free agents and, subsequently, those who used those salaries for comparison in individual negotiations or arbitration. Hundreds and hundreds of players were sure to be hurt.

With no more witnesses, the hearing was adjourned at four thirty. Thirty minutes later the owners called their meeting to order at the midtown Citicorp Club in a long room, partitions removed to fit the crowd.

At PRC meetings Kuhn seldom spoke, sitting and listening, his views already well known. Yet, as MacPhail had testified just hours before, the commissioner exerted much influence. For this owner meeting, he was in charge, at least in title, as chair. After a brief introduction, he turned to Grebey, who brought everyone up to date. Then Williams took the floor. He launched into the problems with PRC proposals and the permanent damage it was creating. Williams grilled Grebey like the high-powered lawyer he was, as Chiles nodded his head in agreement.

"We need to speed this up," Williams insisted. "The whole process is moving too slowly and we will lose the NLRB hearing." Williams had been keeping tabs on the proceedings. He could read Weiles, and clearly the players were going to win this one.

Kuhn listened closely to the feedback of every owner. The eight peaceniks had met for three hours at the Carlyle Hotel before the joint meeting, signaling that their preference was for binding arbitration. The old guard in the National League didn't like an upstart such as Williams making waves and laughed at Reinsdorf and Einhorn, who often voted differently on the same issue (Kuhn had once sent a memo to the combined name of "Eddie Reinsdorf").

Carpenter watched in disgust. He glared at Turner and said the lack of trustworthiness in his colleagues was causing him to sell the Phillies. The outrageous signing of Claudell Washington still bothered him. (Carpenter's own hypocrisy, citing the need for heavier compensation while shoveling bales of money to Matthews and Carlton was shrugged off by Grebey in his testimony, where he pointed to "a certain dichotomy between his [Carpenter's] behavior and his preaching.")

"Emotion becomes too big a factor sometimes," offered Steinbrenner, speaking as an expert in the field. It was hard to keep passions under wraps. The Mariners' George Argyros related with anger that he'd got a call from Seattle infielder/outfielder/DH Bruce Bochte, who told him the owners weren't bargaining in good faith.

Argyros pushed to expand the PRC, to add moderates from each league, and Reinsdorf agreed: "Owners should attend negotiating sessions."

"Then Miller will go into his rain dance to indoctrinate new faces!" Chairman Ed Fitzgerald lashed out. The owners were weakening enough as it was; they didn't need easily susceptible members to be swayed by Miller's persuasive powers.

"We can't walk out of here without saying we back the PRC. Bowie has done a fine job. I will call for vote," said Lou Sussman of the Cardinals.

"No, we shouldn't vote," pleaded Williams, "because there'll be division."

Kuhn smirked as the troublemakers—Williams, Chiles, Steinbrenner, et al.—turned meek when pressed. When it came down to a vote, every owner, even the most outspoken, gave the PRC a vote of confidence and pledged to continue backing their efforts. For Grebey it was a triumphant end to an arduous day. Williams, caught briefly by reporters as he tried to slink out unnoticed, was the big loser, for now.

The NLRB hearing wrapped up on the morning of the 10th. "This is not a case that will be decided on the basis of credibility or demeanor," said the PRC's lawyer, hoping desperately for it to be so. Player quotes were cited, expressions of their belief that baseball was wallowing in money.

Weiles was stunned. "You're showing some players' feelings?"

"These things should be accorded the same weight that you accord, whatever it may be, the owners' statements."

"I'm just wondering about the relevance of statements by players or Mr. Miller to the effect they don't believe the claim," Weiles continued. With the proceedings coming to an end, the owners still refused to grasp the point.

There has to be a claim of inability and a belief in it, the PRC lawyer proposed.

No, no, no, said Weiles. "If the union agreed with the claim of inability to pay expressly made, they don't need any books to support the claim, they already believe it."

Right, but they don't believe it.

"No, no, that's why they need it, isn't it? If they believe the claim, they wouldn't need information to substantiate it."

Weiles ended, "Thank you very much, everybody, the hearing is closed." The legal piece of the strike was over. It would take several weeks until Weiles would render his decision, as he was going away and wouldn't return until August 4 or 5. Later that same day, at 2:00 p.m., full focus returned to the Doral.

After a five-day recess in talks, the parties returned, with Moffett's proposal the center of attention. For three hours they met. Grebey rejected the arbitrator's plan. There was no reason to introduce it; in no way did it address the owners' needs. They had a problem with Moffett's suggestion on cash payments made by a team selecting a player from the pool to the team losing him. For the teams allowed to protect 24 players from their roster, the bill was $200,000; for the teams protecting 30, $150,000.

They also took issue with the three-layer grid of teams. Moffett broke all teams into groups of 9-8-9 based on win-loss percentage. If a premium free agent moved up a group, the losing team would get compensation. If a player moved two levels up, the signing team could protect 24. If players moved one level up, the signing team could protect 30. For movement within the same group, the signing team would only lose their June amateur draft pick. If a player moved down, no compensation. The matrix put forth got into the nitty-gritty on competitive balance and how to strengthen clubs. Weak teams would give up nothing. Still, Moffett's compromise included direct compensation.

The owners could not accept Moffett's plan without change.

A fruitless afternoon was followed by a five-hour recess. It was time to adjourn to the mezzanine-level Crystal Room to meet the press. Though the owners were as interested in positive public relations as the players, Miller ran rings around them. Grebey would be direct: "Based upon the content of the mediator's proposal and the demand of the Players Association to accept it in toto, we reject it." Grebey was suspicious of the press. He told them he'd been sworn to secrecy as to the details of Moffett's pitch, but was immediately contradicted by the mediator himself.

Miller would expound on the issues, more off the cuff, relaxed. "Every time I hear Mr. Kuhn, he bleeds about competitive balance. But every time I raise it, they say it's not an issue." Reporters appreciated Miller's style.

It was back to the Doral at 10:00 p.m. for four hours together and apart, the latest they had met since May 23, 1980, when they settled that dispute at 5:00 a.m. The players accepted Moffett's ideas. It was a gambit by the union—accept the plan, which contained the direct compensation they abhorred, knowing full well the owners would refuse, insisting still on pulling back the full bargaining power of a free agent. It made the players appear, rightfully so, ready to settle and the owners intransigent.

Negotiations lasted well into the night and followed into the morning with some swearing and many exhausted looks. Despite moments of optimism, by 2:00 a.m. all was in shambles. On the one-month anniversary of the strike, talks were at an impasse.

Twenty minutes later Miller updated the press corps, followed by DeCinces.

"The owners are not trying to work with the Moffett proposal," relayed the third baseman/labor leader.

"Jesus, what a liar!" Grebey muttered, grimacing and waving his hand dismissively from only two feet away.

Grebey took his turn behind the mikes to present his view of the day's events, and in a brief pause, DeCinces's cries of "Bullshit! Bullshit!" could be heard from the corner where he stood.

On the way out, Grebey patted Miller's left shoulder, a friendly gesture. In the hallway Grebey told reporters that Moffett's proposal was written by Miller. "It's a setup."

Moffett, his long hair tousled, his jacket and polo shirt rumpled, showed his powerful skill and demurred, stating matter-of-factly that he and a coworker wrote it and that it wasn't unusual for one side to make a claim like Grebey's (though Moffett conceded that his proposal was something of a last resort and not typical).

"It's getting very nasty in there," admitted Moffett.

Kuhn officially canceled the All-Star Game. It seemed that a settlement might never come.

With more time to catch up on work around the house and spend time with friends and family, fans were adjusting to the lack of games. An AP–NBC News poll said 46 percent didn't miss baseball. Only 15 percent said they missed it a lot. That worried Hank Aaron: "People have quit talking about baseball," and "whoever is in charge" should "put both sides in a room." As an ex-player, one of the greatest, and a current executive with the Braves, he understood both the teams' and the players' point of view.

It turned out there were other distractions and Hollywood was most appreciative. Moviegoers crammed into theaters to watch Harrison Ford in *Raiders of the Lost Ark*. *Superman II* was a smash, General Zod and Lex Luthor battling the Man of Steel in what could pass as a strike allegory. It took a baseball strike to help the fortunes of *The Cannonball Run*.

With weeks piling on weeks, more players needed to fill their days. Clint Hurdle of the Royals got a bartending gig, wiping bars and pouring beer, limited by his lack of mixological knowledge. Gaylord Perry, on the precipice of 300 wins and time not on his side, was farming full-time. Valenzuela was still turning out the crowds, appearing before 25,000 screaming worshippers at a Mexico City clinic.

In Boston, Richie Hebner stood waist deep in a hole, shirt off, shovel in hand. The Tiger first baseman and designated hitter had found a singular way of spending the dead time brought his way by the strike. He became a gravedigger. The job in the family business was waiting for him when he headed back East. George "Doc" Medich, now pitching for Texas, had been a teammate of Hebner's on the 1976 Pirates. Medich had gone to medical school while pitching and earned his degree from the University of Pittsburgh School of Medicine. Hebner had approached Medich, now a resident in general surgery at Pittsburgh's Allegheny General Hospital, with a business deal.

"If you screw up," joked Hebner, "keep me in mind."

Billy Martin couldn't help himself from digging a hole of his own. At a minor league game in Hawaii, to watch the A's Tacoma farm club, Martin yelled at the umpire from his box behind home plate. He was banned from those seats the next night.

Newspapers were similarly shown the door, with street sales of the *Los Angeles Times* down, *The Baltimore Sun* and *Evening Sun* seeing declines of 3,000 copies daily. In Philadelphia, beat reporter Bill Conlin wrote imaginary game reports with complete side notes; in Chicago, the *Tribune* covered 1959 White Sox and 1945 Cubs games. *The Columbus Dispatch* covered board games, featuring a matchup of the 1924 Washington Senators and the 1935 Detroit Tigers. Hall of Famer "Goose" Goslin, in left field for both clubs, was quoted after the Tigers won in 15 innings, 10–8—"You win some, you lose some."

Funny, but as empty day followed empty day, and more Baltimore Orioles appeared as weathermen, MacGregor, the first of them, couldn't recall whether pitching was tougher than forecasting. Baseball was starting to fade away.

Outside the Doral, autograph hounds and picketers roamed the sidewalk. One sold T-shirts that said I SURVIVED THE 1981 BASEBALL

STRIKE. A bearded young man wearing a three-quarter-sleeve baseball shirt with THE FAN ironed on the front seemed to be there every day. Not above arguing with the participants, making his points with Moffett or jabbing his finger in the air as he yelled at Belanger, the Fan was both man and symbol, begging the two sides to give him his game back.

The official vote of confidence notwithstanding, Grebey continued battling his own people. A source on the inside said Grebey couldn't say more than four sentences in a row without calling a caucus. Belanger sensed that the owner team was under increasing pressure. And now, undermining Grebey, were rumors that MacPhail would take the lead immediately.

"There's nothing to it," snapped an understandably irate Grebey. "It's nothing but gossip. Gossip columnists should write gossip."

"It's crazy," said MacPhail. The AL president liked Grebey, thought him personable and bright, but saw he exuded a lack of confidence and worry over his security that manifested itself in paranoia. He rubbed owners and Kuhn the wrong way.

Kuhn asked MacPhail to meet with Miller, and as a good soldier, MacPhail agreed. At the Helmsley Palace Hotel, the two met on the 14th and had a constructive discussion, the kind Miller could never have with Grebey. At an impasse with Grebey, Miller felt a shift afoot through the conversation with MacPhail, a slow move toward changing the dynamic.

A real slow move. The sessions on Wednesday, July 15, were a disaster. A four-hour meeting left the players furious after the owners had led them to believe there'd be discussion and further counters to the Moffett proposal but then come empty-handed. Belanger was mad ("This isn't going anywhere! That's horseshit! That's wrong!"). DeCinces suggested that the press should dig more to uncover Grebey's lies. Even the mild-mannered Boone was ticked off. "The owners led us to believe they would give us a new proposal today. Now they say they'll have one tomorrow, so we wasted a whole day."

But the next day was different from others. Secretary of Labor

Raymond Donovan, after a call from Williams for help, arrived at the Doral with Moffett at 2:00 p.m. The "ideal person to initiate a new era of Republican labor relations," according to Counselor to the President Ed Meese, Donovan was country-club pals with the Astros' owner. McMullen had a different take on Donovan's ability. "He's not much, but he's all we've got," he told a reporter at lunch.

"It was like walking into a butcher's cold freezer," Donovan said. He shivered as he met separately and then jointly with the two sides, urging them to come to a solution. His presence was not a message from President Reagan; the White House offered no support for the peace mission. Donovan was out on his own, in the interest of improving the reputation of the administration and himself. The bargaining broke off at 7:05 p.m., to be resumed the next morning at ten thirty. Donovan informed the press, wishfully, that he detected a nicer spirit, but warned the negotiators that if no progress was made, he would summon them to the capital.

Though Grebey would say that the owners had given it their best efforts, his Thursday proposal caused an explosion. Along with a rejiggered set of numbers for the protected-player list, a full page of additional requests was officially presented—players to get pay from the day they reported, a new date, July 30, for the All-Star Game, withdraw the NLRB suit, and service credit to be given from the settlement date, but not for strike days.

Everything had to be brought up, said the PRC chief, and he sent a message to all clubs that service time was not automatic, but, now a matador, he admitted it was a "red flag to the players."

Miller charged. "Stupidity," he clamored. "Bringing up service time now will prevent a settlement," and though Grebey suggested they could go to arbitration on this one issue, Miller snorted, "One does not arbitrate one's life."

The players were willing to go to arbitration on the issue of compensation, as Moffett had been pushing for weeks, and increasingly owners were pressing their negotiators to agree. Kuhn was convinced that if no settlement was reached by the end of the month, then arbitration of the entire matter was the way to go. A telex from Smith of the Padres urged acceptance of the union's offer, not from weakness but from strength.

"If we believe in our position, we should have no trouble convincing a panel of arbitrators that our stance is correct."

The press conferences reinforced Moffett's desire to move from the media circus of New York to Washington. With Donovan pushing the same, there was more pressure to head south. The television crews were particularly annoying, with shouts of "Louder," "Can't hear," and "Hold on, not ready yet."

"That's your problem," replied the arbitrator, but it was his as well. The instant examination by both parties in front of a ravenous press and in the presence of each other, a quasi-negotiating session in the court of public opinion, created its own problems. Without fail the next day's session would begin with the repairing of the damage created at the previous day's press conference. Shutting down the press machine could only help the process.

A day later Grebey and Miller met in DC with Donovan, who said, "Failure to resolve this strike will be a kick in the teeth to the American people," already suffering through a rough economy that July. Donovan asked both sides to come to the offices of the Federal Mediation and Conciliation Service on July 20. The secretary would be there in person or updated through Moffett.

Miller explained to Donovan that his negotiating team had total authorization. On the other hand, Grebey had announced after the recent offer that the PRC were not authorized to go any further. The PRC head had been on a short leash, continually caucusing whenever a certain point was reached, leaving the room to call the PRC board. One owner was shocked: "I thought Grebey had authority." The real powers, those behind Grebey and the league presidents, were removed from federal pressure, Miller explained. They never showed themselves at the table.

Donovan bit at Miller's line. He insisted that the six-person PRC sit at the table. They had never been there as a group. Miller got what he wanted, but wasn't too pleased with the members themselves. Some had potential free agents, which presented a real conflict, and none of them had negotiating experience. The organizational structure that Grebey had been hired to build, narrowing the number of spokesmen, limiting owner representation at the negotiations to a scant few, was falling apart.

A typical steamy, muggy July 17 Friday in Kansas City, and the Tea Dance competition at the new Kansas City Hyatt Regency was the place to be, a weekly event that had taken off, drawing over 1,000 people per night in the two months it had been held. Since its opening the year before, the 40-story building, one of the highest in the city, was *the* classy destination. The multiple catwalks seemed to hover magically above the swinging couples, unlike anything else the partyers had ever seen.

Rich Gale was a solid starting pitcher for the Kansas City Royals, winning 36 games in his first three years in the majors, the kind of ballplayer who would be the 16th man on the roster, ready to be plucked by another team if the owners had their way. When the strike began, Gale thought he would find work in sporting goods or maybe go to medical school. Instead, he was hired as a bartender to work private functions and served as one of three Tea Dance judges, watching through floating stringed balloons as well-dressed pairs sashayed in their pastels and church clothes to the faint strains of "Satin Doll" and other chestnuts. Gale, an inexperienced barman, poured drinks from behind a pyramid of overturned glasses at his station on the opposite side of the lobby. He was a magnet for those partygoers who wanted to meet a real major leaguer.

A few minutes after 7:00 p.m., guests standing on the fourth-floor catwalk, watching the revelers below, heard a loud metallic pop, which echoed throughout the lobby. Instantaneously, the walkway collapsed, spectators from above holding on to the brass railing for their lives. The upper structure smashed into the second-floor catwalk, bringing 64 tons of steel, concrete, and glass to the ground. The room turned black as pitch. For a moment it was eerily silent, but soon screams for help and wails of pain reverberated.

Through the dust and the darkness, Gale waded through the

rising waters spewing from pipes cut by falling debris, pushing aside twisted metal, chunks of concrete and rubble, helping victims as best he could. Along with every other able-bodied person on-site, soon to be joined by numerous first responders, Gale pushed himself beyond the limits of his endurance, helping as many trapped people as he could. Over 100 people had immediately been killed.

Gale saved the lives of many that night simply by being a Kansas City Royal, drawing people to where he worked away from the dance floor to talk about baseball and the strike and to get an autograph. Two of those were the young daughters of Royals beat writer Mike McKenzie, the sisters hanging around the pitcher before the catwalks fell.

The carnage of that tragic evening left its mark. Gale's financial troubles brought on by the strike were now meaningless, and in his post-trauma nervousness, he sliced open his left, nonpitching hand after he dropped a pitcher of lemonade. At the emergency room, he received five stitches, and the ER nurses noted that his pulse was racing at twice its normal rate. The next day, in a futile attempt to occupy his mind, Gale and his wife, Sue, took in the hit comedy *Arthur*. Gale sat stone-faced in the theater. His nerves getting the best of him, he and Sue drove to his parents' house in New Hampshire, far away from what he'd seen.

Making their way past a man dressed as a life-size hot dog and "Super Fan" in a rainbow Afro wig, Moffett and Donovan realized that the circus had folded up its tents and moved to 2100 K Street NW, the offices of the Federal Mediation and Conciliation Service.

Political pressure of the highest order made Miller nervous. The government could apply enormous weight that was impossible to ignore. What would Reagan do? The union didn't have the power in the halls of government that the owners did. When Miller worked for the United Steelworkers of America, the Department of Labor took an active role to end a walkout. Under President Lyndon Johnson's orders, the warring parties were locked in a White House executive office suite. In the morning, LBJ poked his head in; at night he'd check to make sure they hadn't left the room, broiling from the lack of air-conditioning. A settlement was reached.

The owners were not immune either. Baseball had always skirted around the laws of monopoly due to its antitrust exemption, dating back to a Supreme Court decision in 1922, Justice Oliver Wendell Holmes writing, in effect, that physical play is not product, and that baseball was not business—a strange concept, particularly in 1981. Whenever the sport sparked the ire of the public, some congressman or other would threaten to look into the antitrust exemption. It made the lords of baseball jumpy. "Anytime a high US government official with a direct pipeline to the president gets involved, you certainly feel the pressure," said a PRC member. When Tip O'Neill called Bowie Kuhn—and he did often —urging the commissioner to make a deal because the public needed baseball back, Kuhn got the message. "The Speaker of the House is on my case," he relayed to the PRC.

Miller made his first mistake by agreeing to Donovan's request for a press blackout. The media was the only way of getting information out to 650 players all over the country and the Caribbean. It was impossible to inform each and every member, especially in the days before cell phones and answering machines. TV, radio, and newsprint were the only way to send messages. Union members shared updated information as they looked into cameras or answered questions to scribbling notetakers.

With no widespread source of information, a communications network was built. Telephone networks were hastily arranged to get word out quickly.

The system had its weaknesses. "I can't get ahold of some of my players," quipped Dodgers rep Jerry Reuss, "but we have fourteen housekeepers who are right behind us."

It was much easier for the PRC to spread news. Each member was assigned three to four owners to contact. Whether they were getting true accounts of what happened at the table was a mystery; past experiences showed communication was sketchy at best. The DeCinces/Williams relationship was far outside the norm. Most owners got one version of the story.

"Nut-cutting time," as Rogers called it, began on July 20. Kuhn flew Braniff to DC to be near the negotiations. Arriving at the Mayflower Hotel on Connecticut Avenue in secret, Kuhn set up temporary offices where he could meet with his Executive Council and the negotiating committee. A spokesman for the PRC said he had no knowledge of Kuhn's involvement.

The caucus and meeting rooms at FMCS were smaller than those at the Doral. Donovan shuttled from room to room, spending 45 minutes with the owner team of Grebey, Feeney, MacPhail, and attorneys. The secretary spoke at length about national morale and about the necessity to find a solution, pushing the owners to settle.

They were unmoved. One member of the PRC was dismissive of Donovan's efforts—"just there, showing up." Donovan knew that Kuhn, though not present, believed if Miller truly wanted to come to an agreement, he could simply accept the PRC's proposal. Of course quick settlement would result from complete capitulation! Donovan was seeing that Kuhn's opinion was not singular.

"Those no-good SOBs," Donovan muttered, tomato red as he headed to the players' caucus room.

Miller, Fehr, Belanger, Boone, and DeCinces launched into their problems with Grebey, the lack of honesty, the erratic information that was spread to the owners, the delays.

"We get it, we understand what they're doing," the union told Donovan. When Kuhn and the owners hired Grebey from union-busting GE, it set the tone of the negotiations. For every substantive question, Grebey would condescendingly give the players half of the answer that he assumed they could comprehend. The pomposity of Kuhn and the arrogance of Grebey spoke for themselves.

Plus, Grebey absolutely couldn't decide to settle, unlike the players who could, subject to ratification. What the players gave was against themselves because the PRC leader couldn't come back without going to his board. Grebey was just a messenger, and it resulted in little to no movement at the negotiating table.

"Are they ever gonna get there?" asked Belanger.

As Donovan spoke, DeCinces and the others sensed that he was not pro-owner, as they feared. His job was to put an end to the strike. They welcomed that attitude; it signified progress. If Donovan could put pressure on the PRC to move past the stalemate, there could be an agreement.

At four thirty, Donovan brought the two parties together for a discussion, not a negotiation. For one hour they hashed out the background, Donovan speaking at length and sternly. Afterward, before the cameras and microphones outside the offices, Donovan smiled, putting his best face on the day.

On the second day, the players presented a new pool proposal. Instead of 36 players protected throughout an entire organization, they now offered 24, softening it so not all 26 teams would have players in the pool every season. No team would lose more than one player every three years. Further, a team losing a premium free agent would pick a player and pay $150,000 to the club losing a player in pool. There'd be a cap of no more than seven premium free agents in any one year, coming from the top 20 percent of players ranked over two years.

Miller felt that the players addressed each owner problem with this proposal. He wasn't optimistic, convinced they didn't want a settlement. Why would they? Most owners weren't losing money due to the strike insurance. Seventy percent of a team's operating budget was in major league expenses—salaries, hotels, travel. If only they could figure a way to sustain a baseball business without the nuisance of the players and the game.

After hours of separate meetings on the 22nd, the two sides never together, a long lunch break was called at 2:00 p.m. Donovan and Moffett, who had spent the morning going back and forth between the two rooms, chose a local health-food restaurant. The PRC slipped out the back. Miller, Fehr, and five players adjourned to a burger joint across the street. At their checkered-tablecloth table, they waited, Miller propping his chin in his left hand. DeCinces read the paper. The gathered press, seeing nothing was in the offing, dispersed.

With the coast now clear, the three groups made the six-block journey to the Office of Personnel Management. In the fifth-floor conference room waited six men. Forty days after the strike was called, the players finally sat down with the full board of directors of the PRC. They were there, with the full power of all 26 clubs, to take advantage of any progress. Miller had made an issue that not every team had been informed and had that week sent a telegram to them explaining the pool idea. Miller wouldn't trust Grebey anymore to relay the facts.

Nothing constructive came of the clandestine summit other than Donovan's harsh talk, but having all in one room was a step forward. "There was a clearing of the air. It was a good open meeting," said one insider, confirming Moffett's hunch that there was less chance to tense up with a surprise meeting. Phil Garner, in DC for support, saw in the faces of his friends the grinding tension, the weight of the world on their shoulders worse than the strain of a 16-inning game. Talks were to resume the next day at nine thirty, now with a glimmer of hope.

The day began earlier for the owners' team with a 7:00 a.m. meeting at the Hay Adams Hotel to review a proposal to present to the players. The latest union offering was something they could work with, and though they'd rejected Moffett's ranking of clubs by win-loss record, they saw in it some merit. After two and a half hours, they were ready. The pool was moving forward.

On July 23, the owners gave up direct compensation. Though a pool plan was anathema to them, it was becoming more appealing than the loss of the entire season. Kuhn had been explaining why he came to this conclusion in his daily talks with the PRC. They presented their own variation of Moffett's grid, and in their plan, five teams could be exempt and remove themselves from the free agent draft; other teams could protect 24 to 28 players from the entire organization. Teams not signing a free agent could only lose one player in the pool over three years unless they signed a premium free agent in one of those years. If you signed, you lost.

Grebey informed the press of some details, that signing teams could protect 24, nonsigners 28. He offered no further details on how the pool would work. The owners' pool proposal was a myth, rebutted Miller, who still wanted signers to protect at least as many as nonsigners. Any other calculation penalized the signing team, and, directly, the player looking for maximum bargaining power. In the owners' proposal, a team would get $150,000 if it lost a player to the pool and didn't sign a free agent, and nothing if it had signed a player, another punitive step. The issue of credit time was also still up in the air. MacPhail was shocked that the players didn't accept the owners' plan in full. He thought that's where Miller was after their backroom talks; it was the sense that he'd passed on to the PRC and Kuhn. There was much to chew on.

The morning session had gone well enough that word had spread of an imminent settlement, one general manager going so far as to have his secretary find player addresses to get them back. In the afternoon, MacPhail took over the lead, asking questions about the players' pool. DeCinces thought to himself, "Something's gonna move."

"Would a club have to contribute to the compensation pool if they didn't draft any free agents?" MacPhail inquired. He'd been taking diligent notes on the pool idea during sessions, trying to come up with a form that would satisfy both parties. Though he hadn't wanted to take over, he did, especially with dissident owners demanding a meeting during the next week.

As MacPhail spoke, someone came in to the room and whispered in Grebey's ear. The midday break brought the newspapers and trouble.

"That's it, don't say anything more," Grebey called out. "This meeting is over. Everyone out of here."

MacPhail turned to Grebey in confusion, saying something the players couldn't hear.

"We are going to recess," Grebey confirmed. "No more discussion."

"Excuse me," asked Donovan, who had attended all four days' worth of sessions, "what's going on?"

"We're going over here," answered Grebey. "Come see us."

"You're right I'll come see you," said Donovan as he headed to the owners' caucus room.

The union was flummoxed at the stone wall that had dropped and unaware of why the owners had withdrawn. MacPhail, gentlemanly as always, had been making strides toward settlement and, in midsentence, had the rug pulled from under him. They waited in their caucus room near the main negotiating room.

In time, Donovan came in. "This is about what Davey Lopes said." The morning's West Coast news had made its way east.

"Do Doug DeCinces and Bob Boone have legal backgrounds?" the Dodgers second baseman told Chris Mortensen of the *South Bay Daily Breeze*. "The last thing I want to do is pick up a paper and read Doug DeCinces's synopsis about the players' feeling because he is not qualified and he doesn't know what he is talking about." Lopes was peeved. "It's my life, it's my livelihood." Lopes was sorely pissed off at his teammate Garvey, who was still getting paid during the stoppage (as were a growing list of players, including Winfield and Carlton).

Testifying back on July 8, Grebey had said that outside owner chatter was as interesting and irrelevant to the process as outside player chatter, but with Lopes's comments, suddenly comments made off the table were pertinent. The PRC leader saw the players falling apart, the solidity falling to pieces, and now he was in no rush to settle.

Lopes wasn't alone. Tiger pitcher Dan Schatzeder wanted a stronger voice for all the players. Reggie Jackson might have his Panasonics to shill, said Schatzeder, but a nonstar such as himself had no advertising income. "I won't be a martyr and give up $200,000 so Steve Kemp can become a free agent," Champ Summers said of their fellow Detroit teammate.

It was the natural fallout from the press blackout. The rank and file weren't getting the news they needed. Miller told Donovan that he couldn't keep it going. The secretary understood; he'd seen that Miller was sincere in his efforts to achieve a settlement.

The session was over, and though Donovan felt that his presence over 24 hours of meetings was worth it, the DC phase was a failure. Miller looked haggard and tired, slumped in his chair. What hurt most was that a deal was in his grasp, free agency saved, and it had been yanked away. The ripple caused by a few drops of player discord could quickly turn into a tidal wave. The press loved the idea of the players eating their own, slamming DeCinces and Boone, who were out on a limb, undeserving of scorn. Miller and Belanger doubted that the season could be saved. Boone and DeCinces had another idea.

"We are going to have three meetings with all the players," DeCinces said. "This is a pivotal point, we need to hear from them. *I* need to hear them and speak to them."

"Doug, this isn't the time," Miller said weakly.

"Marvin, this is the time."

"There's not *enough* time. When do you want to do this?"

"Next couple of days," answered DeCinces.

"Maybe we should wait," said a hesitant Miller.

Waiting was not an option. "Don," said DeCinces to Fehr, "get us three meetings—O'Hare Airport, LAX, and New York. All players have to pay their way to these meetings."

It was time to take this show on the road. The players were as tired as Miller. DeCinces had hardly seen his wife and family in six weeks. Rogers, there nearly every day, flew back and forth to Montreal constantly, at times getting direct feedback from angry fans, one of whom cut his leather hanging bag with a knife. But they had to go on, they were so close.

DeCinces went to stay with the Boones in New Jersey, meeting with some other Phillies, playing golf and talking about what was to come. Then it was off to Chicago on the 27th to face the players.

For the next few days, Miller was alone or in conference with Fehr. The owners didn't understand where Grebey had put them. Anything short of a victory would be Grebey's undoing. Anything short and the owners would wonder why they went through this. Yet many owners wanted to hold out. Kuhn played his tired old game of impartiality and mock outrage. Slamming Miller while seeming to defend the players, Kuhn spoke out. "This information gap is deplorable," Kuhn lamented. Every one of the 650 should know what's going on; they're entitled. "I have been assured" the 26 clubs know what's happening. Assured? He didn't know? That information had been disingenuously spread among the owners was well known. Kuhn urged clubs to send their offer directly to the players. The Red Sox, White Sox, Mets, Yanks, and Dodgers did just that.

The union was further pilloried when Miller said it was the players' Executive Board, not he, who had the power to accept the owners' proposal. All along the union had slammed Grebey for having no power, for needing to conduct a 26-owner fire drill to arrive at a response. We have the power to approve, the union would say. Now Miller was backing away. His reasoning was sound—as long as he thought the owners' pool proposal had all the trappings of direct compensation, he couldn't approve it on his own. It wasn't what his constituents wanted. Still, it was grist for the mill.

Miller grew so tired during his days spent in solitary thinking or with lawyers and some players on the negotiating team. The long sessions, the pressure of Washington, and now cross-country plane trips? It was not the life for a 64-year-old man. He had grown thinner, eating less, smoking Marlboros more.

Unlike Kuhn, who kept only his side of correspondence, Miller saved his mail. The public fury that poured into his office wore on him. Nasty or not, he took them to heart. Most were about the money, not the principle. Many offered solutions.

"Dear Mr. Miller, get your ass in gear! Thank you."

"You're an asshole if there ever was one."

On the morning of Saturday the 25th, Bob Fishel, the AL public relations director, brought 12 copies of the PRC's July 23 proposal to Miller's apartment. The owners suggested to the press that the current recess was for the players to consider their pool proposal. After days of consideration and conversation, Miller had a new proposal that he hoped would end this once and for all.

Before heading to Chicago on the 27th, Miller called MacPhail.

"Lee, I have some ideas and I'd like for you to jot them down." Miller relayed eight points for MacPhail.

"All right, Marvin, I've got them. What should I do with them?"

"If the owners propose this package, I'll strongly recommend the players accept it."

"Is our side able to make any changes?"

"Of course, that's your right, but if you make any major changes, then my commitment to you doesn't stand."

"How can I use this material? Do I tell the PRC that this came directly from you?" MacPhail asked.

"That's entirely at your discretion. I think you should follow your best judgment on the matter." Miller liked MacPhail and trusted him. He had always been honest and decent. The dialogue was nearly over when Miller reiterated a key point.

"One thing, though: the *PRC* has to propose this. If I propose it, it has no chance in hell of being accepted." Miller and the union had been shown over and again that the owners could never agree with each other enough to give a solid proposal. The compromise Miller presented solved what the owners said they wanted to accomplish, but didn't gut free agency, which in reality was what they wanted. If Miller proposed it at the table, Grebey and company would never agree to it. It had to be done in a roundabout way. Miller gave MacPhail what he needed for a settlement.

O'Hare Airport was abuzz with talk of a possible air traffic controllers strike. At the O'Hare Hilton, the players' Executive Board, with a side trip to *The Phil Donahue Show,* met with over 50 players who could easily get to Chicago. Not everyone was on board when they arrived.

"I'm gonna tell them this bullshit has to stop. The union is being unreasonable," White Sox slugger Greg Luzinski told Reinsdorf before heading out.

"Don't be a rabble-rouser. Don't fight the union," advised the Sox owner. Reinsdorf told "the Bull" what he thought, that the union was wrong, that it had enforcers to keep guys in line. Cubs pitcher

Mike Krukow was impatient, ready to go off on Miller and the union. His teammate, first baseman Bill Buckner, had grown uncomfortable sitting around and waiting. He wanted to get back on the field.

Boone and DeCinces gave a recap, the latter struggling, walking and sitting with difficulty due to another flare-up of back pain. Miller, acknowledging the terrible information gap that came from the blackout, explained the owners' compensation idea and his own view that it was a punishment for signers. Then he discussed the union's pool, which addressed competitive balance but didn't hamper free agency. He put both sides' proposals out for discussion.

"If you had to take a team vote today," Miller asked the 26 team reps, his voice a little scratchy, "do you think the clubs' proposal would get majority support?" Not a chance, replied 24 of them. There was unanimous support for Miller and the players' position and rejection of the owners' latest offer. After five and a half hours the meeting was adjourned at 11:00 p.m., and the players met the waiting press. Each and every quote backed up the union. Krukow and Buckner said they were going to look for new jobs. Buckner went further: "I'm behind the negotiating team one hundred percent. Now I can sit out the season and not feel quite as bad." Though Summers stayed away, Schatzeder was there. "I mostly sat by and listened, but the meeting enlightened me," he told a reporter. The five or six dissidents that came had heard the good news and were instantly converted. Miller felt invigorated.

Good thing, as he had to hop on a plane bound for Los Angeles the next morning. He'd have time to rest before meeting with a new set of players at the Marriott near the airport on the 29th. It was a reunion of sorts for 70-plus Southern Californians. Nearly all the Dodgers who lived in the area were there. What was calm in Chicago blew up in laid-back LA.

From the dais at the head of the hotel ballroom, the player reps began their briefing, Miller staying mum, watching.

"We're here to listen," said DeCinces, who then asked for comments.

Reuss, who had also been slammed by Lopes in the press, looked at his teammate. "If someone has an objection, damn it, say something."

"Can I say something?" Reggie Smith stood up and, without a microphone, could be heard by all. "Who in this room isn't with the Association?" Smith, who had voted against striking in 1972 as a Red Sox, saw a chance to redeem himself. He ripped into Lopes and everyone who didn't understand what this was about. He had seen much in the last ten years, even more stretching back to 1966, his, and Miller's, first year.

Lopes backed down from his previous comments. Under pressure, he stood up, apologizing while maintaining a degree of innocence, saying he was taken out of context. He was still pissed off that some players were getting paid while others weren't. Angels second baseman Bobby Grich objected; everyone had had the chance to have a stipulation included in his contract to be paid in a strike.

The mood was changing fast, getting especially rowdy after hearing the story of how close they were to a deal before Lopes and Schatzeder roiled the waters. DeCinces was worried this would turn into a melee. Miller calmed them down. "We need to discuss the facts." Once everyone settled down, the questions came and Miller answered. He was nonemotional and straightforward, providing the right tone.

After two and a half hours Rod Carew called for a voice vote: all ayes in support of the union. Lopes made his way over to DeCinces and told him how sorry he was.

"I appreciate it. Thanks for coming to the meeting." DeCinces shook Lopes's hand graciously.

The press horde could hear the yelling from inside the ballroom and could hardly wait to confront the players.

"He [Miller] wanted to get feedback, to clear up a lot of things that had been going on," said a chastened Lopes. "By doing this, it makes everyone feel a lot better. It makes me feel better. I just wanted to see what was going on. I now feel we're stronger collectively than we were when we started this thing."

"The decision we made a long time ago to strike was the right one. Without a doubt, it's therapeutic," said Smith, still hot. Ted Dawson, of Channel 7, provoked the Dodger outfielder, who was in no mood to be challenged. Suddenly the two were being separated and the lobby/pressroom was in chaos.

The owners believed they cared for the game in a uniquely special way. Perhaps that was true when it came to the business side, perhaps not. The players loved the game and loved to play. They might not love each other, but as teammates they were bound together to win. In the labor fight they were all loyal and committed teammates. The owners never recognized that.

"Here we are," said a pleased Williams to his fellow American League owners, starting 90 minutes earlier than the time the players were to begin in Los Angeles, "arrayed politically from Genghis Khan [pointing to Calvin Griffith] to Mahatma Gandhi [placing his hands on his chest angelically]." Eight of them had called this meeting with Williams in the lead. All eight wanted to accept the players' offer of binding arbitration. MacPhail, more in the know than any of them, was displeased. He urged Williams to stop talking to every writer who crossed his path and stop trying to run MacPhail's league. He was the president and he would call meetings.

"Baseball is under fire," intoned a serious Kuhn. He'd been in telephone contact with some of the PRC and his own Executive Council, trying to convince them to hang tough. "We must maintain unity."

MacPhail gave a full recap of how they'd arrived to this dreadful place. "When it's over, we must examine and reorganize our negotiation procedures," MacPhail concluded, a clear sign that Grebey's, and perhaps Kuhn's, days were numbered. Chiles picked up on it right away, pleading for a change in the commissioner structure of the last 60 years and pushing for an analysis of how this mess happened and who was responsible.

Despite Grebey's claims that there had been good collective bargaining the last two weeks, Williams knew, and said, it had not worked, that binding arbitration was the only way.

"Miller wants to go to arbitration," MacPhail disagreed. "That's why he has been dodging settlement."

"We are facing an economic and psychological disaster," said the A's Roy Eisenhardt, before making a motion to support arbitration. One by one the octet was ready to vote aye.

"The National League won't go for arbitration," Royals owner Ewing Kauffman interceded.

"Our feeling ought to mean something to the National League," hoped Williams, still new enough to underestimate age-old rivalries.

"It's time to vote on the issue," Reinsdorf interjected, "and not concern ourselves about the National League."

Fitzgerald pushed back. "The PRC wants to continue collective bargaining."

MacPhail pleaded for more time, explaining the progress he'd made since emerging as leader. Williams put forth a deal—"If arbitration proponents don't seek a vote on the resolution today, then, if there's no agreement by Monday, we go for arbitration." Once Williams went along, it was easy for all the rest to agree. Refusing a request from MacPhail, whom they all revered, was not easy. It didn't really matter though; the dissidents had won.

When the National League owners caught wind of their rivals' get-together at the Bankers Trust building on Park Avenue, they assembled at one thirty at the Citicorp Center. When two NL owners (McMullen and Smith) joined the AL eight, the rest of their league brethren were furious.

For only the second time, a joint meeting of them all would take place, Williams and crew heading to join the National Leaguers on their home turf. Though Grebey had scoffed at reports of owner discord, mocking Miller for his cross-country dog and pony shows, it was impossible to deny the reality of the situation. With one-half of the major league teams pushing hard for a settlement, the hard-liners could not hold out.

MacPhail distributed a single sheet, <u>MILLER INPUT OF JULY 27TH</u>, and revealed what he and the union chief had discussed. The owners were meek, except for Turner, who, in a Moral Majority turn of a phrase, suggested they "get rid of these guys and get new ones. That's what the Lord did. He drowned them all and started over again with two of each kind." The rest of them calmly discussed the merits of Miller's outreach, saw in it enough room to work and save face. That, plus the impending final installment of strike-insurance money from Lloyd's, created an overwhelming desire for a quick settlement that permeated the room. Instructions were sent to the PRC to get it done. The PRC at last understood the will of whom they represented.

The owners' silence as they shuffled out after two hours stood in stark contrast to the raucous player passion in Los Angeles. They'd begun the day thinking the players were crumbling, but were now getting reports of their vociferous unanimity. The strike was over that day.

While the world watched the royal wedding of Prince Charles and Diana Spencer, Miller turned on the news. Back in New York he saw on TV a very different owner tone, the macho posturing and false bravado gone. Chicago and Los Angeles showed powerful solidarity, giving Miller a huge boost. His devotion to the cause was revived, his talk with MacPhail had been productive, and the coming end of the insurance money on August 8 made all the difference in the world.

He arrived home to a ringing phone. It was MacPhail asking Miller if they could meet in the National League office in the morning? Curious, Miller said yes.

The end was near.

Chapter 6

START ME UP
JULY 31–AUGUST 9

The *New York Daily News* was the first to report it—"PLAY BALL."
It was over—baseball was back.

A little after 6:00 a.m. on July 31, Miller, visibly exhausted,
moved slowly to the microphone in the Crystal Room.

"We have indeed made a settlement, subject to ratification by
each side."

That was it. After 49 days the strike had ended. Belanger shook
MacPhail's hand.

"It didn't have to happen," said the weary Orioles shortstop.

"Let's not let it happen again," answered MacPhail.

There would be no peace-treaty picture between the two main
warriors.

"I don't think you should pose with him," DeCinces, still angry
at Grebey, advised Miller, pulling him aside.

The union head agreed, telling cameramen, "I don't go for posed
pictures," though he had in 1980. Back then, Miller wasn't consumed
by the lack of trust and scorn that he now had for his foe.

Grebey sought out Boone, whom he respected. They shook
hands. Seeing a connection between them, Grebey, in all sincerity, told the Phillies catcher, "You know, Bob, I'm sorry you were

involved in this. You're really a good guy. I'm sorry you and I had to be on opposite sides of the negotiation."

Boone was gracious but couldn't wait to find DeCinces.

"You wouldn't believe what he told me," Boone began before relaying what had happened. They both burst into laughter. Grebey had totally misread Boone's calm as sympathy.

Looking for other hands to shake, Grebey spotted and approached Staub. Noticing being noticed, Staub took off, with his former nemesis in a hot pursuit around a table.

"You're a liar. You're always going to be a liar and you're not going to be my friend," shouted the orange-haired Met. The pair wouldn't be working on any crossword puzzles together in the foreseeable future.

At the press conference, Miller smiled as he paid tribute to his players. "It was a victory for the spirit of the players." He was so proud of them, this dedicated group of self-advocates standing up for the principles they held dear. He wasn't as vital anymore, reminding all that this would be his last negotiation before retiring after 15 years as executive director of the Major League Baseball Players Association.

The scene had been set in motion by MacPhail's phone call. At the July 30 meeting the American League president had requested, the participants were Miller and Fehr, MacPhail and Grebey. Hoping they could have a one-on-one session, Grebey had made a last-minute call to Miller that morning, but Miller was through with that. He offered the two-man committees, no less.

"We're here to make a settlement," MacPhail announced.

For four hours, from 1:00 to 5:00 p.m., the quartet haggled at National League president Chub Feeney's office in Rockefeller Center. The setting was more conducive than the sterile rooms at the Doral. No tables separated the two parties. In the warmth of the wood-paneled work space, with its view of the skating rink below, Miller sat on the couch, apart from the other three.

When Grebey tried to speak, MacPhail shushed him. Grebey accepted his spot in the backseat with stoicism. It was sad. Grebey, who'd only done what was asked of him by the owners, was silenced, his legs cut out from beneath him. He could only watch. When the businesslike MacPhail attempted to make changes to the union proposal that Miller had given him, Miller cut him off. He was so angry that he wanted "complete and unconditional surrender."

Moffett had originally scheduled a bargaining session for 2:00 p.m. in Room 1706 at the Doral. At 2:15 he was informed the negotiators wouldn't be joining him. Only then did he know a deal was in the works. The imperturbable and persistent mediator, realizing that he was the only one who wanted to meet, was glad to be stood up.

Shortly after 5:00 p.m., the parties broke to hold caucuses with the other members of their negotiating teams. MacPhail and Grebey adjourned to the NL legal offices on the 47th floor at Citicorp Center to meet with Feeney, Hoynes, and the full PRC. Back at his Rockefeller Center office, Kuhn was going over the details. Miller and Fehr headed to the players' association headquarters on Sixth Avenue. Along with attorney Rose, Belanger, Garner, and Rogers, Miller and Fehr recounted the last hours of productive talk. Miller explained that he saw a change in attitude, professional and practical, not a hint of stall or delay. Though far from definite, the indications were good.

The four principals met again at six. At nine, MacPhail and Grebey went to dinner with their lawyers; Miller and Fehr returned to their offices. Boone and DeCinces had arrived. DeCinces had stayed with his parents after the Los Angeles players' confab and taken a late flight to New York. Things were happening so fast that he couldn't get there in time.

Around midnight, the full committees assembled at Hoynes's office at Willkie, Farr and Gallagher, with Kuhn and his Executive Council there as well. As they talked out the agreement in principle, a 22-page Memorandum of Agreement was typed out. By one thirty in the morning of the 31st, it was clearly over. PRC members called their owners and word began to spread. Eisenhardt got word from Clark Griffith at 11:28 Pacific time. After all this time, Eisenhardt didn't even ask about compensation.

Nothing was official until five thirty in the morning when a tentative agreement was signed and the negotiators made their way to the Doral, arriving after six to announce the agreement. By then everyone knew. Grebey's holding the late-edition *Daily News* made that plain to see.

Except for one numerical change and three addenda, the deal was what Miller had dictated to MacPhail before boarding a plane to Chicago. The owners got most of their definition of premium players and would get significant compensation for 7 to 9 free agents each year. Though it would come from a pool and not directly, it was still a giveback by the players. Teams that signed free agents could protect 24 players, nonsigners, 26.

The players felt this small amount of compensation, though more than previously, would not be a hindrance to signing. The pool addressed owners' concern on competitive balance as teams would be able to protect major and some minor leaguers, resulting in only five or six players from the major league roster becoming exposed. Even the better teams would lose some players, unless they were part of five "conscientious objectors" who chose not to draft free agents. Allowing five teams to voluntarily opt out of the draft was meaningful, a major selling point.

The extension of the basic agreement was also important. MacPhail had asked Miller if the owners could get that in return for other concessions. Miller didn't rule it out and eventually accepted the new expiration of December 31, 1984. On his copy of the agreement, Miller wrote, "Significance? Not anxious to do battle again."

Service time had become more important to the players than compensation, and it was secured in full. It was a must for Miller though subject to barter. MacPhail asked if the owners could get the NLRB hearing dropped in a trade. Miller agreed.

The settlement still needed to be ratified by both sides. The Executive Board of the players' association was to meet in Chicago on August 1, followed by a poll early the next week of all the players, conducted by the player representatives. The owners scheduled a ratification meeting the following week, also in Chicago. At that meeting they would decide whether to adopt a split season or pick up from where it left off when the strike began on June 12.

Since that day, the damage to the game had been devastating. The players lost an estimated $28 million in salary. Winfield dropped $385,000, while those at the bottom saw $11,000 vanish from their minimum salaries of $32,500. The owners lost approximately $116 million in tickets and concessions with the cancellation of 712 games. Cushioning the blow was $44 million of their $50 million in strike insurance. That the strike ended six days before the insurance money ran out was not a coincidence.

New York City lost $8.4 million in business and wages, an estimate not counting those dependent on baseball itself. In Pittsburgh, the Chamber of Commerce quoted a loss of $11.5 million for city businesses based on the $34 million impact of baseball on the economy for the whole season. The Rangers estimated $3 million in losses, the Dodgers $7.6 million, the Twins $1.6 million. It could have been worse. Calvin Griffith boasted that the strike prevented a $2.5 million loss, the combination of strike insurance, nonpayment of salaries, and the lessening of expenses easing the financial pressures that had pushed him to considering selling the team. In fact, with the Twins' new Dome expected to be ready in 1982, he was now looking to buy more shares. The franchise was sure to rise in value.

In the immediate aftermath much praise was heaped on MacPhail. His role was hugely significant, though he demurred. "I was a messenger boy," he said humbly, working solely at the direction of the PRC and Grebey. The filtering of the strident voices of the American League dissidents through MacPhail's even temperament was effective. "Lee's role was a major necessity," declared Miller.

Raymond Donovan was also acclaimed. Hours after the announcement, Kuhn sent a telegram, hailing the secretary: "Your involvement was a vital contribution to the solution." The federal pressure had its impact and the move to DC had, over time, worked. Donovan brought out our bottom line, DeCinces said, while Rogers was more generous: "Secretary Donovan came into this thing a little naïve; he really didn't know what was going on. But he busted his rear." He had helped, which was more than could be said for the commissioner of baseball.

The "clubs and players have learned a bitter lesson," Kuhn asserted, both less likely to incur stoppages in the future. He'd done all he could, and though he supported the 1980 solution that resulted in the strike of 1981, in hindsight he wished the sides would have come to a compensation deal then.

In retrospect Kuhn saw he could have exerted pressure on owners, but he didn't disagree with their position, seeing "legitimate interests on both sides." On the positive side, the two sparring parties "came out of this with a great deal of mutual respect."

Rogers didn't wait long to lash out. "Mutual respect? Bat guano! I have so little respect for the owners it's unbelievable." The wounds between players and owners went deep. "Anytime you stand toe-to-toe with illogical viewpoints and you try to use logic, there will be frustration. And frustration breeds bitterness," a still-upset Rogers told a reporter. Said Staub, "It was a destructive thing to our game. . . . [The owners'] all-out attack was to get exactly what they wanted or break the Players Association. I am very displeased about that."

The players were more united at the end than at the beginning. Grebey and Kuhn's early belief that the players would fall apart, that they'd never go on strike over compensation, had blown up in their faces. "Owners won't underestimate the players anymore. That's probably the most important thing to come out of the strike. If there was a victory, it was a victory for the spirit of the players," asserted Miller.

"I very seriously doubt that the owners will try to challenge the players again," crowed DeCinces.

Between the owners themselves the gashes were wider. "The most insane, inane, asinine strike," cried Reinsdorf. He saw no reason from an owner's standpoint for the strike to have happened. It was all the fault of the old guard, the "Neanderthals" as Reinsdorf called them. He had been ready to give up right away.

Chiles saw how the players behaved and wished his side had

performed likewise. They "hung tough, strong stuff, gotta be proud of them," he said wistfully. The owners' attempts to put the players in their place hadn't worked, and the result was self-reflection and recrimination.

Grebey and Miller spouted the same cliché, that there were no winners and no losers, but the players had clearly won. The deal was basically what Miller had proposed before spring training. The owners had gained little and the hard-liners were vanquished. The impact on all professional sports was huge. Had free agency been disemboweled in baseball, then free agency would have been nonexistent or extremely watered down in all other team sports. Baseball under Miller had set the labor trend for all of the other professional leagues.

The players were grateful to be returning to the field. After a week of workouts, the season would begin again with the All-Star Game on August 9, regular play the next day. In the meantime, baseball took its annual trip back to simpler days.

Cooperstown, then and now, is an oasis for baseball fans. The hundreds of thousands who visit the central New York village at the base of Otsego Lake, the site of native James Fenimore Cooper's classic American tales, are immediately struck by it.

Unlike the cities and suburbs from which most visitors hail, Cooperstown is part real, part fantasy, an actual working village with a vintage beauty that, for baseball fans, doubles as theme park and shrine. Induction weekend in 1981 paired a Sunday ceremony to honor the newly selected greats—Johnny Mize, Bob Gibson, and Rube Foster—with the annual Hall of Fame Game the next day.

Since 1940, it was the only midseason exhibition of major leaguers other than the All-Star Game. Two teams wound their way by bus through the back roads of rural upstate to the inconveniently located home of baseball and played for fun on one of their few days off. The coming matchup was exciting—Martin's Oakland A's versus Seaver, Bench, and the Cincinnati Reds. Sure, the big stars played little, but their presence in the middle of the village on Doubleday Field—the purported site of the birth of baseball, where fiction would have it that Civil War general Abner Doubleday laid out the rules of base-ball for a gaggle of Cooperstown kids in 1839—was thrilling.

The months leading up to induction were typical—all area hotels were booked, the game was a sellout, and the Cooperstown High School senior class of 1982 were ready to sell concessions to the hordes of visitors. The seniors were traditionally given exclusive right to sell food and drink to the 10,000 or so who would cram into the Double-day Field grandstand and bleachers. It was the main fund-raiser to finance their senior trip to Washington, DC. The Hall of Fame, Main Street merchants, and high schoolers were only slightly worried at first when strike talk emerged, but, until the official announcement that the strike was on, didn't believe it would happen. When it came, shock set in as the money that poured into Cooperstown annually like an annuity was at risk.

As the August 2 induction drew closer, the Hall of Fame game was canceled, the first local victim of the stoppage. It was replaced by a minor league contest, a New York–Pennsylvania League matchup between the Class A Oneonta Yankees (where June draft choice John Elway would be assigned) and the Elmira Pioneers (in the Red Sox chain). No Hall of Fame Game had ever been canceled in advance, though there'd been rainouts in 1944 and 1962, and in 1945 a post-ponement due to World War II travel restrictions. Until 1981 it had taken Mother Nature and Adolf Hitler to put a stop to the classic.

The senior class faced the loss of their primary fund-raiser head-on. A rash of bake sales put a slight dent in the $20,000 to $30,000 needed to send nearly 100 students to the nation's capital. The class turned creative. Admission was charged to watch the seniors take on the teachers in donkey basketball. The locals howled as they watched the players shoot from the backs of the donkeys, some of which would suddenly bolt down the gym floor. Other animals lay down, immovable, doing their own interpretation of the labor nego-tiations. Not a lot of money was made but it lightened up a difficult situation.

The big money, the ace in the hole, was an auction that centered on donated items from Major League Baseball. Used cleats from Nolan Ryan, a 1971 World Series Champion Pittsburgh Pirates autographed ball, and game-used jerseys and gloves were displayed in the gymnasium to gin up interest ahead of the event.

Despite the strike and the cancellation of the game, preparations for the marquee weekend went on as usual. At Doubleday Field, padding was installed on the iron rails in the outfield, and the warning track was leveled off. At Cooper Park, a private space adjacent to the Hall of Fame library where the induction ceremonies would occur, wires and stands were set up for television, radio, and newspaper reporters. Representatives from United Press International and Associated Press were given telephones and darkrooms in the library basement and equipment to transmit photos. CBS was there with cameras, as was the not-quite-two-year-old Entertainment and Sports Programming Network, there to broadcast the day's event. WCBS radio and Sports Network TV were on hand to cover a new way of doing the ceremony, each Hall of Famer introduced individually. Cooperstown police chief Henry Nicols said the local force would work, as they always did, with the assistance of state troopers and the county sheriff. The weekend was generally crime free, noted the chief, who cited the biggest challenge as "taking twenty thousand people and turning them loose in a village that is used to twenty-five hundred."

With the strike ending in the wee hours of July 31, two days before Induction Sunday, there wasn't enough time to make the weekend whole. The Hall of Fame Game could not be reclaimed; refunds were already in full swing, and the players were in no condition to return to the field so quickly. Would more fans descend on the village with the season now on its way back? One, Mets manager Joe Torre, had been ready to make the over-three-hour drive from New York to Cooperstown to watch Gibson, his former Cardinals teammate and present Mets pitching coach, receive baseball's highest honor. When Torre heard on the radio that the strike was settled, he instead returned to Shea Stadium to get some work done. What would the reaction of the fans be now that baseball was back? Jack Buck, the emcee of the festivities, was about to find out.

After the Hall of Famers took their seats, and new inductee Johnny Mize sat down, with Bob Gibson to his left and Earl Foster, Rube's son, to his right, the Cardinals announcer began.

"Isn't it fun," asked the buoyant Buck, "to think that a week from today we'll be watching the All-Star Game?"

"BOOOOOO!"

"Now, you didn't come here for that, did you?" asked the shocked Buck. He valiantly forged on, "And your favorite team will be in action the following day."

Louder *Boooooo*s erupted from the fans standing outside the green snow fencing that surrounded the ceremony.

Buck gave up. "I know how to stop your booing," he mused aloud. "By introducing some of your favorites enshrined in the Hall of Fame."

The crowd settled down and loudly cheered their heroes, the men who, in their eyes, would never have struck and walked away from them in the middle of a season. When the introduction of the older Hall of Famers was over, Hall president Edward W. Stack came to the podium with the most dangerous task of the day—the introduction of Bowie Kuhn. Stack tried his best.

"Here is a man who has been very intensely involved throughout the successfully concluded labor negotiations and who had to get by with only five hours of sleep a night during these last few months."

Most observers would have been surprised by that assessment, since Kuhn had been noticeably absent for the last few months. The savvy fans in the crowd had no sympathy for the weary commissioner.

"Awww," mocked the crowd.

As the boos crescendoed, drowning out a slight scattering of applause, Stack presented the commissioner of baseball.

Kuhn tried his best, offering that "the anguish, the pain, of the experience is still terribly fresh in our minds. In my judgment, this too shall pass." A genuine romantic when it came to baseball's past, Kuhn's eyes had welled with tears during the introduction of the game's greats. "These memories ultimately will outlast the nightmare we have endured this summer." Or so he hoped.

After the hostile reception, Kuhn, who loved the game's past and treasured Cooperstown, was, for the first time, thrilled to leave, flying out of little Oneonta airport, twenty miles away.

Foster, Mize, and Gibson made their speeches, and the day's events concluded. Gibson left town that night due to the threat of the air traffic controllers' strike. The next day would be the minor league game, a letdown from the usual major league fare.

It was clear by Monday morning that game was an attendance disaster. Where usually 10,000 would show, Doubleday was one-third filled. Businesses on Main Street suffered, with one bar, the Bold Dragoon on Pioneer Street, hanging a banner from their second-floor balcony: DEAR PLAYERS AND OWNERS, THANKS FOR NOTHING. Mrs. Woods, owner of one of the few dedicated baseball-souvenir shops, said business on the street was pretty spotty. On the plus side, the Hall of Fame gift shop's entire line of shirts and earthenware, with HALL OF FAME GAME, A'S VS. REDS with a block-letter CANCELLED stenciled over it, was sold out.

The Hall of Famers still on hand for the game had mixed reactions to the freshly settled strike. Some were predictably out of touch, such as second baseman Billy Herman, who said, "In 1946, some guy came to the [Boston] Braves clubhouse to talk to us about forming a union. We kicked him out in a hurry. So did all the other clubs."

Others were supportive, though grudgingly. Tigers legend Charlie Gehringer thought the strike was "for the birds. I guess if I was playing, I'd be right in there with 'em."

Robin Roberts, instrumental in recruiting and hiring Miller back in 1966, saw the issues keenly, citing it as "the silliest strike I've ever seen. The owners acted as if compensation was the issue, but it was really money—and trying to give Marvin a loss before he retires."

And 87-year-old Burleigh Grimes, the last legal-spitball pitcher, was fit to be tied, spluttering that when the fans booed the modern players on Sunday, "I was as mad as I used to get on the mound."

The Alabama drawl of Mel Allen, unchanged despite his decades in New York as the Yankees announcer, warmed the 3,200 that came to watch the minor leaguers play at Doubleday. As Allen introduced Stan "the Man" Musial, hobbling from recent knee surgery, he took his place in the batter's box, wiggled into his famous corkscrew batting stance, and took a mighty swing at an imaginary pitch, pointing to deep right field where the ball was supposedly heading. Take that, Pete Rose!

Mize threw out the first ball (ironically, Mize had played for Elmira in 1932, batting .326 and switching from the outfield to first base, embarking on his now Hall of Fame–worthy career). Oneonta won 8–6, homers flying out of tiny Doubleday. The high school seniors hawking hot dogs and soda to the sparse crowd raised $2,500 that day, much less than half of the previous year's take. Not to worry; by the following spring they'd raised enough money to go to Washington, as usual.

The question for baseball, with the strike settled and the All-Star Game six days away, was would the game continue as usual?

A smiling Joe Torre sat with his feet up on his desk. He was back to work, back at Shea where he belonged. With the strike over, normalcy returned. The owners seemed unconcerned that the strike could prove damaging. Calvin Griffith was not at all worried that the fans would disappear. In Toronto, Peter Bavasi said that any talk of the strike's being ruinous was shortsighted. Einhorn conceded that in the long run there'd be no effect from the strike. What of the short term?

Former Cubs pitcher Ken Holtzman predicted 40,000 would flock to Wrigley Field when play resumed. It was a pretty optimistic forecast for a team toward the bottom of the attendance standings. Holtzman was a tad off. Only 1,000 arrived at the corner of Clark and Addison on August 1 to see the Cubbies work out. The good news was that during the strike only two of the 1,500 season-ticket holders canceled. The *Tribune,* proud new relatives of the Cubs, devoted 70 percent of the sports section and 25 percent of the front page to baseball's renewal.

Over 4,000 turned out at Tiger Stadium to watch sprints and calisthenics, and in West Palm Beach fans made their way back into the sun, squinting as the Expos loosened up at their facilities. The Reds jogged at the University of Michigan in Ann Arbor, having been rendered temporarily homeless by the Kool Jazz Festival, which had been booked for Riverfront Stadium.

Baseball—the game, the history, the food—proved impossible to give up. Ticket sales, which had been 1 million ahead of the 1980 pace before the strike, were strong, fans gobbling them up at newly opened box-office windows, like Pac-Man eating dots. A five-figure crowd descended on Dodger Stadium, straining to see the recognizable physique of Valenzuela running on the dirt track, smiling, an obvious skip in his step. Garvey left his stint on the *Hollywood Squares,* happier doing sit-ups on the grass than answering questions from a box. Spring training take two, held in major league home ballparks, was an odd sight.

It was nothing compared to the eccentricities that came with the owners' meeting for ratification of the settlement on the 6th. They could see the underutilized runways of O'Hare from their room at the Hilton, the PATCO strike that began three days earlier playing havoc with air travel.

Ratification was a foregone conclusion. The players had already affirmed the pact, 11 of the 26 teams unanimously, the total tally 627–37 with 3 abstentions, when only a majority was needed. The owners needed to simply approve what had been drawn up in New York.

The room resounded with a repeated banging. August A. "Gussie" Busch, beer baron and Cardinals chairman of the board, pounded his cane on the floor for attention. "Gentlemen, I am here to speak to you today because, in all my years, both business and personal, I have never been more disgusted, angry, and ashamed of a situation in which I was involved. Once again we are ridiculed by everyone—inside and outside sports."

The mix of new and old owners sat silent.

"When we 'folded' in 1980 to get what was promised as compensation, we had already given up our bargaining chips for 1981. What did we end up with? If the Cubs lose a player to the Phillies through free agency, then possibly I have the honor of giving the Cubs my twenty-seventh-best player—marvelous compensation." It was the clearest explanation of what the owners had bumbled their way into.

"In the future, credited service time will no longer be an issue. A precedent has been set. A horrible contract has been extended for one year. In return we have the privilege of increasing players' minimum salary to forty thousand dollars in 1984 with nothing in return regarding pension contributions. We will never again be in a position to get strike insurance. We have made the union our partner. While everyone must share the blame, the major blame lies in this room." Busch scowled, casting his eyes round the room. "The owners who forced this settlement by their actions at the meeting in New York sold us out because of their individual problems and egos. There are owners who undermined the PRC and shamefully cheated and deceived us all." Busch would have turned his baleful glare at Williams and Chiles, but they weren't there.

"They think they are the future leaders of baseball, but, believe me, they are not worthy to even carry the briefcase of a Walter O'Malley, Phil Wrigley," and others, dead or gone. "I have been in baseball in good times and in bad, but none so shameful. If you have any courage left, I urge the men of integrity here today to vote no on this contract. If nothing else, it will show that the entire ownership of baseball is not insane."

This stunning attack was the last gasp of a struggling dinosaur. The new breed—Reinsdorf, Steinbrenner, et al.—watched; it was something to see.

After one hour the vote was cast—21–3 in favor with 2 abstentions. The Reds, Cards, and Twins voted no. Cincinnati club president Dick Wagner refused to rubber-stamp the agreement. Griffith, instructed by his son to vote yes, voted no.

The leagues then met separately on whether to simply resume the season or to develop a split-season plan. If they split, they'd get new pennant races. Kuhn thought a split would spice up the second half, from a marketing point of view if not from a baseball purist's. The players had agreed that the owners could decide how to finish the 1981 season.

They came up with this: a second race in all four divisions, followed by a best-of-five-game series between the two winners of the halves, if different. If the same team won both halves, they would have to play a wild card, which would be the team with the second-best record over the entire year in the division.

Wagner immediately saw the problem. What if his Reds, who, despite their June tear had finished half a game back of Los Angeles in the first half, should finish half a game behind Houston in the second half and not make the playoffs? Wagner suggested the second-half winner could play the overall winner, an idea that would enable a new pennant race while rewarding the best team.

The Yankees preferred a bye setup, Steinbrenner assuming they'd take both halves. Five clubs favored a straight resumption of the year. Creating a split season, with each team playing a different number of games as a result of first-half differences in schedule and early-season rainouts, would be a disaster. After the strike of 1972, the season went on as usual, and the Red Sox lost their division to the Tigers by half a game. They also played one fewer game. Had that been scheduled and Boston won, there would have been a tie at the top. Now, the same situation was being created. The Reds had played one less game than the Dodgers, and a vote crowning Los Angeles division winners was in the offing. The American League, following two hours of discussion, approved the original scheme 12–0, the White Sox and Angels not voting.

National League rules required a three-quarters vote, and they barely made it, with the Reds, Cardinals, and Phillies voting no.

The Phillies were the only first-place team that went against their own interests. Carpenter had been convinced by his manager that it would be good for the game to start fresh and rebuild fan interest. A bit disingenuous. It would be good for the Phillies, who had now clinched a playoff berth. The other first-place teams, the Yankees, A's, and Dodgers, also voted in the affirmative. At least Fred Wilpon, president and CEO of the Mets, copped to a partial truth, knowing his team didn't have a fastball's chance in hell to make the playoffs if the season was resumed in full. "It's self-serving," he said of his club's vote to split, "but I'd feel that way even if I weren't with the Mets."

Kuhn was ecstatic, counting on the enthusiasm for a split-season format to pave the way for a permanent wild card. The current television contracts with ABC and NBC already gave owners the right to create a third tier of playoffs. He'd informally polled all the clubs and got only mild resistance. MacPhail, as to be expected, was more tempered, understanding that the new split-season plan "may not be completely fair to all teams." Wagner protested, "We don't care for it, for fifteen or twenty reasons. And they start with integrity. Circumstances could lead a team that won the first half to pick its own opponent, in effect, in the second half." Like the Amazing Kreskin, he saw the future plainly.

In the week leading up to the All-Star Game, fans were turning out in droves for exhibition games to see what they had sorely missed. In Philadelphia 8,422 paid $3 to see the Phillies beat the Orioles 4–3 in seven innings. DeCinces (single) and Boone (game-winning RBI) were thrilled to be back on the artificial turf, playing, rather than arguing. For the same $3, over 9,000 came to see the hometown Brewers maul the Braves 15–4. The Indians went the other way, charging regular-season prices for a Tribe vs. Pirates exhibition. Still, 6,729 came out for the game. At the prodding of Mayor Jane Byrne, the Cubs and White Sox agreed to play their first charity game in 10 years, 75,000 Chicagoans expected to bridge the North Side–South Side divide over the two-game series.

In San Diego, 19,000 were ushered in for free to watch the Padres and A's square off for nine innings, until Oakland had to catch a flight. The Padres front office was mulling over various ideas for the comeback, but Ray Kroc had his own thoughts, the owner announcing in an impromptu press conference that Reopening Day against Atlanta would be a freebie as well. Over 35,000 packed Arlington Stadium to see the Astros defeat the Rangers. The scuttlebutt was that J. R. Richard would make his return, but that possibility was denied by Houston skipper Bill Virdon, who, though seriously considering the dramatic return, didn't think Richard was ready. George Steinbrenner vetoed a two-game series with the Mets.

Dodger Stadium held 45,000 fans, who watched, for free, the minor league Albuquerque Dukes squeak past the parent Dodgers 2–0. Obviously, the big leaguers needed some more time to get in midseason form. National criticism arose that players wouldn't be close to ready for Sunday's showcase. In Cleveland, *Plain Dealer* writer Hal Lebovitz complained, "What an utter farce, to charge top prices for what has to be a charade, a workout."

The Yankee Stadium signboard hanging high above the Major Deegan Expressway touted OPENING DAY/TEXAS RANGERS/MON AUG 10. Reggie Jackson wasn't so sure he was ready to return. The strike had been a blessing, a chance to relax, to leisurely work on his swing, to enjoy his car collection, to grow a beard, to shave it off. Time away from New York and Steinbrenner was quality time indeed.

He had much to prove in the second half, to himself and the owner. The first-half fights with the Boss, the insult of designated hitting, Winfield's success, the May slump, the injuries, his contract squabbles that stung his pride—he hoped they were relegated to the past. It was impossible to shake getting older. A former teammate had watched Jackson flail in the first half and was stunned. "I see him miss pitches right now, pitches he used to cream, and I just can't believe my eyes." In his heart, Jackson knew he had something left to show.

Steinbrenner was back in midseason shape, slamming Jackson and hammering away at his star's shaky confidence. "It's his head that's all screwed up. You know what's eating away at Reggie

Jackson? He's playing in an outfield with the greatest athlete in baseball today. Dave Winfield runs better and throws better and hits for average better. Don't you think Reggie sees that? Don't you think he knows that? It eats him alive." Of course, though, "I'm still in his corner," said the schizophrenic Steinbrenner.

With a lock on the postseason, and the starting staff healthy following the layover, the next two months looked like easy going for the Yanks. The Brewers had a tough schedule ahead; 31 of their 53 games would be on the road. The Orioles were sure to be tough, though how the months of negotiation pressure would take their toll on Belanger and DeCinces remained to be seen. If DeCinces faltered, the Orioles were prepared. On August 8 they brought up Cal Ripken Jr.

In the West, Martin's A's were now semi-champions. Oakland had played 5 more games than second-place Texas, and 7 more than the White Sox, $2\frac{1}{2}$ games behind in third place. The ChiSox had one fewer loss than the newly crowned Athletics. White Sox manager Tony La Russa howled at the inequity of the split season, remarking that if the Yankees and Dodgers hadn't finished in first place, the plan would never have been considered.

The Royals were happy to have their first two months expunged from the record. It had been horrendous for the 1980 pennant winners. Their World Series loss had exposed their weaknesses. Scouts told American League teams to do what Philadelphia had done: keep fast guys such as Willie Wilson, U. L. Washington, and Frank White off base with hard-thrown fastballs, and stop George Brett from beating you. It had worked, so much so that Washington had given up the ever-present toothpick that hung on his lower lip in a futile effort to change his luck.

Brett's frustration had erupted in multiple explosions, including an attack on a UPI photographer and an assault on the bathroom in the visitors' clubhouse in Minnesota. The team was fraying at the edges. Manager Frey screamed at Wilson for not wearing a jacket on a team flight to Seattle, and Wilson responded by leaving the airport. First baseman Willie Mays Aikens was furious at Frey for not picking him to go to the All-Star Game, Frey knowing full well that Aikens had a bonus clause. Designated hitter McRae wanted to be traded. Still, the fifth-place Royals were the reigning league champs, and that couldn't be discounted.

Fernandomania seemed like a long time ago as the season was set to resume. The Dodgers had their troubles—Lopes hitting .169, shortstop Bill Russell not much better at .196, though injuries had contributed to their dreadful first half. But this team had a certain something, a magic that surrounded them. Dusty Baker saw it: "We got a great mix, the right balance between veterans and kids. It's the closest team I've ever been on." The Dodgers had a sense of inevitability in this Year of Valenzuela, but the Reds, sore at the theft of their stellar first half, were determined to win, and with Seaver at the top of his game and Bench recovered from his ankle injury, the Dodgers' sense of destiny would not go unchallenged.

The Expos, Cardinals, and Phillies were certain to continue their three-way dogfight in the second half. It was hard to conceive of the Mets, Cubs, or Pirates putting up much of a fight. As long as Montreal could live up to its potential, St. Louis focus, and Philadelphia avoid complacency, the trio were bound to duke it out. And with Rose one hit away from Musial's record, the Phillies had the spotlight.

Before Rose, Schmidt, Dawson, Valenzuela, Winfield, Jackson, Brett, and Seaver had their chance to fight it out on the road to the postseason, they had to make a short detour to Cleveland.

Cavernous Municipal Stadium was so large that you could fit in a completely sold-out Wrigley Field and still have room for a completely vacant Arlington Stadium. The 52nd All-Star Game was Cleveland's big chance to pack 'em in and show the baseball world this symbol of down-on-its-luck, rust-belt decay was on its way back.

With typical Cleveland luck, there was almost no game, but downtown events proceeded as scheduled—a 1940s musical revue, a four-day "All Nations Festival," a regatta, parties on Public Square, and the opening of the observation deck at Terminal Tower, lit for the first time in 51 years. Cleveland tried, desperately, to convince anyone paying attention that they were "the Comeback City."

It was clear early on that the game was not going to be played as originally planned, the owners voting on July 9 not to resume the season with the All-Star Game. Still 15,000 Clevelanders had turned out four days later, the day before the originally scheduled game, just to boo cancellation. Attendees shook their fists and jeered, loudly, reaching 130 decibels. A local band, Wild Horses, played "(I Can't Get No) Satisfaction," the unofficial theme song of the summer.

Some simulated action occurred on July 14. An oversize Strat-O-Matic board game was set up at home plate, the idea of two local television producers. Cleveland favorite Rocco Scotti, whom Kuhn had ousted from the real game for not being famous enough, sang the national anthem, his eyes tearing up as they always did. Indians Hall of Fame pitcher Bob Feller tossed out the first dice.

"Wait a minute, Bob. My battery just went dead," interjected a panicky photographer.

"Mine has been dead for years," Feller quipped.

The imaginary game began in front of almost 60 people lazing around in the lower level of the park, surrounded by 76,625 empty seats. Six reporters, looking to cover anything baseball-related, watched, pad and pencils out, and pictures were snapped of rolling dice and flipping charts. The center-field scoreboard posted the inning-by-inning action as the play-by-play was announced over the public address system, echoes booming from section to section.

Although there was some solid pitching, hometown favorite Len Barker matched with Steve Carlton, it was a virtual slugfest, the National League coming out on top behind 2 Manny Trillo home runs and a 422-foot clout by Dave Parker. The NL set a record with 7 runs scored on 7 hits in the top of the seventh inning. Not a real record, but a sort of record.

As the strike went on, dates for the real-life game were pushed back: July 15, July 30, mid-August, and even a rescheduling for 1982. Mayor George Voinovich hoped for a shift to the following year to showcase, not rush, his city. When the strike was settled, and it was agreed that the players would be granted some time to work out, the decision was made to start the second half of the season with the All-Star Game on the night of August 9.

For Cleveland, the date posed a problem. The famine of mid-July was replaced with a feast of activity in the city. A Browns-Steelers football exhibition game, a Roberto Duran–Nino Gonzalez prizefight, and the 2,000-person American Bridge Association convention were in town. Rooms were scarce. Still, the game was on, baseball was back, and, despite the worries about fan anger and apathy during the 50-day stoppage, a record 72,086 turned out.

How would the fans react at first sight of the players who had so recently gone on strike? There was no avenue to boo the owners. One by one the players were introduced, singular targets for wrath, but the catcalls were selective. Dallas Green, manager of the National League, was booed, but he was the other team's skipper in an American League home park. Understandable.

Jim Frey, manager of the AL squad, was also booed. Frey had incurred the ire of Clevelanders, picking Tiger Jack Morris to start over hometown hero Barker and selecting Blue Jay Dave Stieb over Indian Bert Blyleven. The fan reaction was excusable. Reggie Jackson was loudly jeered, but that was because he was Reggie Jackson. In fact, all the Yankees were booed. Everything seemed to settle into normalcy. Old-timers Warren Spahn, in a vintage Milwaukee Braves cap, and Feller, straight off his stellar dice-rolling stint, slowly jogged out to loud applause. As Bob Hope and Bowie Kuhn watched the fireworks explode high over the stadium, and Vice President George H. W. Bush prepared to throw out the first pitch, it was nearly time for baseball. It had been a long wait.

All-Star Game victories were the near-exclusive domain of the National League. Since 1963 the senior circuit had won 17 of 18 and was on a 9-game winning streak. The last time they'd lost was 1971.

Valenzuela did his job in the first, not allowing a run. Seaver, entering the game in the bottom of the second, was rudely greeted by Orioles slugger Ken Singleton, who knocked a home run. With a

1–0 lead, the stage was set for Barker, who made his way to the mound for the top of the third inning accompanied by the deafening cheers of "Len-ny! Len-ny!" by the hometown faithful.

From the corner of his eye Barker could see, scampering onto the field, a big-chested blonde, jiggling her way to the hill in a fringe top with an Indian headdress printed on it and satiny blue shorts with two stripes on either side. A dancer manqué, Morganna had been crashing sports events since the 1970s. Arms outstretched, she introduced herself to the smirking Barker.

"I'm Morganna, the 'Kissing Bandit.'"

"I know," replied Barker.

The cops quickly rushed out to drag Morganna away. It was all in good fun until she found herself facing a night in jail.

Carter's homer in the fifth was followed in the sixth by a crushing solo shot by a puffy Parker, who'd gained 20 pounds over the strike. "The Cobra" mirrored in reality what he'd done a few weeks before in simulation. "All right!" whooped Bench from the bench as the overweight Parker chugged his way around the bases. The National League was in front, a position they were quite used to. But this American League squad wasn't going down lightly.

In the bottom of the inning, three straight singles by Singleton, Dwight Evans, and Fisk loaded the bases for Fred Lynn, who singled to right for the game-tying run. It was almost a pure Red Sox rally, except that Fisk and Lynn were no longer in Boston. Buddy Bell put the American League ahead with a sacrifice fly that sent Evans home. Eddie Murray pinch-hit and forced Lynn at second. Brewers catcher Simmons was sent in to bat for Willie Randolph, and Simmons put another run on the board with a single, driving in Fisk. The American League was set to blow it open.

Al Oliver came to bat, facing a new pitcher, Burt "Happy" Hooton of the Dodgers. Oliver sent a shot that looked as if it would fall for a hit, but Dusty Baker, playing hard-nosed NL baseball, dove forward for a spectacular catch, ending up with a dreaded strained groin. All for the sake of winning a game that counted for nothing but pride. The rally was stopped dead.

What happened to Lynn after the sixth? While sliding into second, Lynn twisted his left knee and removed himself from the game, disappearing without telling his manager. Frey sent in Tony Armas, an unexpected roster move with the game heading into the late innings, when every player counted.

Carter's second home run made it a 1-run game, 4–3, still in favor of the home team. As soon as he connected off Yankee reliever Ron Davis, Carter knew he'd hit the ball hard. Winfield went back, back, back below the soaring ball, futilely scaling the wall. The play so far had been sloppy, with some fielding flubs from major leaguers who hadn't played competitively in two months. Carter's hitting may have been back in sync, but his home run trot needed work as he stumbled and hit the dirt rounding first.

A weary Rollie Fingers entered the game, as sure a person to hold the lead as any. Fingers had had a difficult trip to Cleveland. He and his wife, along with Simmons and his wife, arrived at O'Hare Airport on Saturday, after a Brewers workout, only to find their flight to Cleveland canceled due to the PATCO strike. On August 3, the nation's air traffic controllers walked off the job. After they refused to return two days later, President Reagan fired all 11,000-plus of them. The Reagan Revolution had begun. Baseball owners, so recently vanquished, looked on with envy.

The Brewer All-Stars waited it out at a Chicago hotel until Sunday. Finally, the players made it to Cleveland on separate flights, Fingers arriving only five hours before game time. As if that wasn't bad enough, Fingers felt as if he were pitching at the level of the second week of spring training. He certainly wasn't up to snuff when he started off the top of the eighth.

Four batters—a walk to Ozzie Smith (later thrown out at third base), a walk to Mike Easler, a homer by Mike Schmidt almost to the exact spot of Carter's second, a single by Baker—and the premier reliever in the American League was gone, as was their lead. The National League was up 5–4, and they weren't going to give that up.

After a scoreless bottom of the eighth, Fingers' National League counterpart, Bruce Sutter, came in to shut the door in the bottom of the ninth. With one down, Frey sent Stieb to hit. Yes, *pitcher* Stieb. Because Lynn had flown the coop, Frey was out of position players. (A record 56 were used.) He was so unprepared to hit that he did a quick scramble for parts, using Rick Burleson's bat, Bell's batting gloves, and Tom Paciorek's batting helmet. Stieb quickly struck out. The crowd booed mercilessly. Winfield flew out to left and the NL had won again.

Vida Blue got the win for his one inning of work, becoming the only pitcher to win All-Star Games for both leagues. Gary Carter flashed a broad smile as Kuhn handed him his Most Valuable Player award. Though disappointed that he never got a shot at an unheard-of third home run, Carter was jubilant leading the National League to its 10th straight victory. Like Fingers, he didn't feel right physically. Unlike Fingers, he performed exceptionally well.

Though marred by sloppy play, the All-Star Game was an exciting return. Two months of labor haggling and vitriol were over. Two months of the American public looking for ways to fill the void that baseball's disappearing act had created was gone.

The real season would start in less than 24 hours.

Chapter 7

Pete Rose missed baseball. Yes, he supported the strike, even though it meant he couldn't play and stopped his pursuit of Musial's record in its tracks. For a man in perpetual motion, a halt was beyond comprehension. The 200 swings he took every day during the strike were nothing compared to the real thing, the intense competition.

Veterans Stadium was packed, as it was in the last game before the strike, 60,561 strong, sure that this would, finally, be the night that Rose broke Musial's hit record. A national TV audience tuned in. The frenzy surrounding the event spread throughout Philadelphia. Wagering on the Big 4 lottery was stopped by the state due to the heavy betting on 3631. The Rose magic number had a potential payout of almost $5 million. If the number hit on August 12, Pennsylvania would have to give 12 times the $400,000 in total bets on all numbers, paying $5,000 for every $1 waged. The state may have been the only group rooting against Rose on the first day back.

After visiting St. Louis got off to a quick 1-run lead in the top half of the first, Rose and his 10-year-old son, Petey, batboy for the night in Phillies cap and maroon shirt with ROSE 14 on the back, knelt in the on-deck circle, watching Cardinals righty Bob Forsch warm up. When the home plate umpire signaled, Rose strode to the plate. He tapped his helmet, pushed back his hair, and descended into a crouch. He was ready.

Shortstop Garry Templeton broke toward the front of the second-base bag the moment he saw Rose's bouncer up to the middle. The high hopper off the hard turf proved too hard to handle. As Templeton bobbled the ball, Rose passed first base. Even a clean play wouldn't have caught him.

"Go, go, go," the man in charge of fireworks heard Phillies vice president Bill Giles shout. Buttons were pressed and explosions sent up over the ballpark to the roar of the crowd. He'd done it! They'd seen it! Jubilation.

Except Templeton's misplay was ruled an error. Giles, aware that the grounder might not be called a hit, had screamed, "No, no, no," not "Go, go, go." The premature celebration was a bigger gaffe than Templeton's. Rose was fine with the call. He didn't want a cheap hit for the record breaker.

In his second at bat Rose hit a hard comebacker to the mound that Forsch fielded cleanly. In his third at bat Rose was put out, second to first. Petey grew worried. When the older Rose said his bat was too slow, the younger attempted to calm him.

"Ah, Dad, don't worry about it. If you don't get it tonight, you'll get it tomorrow."

Before leading off the eighth inning, Rose took a few practice swings and then hit the knob of the bat on the ground to dislodge the heavy batting doughnut. He bent over to pick it up and, while giving it to Petey, put his hand on the boy's shoulder. Rose leaned in to whisper. "Watch. This time I'm going to get the hit," he boasted in an attempt to cheer up his anxious son.

Forsch was out, replaced by Mark Littell. After a first-pitch fastball for a strike, Littell, whose best pitch was his slider, attempted to sneak in another. Rose whipped his bat around, lacing a solid shot between short and third. Ken Oberkfell dove for it, Templeton reached for it, but the seeing-eye hit found its way into left field for a single. As he streaked toward first base, holding his helmet down midway to the bag and giving one hard clap to himself as he rounded the base, the Vet exploded in a standing ovation and fireworks. Upon receiving the prized baseball, Rose handed it to his son for safekeeping. A new set of 3,631 colorful balloons were released high into the night air. Rose's teammates came over to congratulate him.

Musial, in attendance again, made his way from his box seat behind the Phillies dugout to first base to congratulate the man who'd passed him. The Man had told Rose after the 1980 World Series that he'd be happy to be there in person whenever his record was broken. Musial, cool in a cream-colored jacket and light blue slacks, shook and patted Rose's hand and put his arm around him as Rose lifted his helmet to the fans.

Rose stood for a full four minutes acknowledging the adoring crowd. Thirteen minutes later they were still whooping it up as Rose scored on a Schmidt single to center. Emerging from the dugout waving a white towel, Rose paid tribute in return. In the bottom of the ninth, Rose grounded out against Sutter, and the Phillies lost 7–3. No one cared.

After the game, in a special interview room set up with a red telephone on a podium in front of a large Phillies banner, Rose held court. The phone rang as he began answering questions.

"Tell the president to wait," Rose joked to the uproarious laughter of those assembled. Behind him stood Musial and Kuhn, who found Rose's enthusiasm delightful and laughed along.

Rose picked up the receiver with his batting-glove-covered left hand. Reagan was calling to congratulate Rose and there were technical difficulties. After a series of failed attempts at a connection — "One moment please"; "One moment, sir"—Rose said, "Maybe the operators were on strike." After the hilarity subsided, he followed with a Cold War one-liner: "It's a good thing there ain't no missile on the way." Rose was asked by the switchboard to hang up and they'd try again, but after two more tries it was getting ridiculous. "I'll give him my home number," Rose wisecracked, grinning his gap-toothed smile.

"Hello, Pete Rose? Listen, this is Ronald Reagan."

"How ya doin'?" More laughs.

"Well, I don't know. I'll tell you, I had as much trouble getting this line, I had to wait longer than you did to break the record."

"We were gonna give you five more minutes. And that was it." Genuinely funny, obviously having a good time. The world was Pete Rose's.

There was a full schedule on August 10. In Minnesota, the A's starting nine got 7 hits in losing to the Twins 7–2. That gave the entire lineup 3,191 career hits, not even close to Rose alone. At the reopener in San Diego, all 52,608 patrons, the largest turnout in team history, were admitted free, first come, first served. Kroc apologized to the fans for the strike, and getting into the spirit of contrition, Padres starting pitcher Juan Eichelberger gave up his salary for the day, approximately $300 of his $50,000. Not everyone was so generous. Ted Turner insisted that the Braves get their visitor share of a normal gate of 12,000 and was paid $4,800.

The New York baseball season got off to its second start with a daytime 13-inning Met win over the Cubs at Wrigley. The Tribune's purchase, now officially approved in an 11–0 National League vote, was looking bad when starter Krukow balked in the first run of the new half. In the 11th, the lone Met All-Star, Joel Youngblood, finally arrived from Cleveland. With not a plane to be found, Youngblood drove the five hours from Ohio. He flew out to center before Kingman reached outside the strike zone to pull a Rawly Eastwick pitch far out of the ballpark and down the street for a 3-run home run and a temporary New York lead. The Cubs came back with a trio of runs in the bottom of the frame, and after the teams exchanged single scores in the next inning, the Mets went ahead for keeps when Youngblood, who had doubled, scored on an Ellis Valentine single for the go-ahead run. Perhaps the split season would be good for Torre's squad, who jumped out to a 6–2 start.

That night, Secretary Donovan threw out the first pitch as guest of honor at Yankee Stadium and had his photo taken with some of the players. There was a smattering of boos, some for Donovan, others not strike-related. The bad news was Jackson was hitless again. The good news was that his stolen Mercedes-Benz had been found in Canarsie during the strike. Some of it at least. The doors, trunk, and wheels were missing, but the engine, transmission, and frame were intact. The rest of the season would be a rebuilding project for car and owner. The fully intact Yankees beat Texas 2–0, and Tommy John became the only starting pitcher in history to win two openers in one season.

Valenzuela didn't get to open the second half, that honor going to Reuss, as it was supposed to in April. Before the strike, the Dodgers drew 46,000 on average and sold out when Valenzuela started. It was a slightly disappointing crowd of 45,817, far short of the 56,000 capacity that came out to see the Dodgers vs. Reds for the second game. Attendance wasn't the only thing that was off. Cincinnati pounded the rookie, scoring three runs in $4\frac{1}{3}$ innings before Fernando was pulled.

The first week back was a good one for the National League, which averaged 22,617 fans per game, slightly higher than in the week leading up to the June 12 close. Deceptive numbers, as the total included Rose's record breaker and the Padres open house. The real story could be seen in the American League, where a massive shrinkage took place, from almost 23,000 to nearly 16,000, but the business of baseball was about to take a backseat. If the strike put baseball squarely in the cynical realities of the real world—money, bosses, workers—what happened in New Jersey brought perspective to one pitcher, his family, and his fans.

"Tommy, you've got a call," the batboy told Tommy John as he warmed up in the Tiger Stadium bull pen on the 13th.

Soon after, coach Jeff Torborg came sprinting out. "It's Sally and she's upset," he said, catching his breath.

John threw his glove to the ground and ran to the clubhouse. Grabbing the receiver, he could hear his wife's voice, hysterical.

"Travis fell and he's dying!" she wailed. John felt small and alone, as if seen from the wrong end of a telescope. His heart was pounding, his stomach in pain.

After two months of enjoyable family time, John headed back to work and his family went to visit friends in Bay Head on the Jersey shore. Their two boys, Tommy, four, and Travis, two and a half, shared a room on the third floor, their mom one flight below. Boys will be boys, and Sally, needing to get dressed, remembered to tell the teenage babysitter not to take her eyes off the kids.

The windowsills in the room were low, and Travis sat down in the window, rocking and leaning on the screen. Tommy heard the screen pop out and turned to see his brother's feet as he fell. He ran to his sister's room.

Tami, eight, screamed, "Mommy, Mommy, Travis fell!"

Sally, seven months pregnant, bolted down the stairs to where Travis had landed, his head still against the bottom step to the front door, unconscious, turning blue, blood seeping out of his ear. He'd banged his head on the family car before bouncing on the concrete sidewalk.

Kneeling down, Sally could hear his heart beating, but he wasn't breathing. He'd swallowed his tongue and his mouth was locked.

"He's dying!" she shrieked, suddenly in the middle of every parent's nightmare. In her hysteria, Sally got to work. She was still clutching her nail polish and quickly used the stem to pull open her son's teeth, creating enough space for her to put her finger in his throat and move his tongue forward. The boy gasped for breath.

A cop in the area heard the screams and sped over. They put Travis, groaning and spasming, in the car.

"Mommy's here," Sally soothed her son, not sure if he could hear her. Approaching Point Pleasant Hospital, she begged the cop to drive on the sidewalk to get as close to the emergency room as possible. Once her son was attended to, she called her husband in Detroit.

"Travis fell out of a window and broke his neck," the white-faced John told his team. "He's dying. I'm leaving. I'm going back to New Jersey." How would he get back? Air travel was chaotic.

John called a friend who connected him with a private-plane owner, who flew him to Monmouth County airport. There a waiting police car whisked him to the hospital. It was past 2:00 a.m. John visualized the coming scene, a doctor telling him the grim news that his son was dead, and he prayed that he'd be able to withstand the horror.

Sally collapsed in his arms. Travis had undergone brain surgery, four holes drilled into his skull to relieve the pressure. His neck hadn't broken, but he had a serious chance of brain damage. In the recovery room, freezing cold to reduce swelling of the brain, Travis John lay unconscious, head shaved, connected to tubes and wires. His parents prayed.

As soon as he was able to be moved, Travis was taken to NYU Medical Center in one helicopter, his family in another. The two choppers alit on 34th Street by the East River. In those first days, Travis would open his eyes and fade away, not a glimmer of recognition for those who loved him so. Tommy and Sally were told by a top pediatric neurosurgeon that no irreversible brain damage was found. All they could do was wait.

The press demanded updates, and John simply asked that prayers and love be sent his way. The city and the entire baseball world sent positive thoughts. "Travis has had the Kuhn family prayers," the commissioner said in a handwritten note.

While John was away, the Yankees played on, badly. They dropped three straight to the Tigers, though there were positive signs. From the opposing dugout, Sparky Anderson spotted something. "Reggie's starting to come," said the wise, old manager. "You could see it. His timing is starting to come. It was getting better with each game here. You could see a world of difference from the first game to the fourth. I'm glad he's getting out of here." The Yankees were headed home to face Chicago for a 3-game home series and for Tommy John's return.

John's days at NYU were long, 16–18 hours, where he'd sing, read, do anything to get a reaction from his son, to find any sort of connection. Returning to work on August 19 versus White Sox was difficult. He couldn't get Travis out of his mind, and the team played horribly, committing 2 fielding errors leading to 4 unearned runs in the $3\frac{1}{3}$ innings John pitched.

Emotions ran high. Coach Yogi Berra was on the dugout phone

to Doug Melvin, serving as the "eye in the sky," a football technique that the gridiron-loving Steinbrenner had adopted for baseball. Though John had asked for the outfield to be positioned toward right center, there was no follow-through, and balls were landing in the gap.

John exploded, yanking the phone from the wall. "Here." He handed the mutilated receiver back to Berra. "For all those guys are doing moving outfielders around, you can stand here with a dead phone, because it's not working." Yogi kept the dead phone to his ear, fearing what would happen if Steinbrenner was watching.

In the clubhouse Steinbrenner told his hurting hurler, "You gave one hell of an effort," before attacking his players to the press. Without any sensitivity for a team emotionally reeling from the tragic news, Steinbrenner blasted away. "We've got the highest-paid team in baseball, and we're not getting our money's worth," he callously snorted, canceling the scheduled next day off. It didn't help. The next weeks would be tough ones for the Bronx Bombers.

There was discontent in Pittsburgh. Pirate Parker, on the heels of his solid All-Star Game showing, had become persona non grata at Three Rivers Stadium. The two-time batting champ and 1978 Most Valuable Player was the target of boobirds. "I think I stayed in Pittsburgh three years too long," said the underperforming and slow-moving Parker.

Some teammates saw racism in the negative fan reaction, but it was mostly the result of his huge contract, the five-year, $6.7 million pact that started in 1979, and his poor play. Parker had bad knees, made worse by the concretelike Tartan Turf they played on, but never complained despite the constant draining of fluids. He accepted the hoots and hollers but couldn't stand the assortment of junk thrown at him from the upper deck—mini-bats, nickels, a bag of bolts, bullets, batteries. It was so bad that the Security Department of Major League Baseball, worried about fan anger poststrike, had advised clubs to "avoid any promotions involving giveaways that could be used as a missile."

Kuhn was dodging projectiles too. His beloved split-season

plan was under full assault. What only Dick Wagner had seen at the owners' meeting was now garnering mass attention. A potential scenario that baseball had sought to avoid since the 1919 Chicago White Sox threw the World Series was in place. If the division leader in both halves was the same, they would have to play the team with the second-best record, creating the possibility that a number two team, playing a number one team, could purposely lose to make the playoffs. Take the Yankees and Orioles, scheduled to play on the last day of the year. Suppose the Orioles, second-place finishers behind the Yankees in the first half, were set to finish a close third in the second half behind New York and Boston. If the Yankees trailed the Red Sox by mere percentage points going into the finale, the Orioles, by losing on purpose, could give the Yankees their second title, while ensuring themselves the second-best record and a spot of their own in the postseason.

Kuhn thought the possibility that this would happen was small, but if it did, an adjustment would be needed. An adjustment *if* it happened? A change was needed right now.

Cardinals manager Whitey Herzog, interviewed by Joe Garagiola during the pregame show before the first *Game of the Week* of the new season, made it clear that Herzog's job was to get to the postseason, whatever it took. He told the announcer/humorist, "It is every manager's job, and if that is the only way to get in the play-offs, yes, I would lose a ball game. I would apologize to the public though." Herzog wasn't above activating himself to be catcher and have all his players throw with their opposite hand if that's what it took to advance.

Tony La Russa saw it the same way. The following afternoon, on ABC's Sunday-afternoon game, the White Sox leader announced his team would never lose on purpose, but "would refuse to take the field."

Kuhn was apoplectic. "Why wasn't this anticipated? (This one got bye [sic] lots of people in planning)," he noted to himself, forgetting that it was predicted at the Chicago owners' meeting. "Discip[line] WSox, Herzog," he asked himself before answering, "(nothing—we put them in that position)." Though not willing to crack down on the honest managers, he hurried off notes to Herzog and La Russa seeking clarification.

Kuhn wrote to Herzog that his comments showed "disregard for your obligation to do your best to win games." Whitey didn't care. His job was to get the Cardinals to the World Series, and he felt that the split season was Kuhn's way to stick it to Busch. In a telex response, Herzog held his ground, protesting that he always did his best, but his comments came "because of what I think is a natural confusion over whether winning the pennant or winning a particular game is paramount under the present split season plan." La Russa had a face-to-face with the commissioner and reiterated that his team would never take the field and throw a game.

Letters were sent to team owners as well. Kuhn reminded Einhorn and Reinsdorf that according to Rule 21 their team needed to try their best, and La Russa's forfeit idea wouldn't pass the test. The Cardinals apologized for their skipper's remarks, but Busch was in a tizzy, sending articles to Kuhn that slammed the split season.

It was impossible for Kuhn to keep defending the flawed plan. Internally it was a disaster. He mailed an article that quoted his own National League president vilifying the scheme. "Chub," he wrote Feeney, "for good or ill we have to split season; what earthly good does it do for you to attack the corporate decision?" To Edward Bennett Williams, Kuhn inquired about a recent newspaper quote. "If the integrity flaw in the split season plan was so obvious," Kuhn wrote sarcastically, "please explain how the Orioles failed to pick it up. The plan was widely publicized before the Chicago meeting."

The press excoriated Kuhn. Rifling off a copy of a Peter Gammons column to its author with added comments of his own, an upset Kuhn retaliated that the split season was not "a joke," and though it had an error that needed fixing, "too much has been made of that." For all his talk about the integrity of the game, the commissioner sought to downplay the idea that taking a dive to make the playoffs was worthy of so much comment. But the criticism was too much and had to be addressed.

An owners' meeting was called for August 17 at 75 Rockefeller Plaza to fix the problem. There seemed to be as many solutions as teams. Ultimately Plan B was unveiled: two different half-season winners would face off, or in the case of both half winners being the same, they must play the second-half second-place team. It wasn't perfect, Kuhn realized, but he wasn't sure any result would be fair to all. Wagner, still seeing a problem for his Reds should they have the best yearlong record but neither win nor finish in second place in the second half, was stunned that the necessary surgery was Band-Aided over. And there was still the chance that a winner of both halves could handpick its playoff matchup. The new recommendations were to be presented to the Major League Executive Council the next day, then submitted to the MLBPA and 26 clubs. Miller saw little problem if the new plan made more sense and was rational.

Around 3:00 p.m., after the decision had been arrived at, Grebey came over to the union offices and handed them a piece of paper, asking, "What do you think?" Not surprisingly the owners screwed up the one thing they were given to do, and Miller held them to the fire: "They goofed on this and we're not anxious to hang them on it. They're playing it as if this is their baby, and in a way, it is. We never proposed the split season or anything like it. That wasn't one of our demands. Now they feel embarrassed." The players signed off on the new scheme.

It had been a trying time for Kuhn. As if the strike itself weren't destructive enough, the colossal mess of the initial split-season plan and its creation of a nightmare scenario of teams losing on purpose was an added insult. There were new calls for his firing. Kuhn tried to be strong, filing away a quote from Abraham Lincoln: "I do the very best I know how—the very best I can; and I mean to keep doing so until the end. If the end brings me out all right, what is said against me won't amount to anything. If the end brings me out wrong, ten thousand angels swearing I was right would make no difference."

Angels were hard to find as the twin devils of frustration and anger left over from the strike erupted on the field. The disruption of the season began taking a toll on the players who had walked out; at least the negotiators had an outlet at the table. In Pittsburgh, the quick-to-the-bottom Pirates were already down 5–1 to the second-place Dodgers as the two teams headed into the top of the sixth inning at Three Rivers Stadium. Pittsburgh's erratic Pascual Perez hadn't made any friends with his frequent pretend shootings of batters, pointing his forefinger like a barrel and *bang!* you're out. With his team down, a little chin music seemed appropriate.

Bill Russell led off for Los Angeles and was promptly plunked on the hand. The shortstop scored on a double by center fielder Ken Landreaux. Perez, realizing the message had not been received, hit the next batter, Dusty Baker, also on the hand. Lasorda ran out to argue that Perez was intentionally nailing his batsmen.

In the dugout, Reggie Smith, back from a shoulder injury, was irate. He wasn't going to stand for some twig of a thrower hurting his teammates. Perez turned to the screaming Smith and motioned that they should meet under the stands to air out their emotions. Perez promptly struck out Garvey to finish the business at hand. Perez sprinted from the mound and Smith left the dugout to meet him off the field, behind home plate.

The field emptied, as did the dugouts. The nearly 17,000 had no idea where everyone had gone. Was it another strike? Beneath the stands, players, managers, coaches, 50 people in all, tussled in the tunnel behind home. Perez held a bat tightly in his hand for protection. Like most baseball fights, it ended after five minutes with no damage. There wasn't enough room in the corridor to punch.

A sparse crowd of 7,766 came to Busch Stadium on a Wednesday Ladies' Day to watch their Cardinals, tied for first place with the upstart Mets, host the Giants before heading out on the road. An uneventful mismatch turned out to be a memorable August afternoon at the ballpark. On that sunny St. Louis day, Garry Templeton lost his mind.

Herzog thought that his shortstop was one of the real talents in the game, the most talented player he'd seen since Mickey Mantle. "Tempy" was as troubled as gifted, and his greatest claim to fame was not that he was the first switch-hitter in history to amass 100 hits from each side of the plate in a single season, but his statement of rebellion when he wasn't chosen by the fans for the starting lineup in the 1979 All-Star Game. "If I ain't startin', I ain't departin'," he warned. The tantrum solidified the image of Templeton as an egotistical spoiled brat.

Days before the August 26 game, Templeton went into Herzog's office and dropped himself into a chair, exhausted.

"I don't want to play day games after night games anymore. I'm too tired."

The manager couldn't get over it. The best player on the team saying that? Herzog could add it to the growing list—Templeton hated playing in Montreal, he didn't like playing in the rain, and he preferred not to hit against certain pitchers.

"What's the matter with you? You're *tired*? Get some damn rest!" Herzog erupted.

Templeton listened, but not as his manager hoped. He started playing in slow motion, jogging instead of running, earning the boos of a disdainful crowd. In the bottom of the first inning, Templeton struck out, but the pitch got away from catcher Milt May. The weary batter strolled one-third of the way down the first-base line and turned for the dugout as May completed the play with an easy throw to first base.

The stadium roared in a cacophony of jeers. Heading to the bench, Templeton gave the crowd the bird, not of the Cardinal variety.

"Knock it off," cautioned home plate umpire Bruce Froemming.

Templeton wasn't listening and he wasn't finished. On deck in the fourth, the boos rising around him, the ironically nicknamed Jump Steady proved anything but, making another obscene gesture at the crowd. Froemming warned him again.

"I have a right to answer back," Templeton protested, claiming that ice cubes and racial slurs were being thrown at him. The umpire didn't care, ejecting him from the game. Turning to walk off the artificial carpet, Templeton grabbed his crotch in a pre–Michael Jackson move and shook his parts at the faithful.

Herzog saw all shades of Cardinal red. He'd never before been so mad at a player in his life. As soon as Templeton was near enough to reach, Herzog grabbed his jersey and pulled him angrily into the dugout. The shortstop resisted, bumping the manager backward. Whitey charged back, pushing Templeton against the wall, the rest of the team closing in to separate the two and stop a riot.

"Get out of here. I don't want you on the road trip. I don't want you around my players. I don't want to see you."

Templeton got his suitcase and clothes bag and left Busch under police protection.

"We're better off without him," said a teammate. "I don't think he's got the guts to show up here. Whatever he does, I don't have any respect for him."

The next day it was announced that Templeton would undergo psychological evaluation, expected to check in to a hospital in the coming days for an extended checkup. It was uncertain when he'd return. What was certain was that he was suspended indefinitely and fined $5,000.

Insanity also reigned in the Bronx. The Yankees were near the bottom of their division, looking up at the first-place Tigers. Detroit had turned it on after losing 3 of their first 4 games. Sparked by the passionate play and late-inning homer heroics of Kirk Gibson, a former Michigan State All-American wide receiver, the young team felt a pennant was within reach. Steinbrenner, his team holding a slim lead over the last-place Indians, found a new tactic he hoped would either light a fuse or destroy Jackson. The Boss had questioned Jackson's eyesight during the away series in Detroit. Coach Torborg threw some batting practice to the struggling slugger, who powdered all but two pitches into the seats, many into the upper deck.

"Go tell 'the man' what you think of my eyesight," Jackson told reliever George Frazier, who had witnessed the awesome power surge.

Steinbrenner was undeterred. First, Jackson was embarrassed when Aurelio Rodriguez, well-known for his weak hitting, was sent up to pinch-hit for Jackson against the Twins. Jackson was stuck at .212 and hadn't hit a home run since May 25, but he was still a more potent force than the great-glove, no-bat Rodriguez. It was obvious harassment. Manager Michael wasn't sure that Jackson could produce with the pressure coming from the owner's box.

Then, on the day that all hell broke loose in St. Louis, Steinbrenner ordered Jackson to undergo a full physical examination. Coyly, Steinbrenner said he was helping Jackson find a reason for the season-long slump. Jackson saw it for the humiliation it was intended to be, but he knew he was a mess, brooding over the lack of progress toward a new contract, watching players make his first huge deal look like a pittance. He wanted his big payback and he wasn't getting it. Jackson had no problems with Winfield, they got along fine, and Jackson wished he had a little of the new guy's attitude toward the owner: "Fuck me? Okay. Fuck you." That was Winfield's style, not Jackson's. The money, the criticism, the insults, ate away at him.

Jackson went up to the office of Yankee vice president Cedric Tallis, who delivered the order, a typewritten message explaining that Steinbrenner wanted Jackson to fly to Tampa.

"Cedric, what is this shit?"

Tallis stammered. "Reggie, I'm just following orders." An irate Jackson called Steinbrenner from Tallis's office.

"Look, George, maybe the way I'm playing is my own fault. . . . I'm gonna show you. . . . I'm off to Chicago to do my job, and then it's good-bye." He agreed to take the physical, he had no choice. It was in his contract that the club could demand one, but Jackson wasn't heading to Steinbrenner's hometown for a public verbal spanking. Instead he went to the NYU Medical Center the next day. He was fine, his vision at 20/10 with a slight astigmatism that caused him to wear wire-framed glasses. When he was done with three doctors, Jackson went to Travis John's room to play with him. After two weeks in a coma, the little boy rubbed his eyes and was slowly coming back.

The first-place winners were finding motivation difficult. The Phillies, like the Yankees, were next to last, and their manager tried to fire them up, bumping an umpire and garnering a suspension.

"We already won and don't need to win another game, but we have pride," Green hoped. Even with the picture-perfect, powerful short swing of Schmidt, who clouted his 300th career home run against the Mets, Philadelphia was looking disinterested. From a seat in the stands, Green watched his team lose all five games he missed, mulling a phone call he'd got from the Cubs, who wondered if he'd be willing to come to Chicago.

The Dodgers had climbed back to tie the Braves for first, but inconsistent pitching from Valenzuela was a growing concern. The A's were straddling the .500 mark, enough for a second-place tie behind the White Sox. Armas and Henderson were still pacing the offense, and the bull pen, so disappointing in the first months, was performing better. Martin, like Green, was pushing his players to stay focused. "We deserve [the playoffs] because we were so far ahead in first half," he said without apology, "but we'd like to win the second half too."

Though the A's had nothing to prove and muddled along at a .500 clip, they were still the most exciting team with, as everyone was realizing, the best player in the game. Rickey Henderson was a supernova, muscles bulging past his short sleeves, powerful legs set to burst out of his pants as he sped to another stolen base. His stance at the plate—deep crouch, way back in the batter's box, weight heavily on his right foot, his left tapping the dirt as if suspended— was instantly identifiable by fans, though opposing catchers hated the shrunken strike zone. "Stand up like a man," they demanded.

As August drew to a close, the Yankees' continued mediocrity put them in the middle of an East Division pack, where every team was playing well enough to stay in the hunt. The Indians had been hitting poorly but erupted in a 4-game series against the slumping Mariners. The Red Sox had clawed back into contention with Jim Rice and Dwight Evans leading the way. The Tigers, Orioles, and Brewers were running in a close heat.

In Baltimore, DeCinces was hitting grand slams, driving in runs, and driving "Wild Bill" Hagy and others into a pennant frenzy.

Ripken filled in at shortstop for Belanger, who struggled, again, at the plate, but the rookie couldn't dislodge DeCinces at third. (After September 11, Ripken had no plate appearances.)

While patrolling the hot corner, DeCinces got an earful from third-base coaches. Indians coaches asked Gabe Paul why they weren't to be paid for the new extra round of playoffs. "Blame the players," said the Cleveland owner. "DeCinces and Boone were against you." Word spread.

Miller and the players came under intense criticism, with undeserved claims that the union wanted all the money. DeCinces had been trying to get the coaches in the players' association, but it was an easier story that the players were too greedy.

"Ask my coaches," DeCinces fired back to a chirping opposing coach. "Ask Marvin."

"Yeah, sure" was the usual unyielding response. The on-field sniping didn't put DeCinces off his game, and the Orioles kept rolling.

Back in New York, Gossage came up with a sore arm, which was trouble since he and Davis, "the Gold Dust Twins" in the bull pen, made the Yankees virtually unbeatable after the seventh inning. Jackson had become a target of the fans, but he wasn't dodging the same projectiles as Parker. At Comiskey Park, after singling and tagging up on a deep fly ball by Graig Nettles, then scoring on a Bucky Dent hit, Jackson was showered with coins and bills by an appreciative White Sox crowd. Bending down on the warning track, Jackson laughed as he picked it up, $31.27 worth. The comedy relief helped, and the next day Jackson hit his first home run in 94 at bats.

A renewed Jackson and an assured playoff berth would please any owner, but not Steinbrenner. When he spotted Lou Piniella and Oscar Gamble in the clubhouse lounge, sprawled on couches, watching the game in progress, he threw them out and made the area off-limits during game time. A full-out assault on his manager began. The Boss slammed the skipper for not having his team ready to play. Steinbrenner also demanded that Jackson be benched. Michael was a data-driven guy, with thick notebooks of stats. His decisions were unemotional, but it was increasingly harder for him to keep his cool.

On August 28, when Jackson returned from his physical and John Hinckley pled innocent of attempting to kill the president, reporters swarmed into Michael's office in the visitors' clubhouse.

"What can you tell us about Reggie?" they shouted. Jackson himself would not speak to them on the matter.

"Reggie's fine, I don't want to talk about Reggie. I have something else to say." The last few weeks had been grueling for Michael. After the Yankees lost 6 of 7 games, Steinbrenner called from Tampa, telling his manager that he was on shaky ground.

"You can't expect a veteran team like this, sitting around for six weeks, to do any work when they've won the first half," Michael, a lifelong baseball man, tried to explain.

"I don't know, Stick," said the exasperated Steinbrenner. "This is just unacceptable. I think I'm gonna make a change. You're just too young. You can't get it out of 'em."

The calls came daily. Michael could set his watch by them. When Steinbrenner went after Michael again, Stick snapped.

"I'm sick and tired of your threats, George. I can't take this anymore. If you want to fire me, then get your fat ass out here to Chicago and just do it."

"You just wait. I'll be there," replied the angry owner.

That afternoon Michael was ready for the press. He launched into a prepared statement delineating the full extent of Steinbrenner's threats, the calls that came in the night. The normally stoic manager had had enough. "If he wants to fire me, let him get it over with."

Steinbrenner was at the game that night, ignorant of what was happening in the catacombs below. When the press asked his reaction, Steinbrenner remained stony, but seated with friends who heard along with the owner about his manager's revolt, he was obviously boiling.

In Montreal, the Expos were smoking. A 5-game win streak put them within a game's reach of first. Carter, even with an injured leg, was producing, driving in 10 runs in two games against the Reds, hobbling around the bases after a grand slam. The pitching staff was untouchable, putting up 32⅔ of consecutive scoreless innings, Rogers hurling a shutout against Atlanta. The outfield was on a pace to be the first all-.300 trio since the 1974 Cardinals. Raines had already broken the rookie stolen-base record with his 61st. Dawson was doing it all, the undisputed team leader as they sought their first postseason slot.

August ended with all four divisions hotly contested, as hoped for when the split season went into effect. However, it would have been the same had the season been resumed in full, with entire records setting the standings rather than 20 games. The Royals were thrilled for the second chance. Had the season gone on uninterrupted, Kansas City would have been mired at the bottom, well under .500. As it was, they were close to the lead.

It wasn't enough to save Jim Frey's job. The man who less than a year before had brought the Royals to their first World Series was dumped on the 31st, replaced by Dick Howser, who'd been jettisoned by Steinbrenner after Frey beat him and the Yankees in the League Championship Series the year before. Now Steinbrenner had three ex-managers as possible playoff rivals—Ralph Houk in Boston, Martin, and Howser.

Phil Garner was also sent packing. The embarrassment he'd caused his owner and general manager during the strike was not forgotten. Galbreath and Peterson had asked Pirates players to be a year-round presence in Pittsburgh, and Garner obliged, becoming part of the community, helping to build the team's public image, though uncomfortable speaking in front of an audience. He was hurt to the core when he was traded to Houston, but his parents and other family members were there. Plus, he was going from last place to first.

The Astros also welcomed back J. R. Richard, who was put on the active list. Though he wasn't ready to pitch, the Astros hoped that he'd recover down the line. If he'd remained on the disabled list and not on the roster before November 20, he'd be unprotected.

It was exciting to see him in Astros colors again, but the best return of all was Travis John's. He was moved out of intensive care. In less than two weeks he'd gone from a coma to walking. It was a miracle.

Rolling into September, attendance was improving. Both leagues were only down around 1,000 fans per game. There was a lot to see. In Boston, the Red Sox played a 20-inning game, the longest in Fenway history. In Los Angeles, Valenzuela was back in form, notching his 7th shutout, to tie a National League record held by Jerry Koosman, Grover Cleveland Alexander, and Irving Young, who sounded like an accountant but had pitched his way into the record book in 1905. Fernando belted a 3-run triple in a 5–0 win over St. Louis.

The Angels provided laughs in Cleveland when "Disco" Dan Ford, after swinging at a Barker pitch, watched the top of his bat fly off, exposing a groove cut down the middle that was filled with cork. The bat had been sawed an inch from the top, hollowed out, and packed with the insubstantial substance, making the bat easier to swing, light on the inside, but still hard on the outside. Earlier in the year, the A's had suspected Ford of corking, which led to a brawl. This time he was caught red-handed, ejected from the game, suspended for three days, and fined.

The Yankees were falling apart faster than Ford's bat. For more than a week after his Chicago Emancipation Proclamation, Michael had been left hanging. Most managers who had won the first half and, by September 6, were 2 games over .500 and 3 games out of first place would feel secure, but when Steinbrenner was at his most Steinbrennery, no one was safe.

The iciness from the front office to the dugout was palpable, Michael shut out of all communication. One attempt had been made to clear the air. For 45 minutes the two spoke on the phone, pure playground stuff, with the Boss insisting the manager say he was sorry to avoid getting fired.

"I didn't mean the threats, but you can't take on the boss publicly." Steinbrenner waited for the apology, but it never came. Michael was fired.

"I've got no reason to apologize because I didn't do anything wrong," Michael told the press after he got word. "When you become his manager, it's like your IQ drops by fifty percent. All of a sudden you don't know anything."

"I feel like a father scorned," said the 51-year-old Steinbrenner about the 43-year-old Michael. It was the seventh firing in nine years for Steinbrenner, and he flipped through his Rolodex to find Bob Lemon. In his first stint with the Yankees, Lemon had won the World Series in 1978 after replacing Martin midseason, then was promptly relieved of his duties 65 games into 1979 and replaced by Martin, who was promptly fired after his marshmallow-man fight, to be replaced by Howser, fired after 1980's East Division crown and playoff loss to his present team, the Royals.

Steinbrenner phoned Lemon's house in Long Beach, California. His wife, Jane, picked up and said that her husband was at the barber. Steinbrenner tracked down the shop, called, and offered Lem the position.

"It's nice to be wanted back," said the bulbous-nosed Lemon, "by the only baseball club in the world." Unlike Michael, Lemon went by his gut, thick as it was, relying on the instincts that made him a Hall of Fame pitcher. Like Michael, Lemon had to deal with an increasingly meddlesome owner. Fortunately he was picking up in the middle of a 5-game winning streak. It was after another win over the Royals, with rookie Righetti allowing 1 run to put his ERA at a stellar 1.63, that Lemon took the helm.

The second half was proving to be tough on managers. With so little time to make the playoffs, each loss was magnified. The pressure was intense and there was no time for patience. The Expos, who had led their division at the All-Star break in 1979 and blown it, then had led again in late September of 1980 and blown it, were fighting for a spot in October, $1\frac{1}{2}$ games behind the Cardinals. The Expos were on a roll, visiting listless, last-place Philadelphia, when news broke. Dick Williams had been fired.

Williams, since taking over in 1977, had turned a perennial loser into a first-class contender, whipping a young team into winners.

Bill Lee, who started his career under Williams in Boston, loved his old-school, gruff style. Dawson had no problems either; he kept his head down, played hard, and kept quiet.

Rogers hated the man. The ace pitcher saw a helmsman who ranged from uninterested to nasty. Their rocky relationship had started in 1979, when Rogers was coming back from elbow surgery, the result of his unorthodox motion, in which he almost fell off the mound as he uncorked a devilish sinking fastball. At Palm Beach Airport, reporting for spring training, Rogers ran into Williams and a few coaches, who asked how Rogers was doing.

"My elbow is good, but my shoulder's killing me."

"[If] you can't fucking pitch, I'll get somebody else," Williams growled. It was the first thing he said to Rogers, not even a hello, and in front of Rogers's family to boot.

Jim Brewer, the pitching coach, saw the pitcher's fist clench and held him back. "He's been drinking, let him go."

Williams hated Rogers equally. He thought his number one starter got too nervous in big games, his breathing so fast and labored that he bordered on hyperventilating, always needing to go to the bathroom. His so-called Cy Young–worthy pitcher was an embarrassment, stealing the fans' money by refusing to step it up for the team. The other Expos didn't share this appraisal. Rogers was a solid presence in the clubhouse and the undisputed leader of the pitching staff.

With the heat on in September to avoid another late-season collapse, Williams's confrontations with his players grew. He was down on Dawson, of all people, and even Lee was disgusted by the manager who took to his corner of the dugout, writing things in personal charts (eventually rendered obsolete by the August unveiling of the IBM "personal computer," with something called MS-DOS by some unknown company named Microsoft). Playing tic-tac-toe by himself while wearing golf shoes and sipping Scotch, Williams didn't seem to care anymore. His contract negotiations with the team had stalled and he was phoning it in, staging a virtual boycott, handing in his lineup card and tuning out. With all his troubles with the team,

Williams had one person who he truly despised, Rogers, who bitched about Williams constantly.

When Cardinals outfielder Tony Scott slid and tore the muscle from Gary Carter's calf in an August 30 matchup, the catcher shrugged it off, layering himself with tape. He could squat, but he couldn't run. With the score knotted at 4 in the 11th inning, Carter walked. Normally Williams wouldn't use a pitcher to pinch-run, but he sent in Rogers, who was coming off a shutout two days earlier.

Warren Cromartie grounded to first, behind Rogers, who, with good speed for a pitcher, went hurtling into second. The tough pitcher slid into second to break up the double play, kicking his feet out but close enough to reach the bag to avoid an interference call. The shortstop was rattled, and his throw to first sailed into the dugout, allowing Cromartie to reach second.

Rogers headed to the showers, out of breath. "Dang, I can't breathe," he told teammate Woodie Fryman. "I'm hurting." Under the spray, Rogers coughed repeatedly, horrified as he felt blood rush up and out to the shower floor. He'd cracked a rib and punctured his lung. Though he didn't go on the disabled list, Rogers was out of action at the most inopportune time. By September 3, Montreal fans were chanting, "Dick must go." Beyond being blamed for Rogers's injury, Williams's ambivalence about his job, his mishandling of the bull pen, his refusal to use new reliever Jeff Reardon, and his lack of communication with his players made it obvious that his time was growing short.

On the morning of the eighth, Williams, in his hotel room, got a call from CEO John McHale, who asked the manager to come down to his suite. Williams knocked and the door opened.

"Good morning, Dick, we're making a change."

"Lord, John, why are you firing me?" Williams was shocked, fired in the hallway and left there like a tray of dirty dishes.

A bigger jolt came in his replacement. Jim Fanning had last managed in 1962, at Eau Claire in a Class C league. He did take the team to a Northern League championship, but that was long ago and far down the ladder. He was a front-office guy, brought to Montreal by McHale as general manager in the team's first year of 1969 and, until he got the call on September 7, vice president of player development. When McHale rang, Fanning was typing a four-page, single-spaced report on the minor league Denver Bears. Fanning was as surprised as anyone that he got the job.

The players knew him well. The farm system Fanning had created had brought Cromartie, Dawson, Carter, Raines, third baseman Larry Parrish, and four of the starting five pitchers to the big leagues. These were his boys, he loved them and they loved him. Rogers, lying on his couch, nursing his sore rib, was ecstatic about the move, a positive step. Fanning had the fire, was competitive, but his demeanor was the polar opposite of his predecessor's. Williams hadn't shown much care in his last days; Fanning cared about every detail and every person on the field. It was addition by subtraction.

The first two games produced two quick losses to the Phillies. The Philly papers called Fanning "Alice in Blunderland," and Harry Caray in the other league harped from the White Sox broadcast booth that the "Expos haven't won since replacing Dick Williams as manager. Nice going, John McHale." Fanning, out of his element, not even sure where the flap of his baseball shoes should go, was adjusting to the game, so much faster than it looked from a desk. He was unsure how much to anticipate, relying on his staff for advice and counting on the understanding of his players. He got it from most, but not from Lee. "Fanning flat out can't manage at all," he told the team. Lee saw Fanning as hyperactive, panicky, and disorganized and suggested the players take over and make their own decisions.

The players thought Fanning could only be temporary until a more experienced manager was found. He still approached the game from a farm director's point of view, going out to talk with hitters in the on-deck circle as he would in the instructional league.

When Rogers returned on September 12, throwing 6 scoreless innings against Chicago before leaving when his rib began to ache, it set the Expos on a new momentum that would erase any issues surrounding their novice manager.

•   •   •

Travis John smiled and blew kisses as he left the hospital on the 10th. In the car, driving across the bridge to New Jersey, Sally put in his favorite cassette, the *Muppet Movie* sound track. "Who said that every wish would be heard and answered when wished on the morning star?" she sang through tears.

As they pulled into the driveway, Travis saw his tricycle. "Bicycle, Mommy! Bicycle!" he squealed. He'd made it home. It was the comeback story of the year.

By mid-September all four divisions were hotly contested, every team but two (the Pirates and the Padres) within 5½ games of the lead. The Tigers were the story in the American League East, holding a 3-game advantage over the Orioles, Yankees, and Brewers, all tied for second. Gibson was hitting over .400, and Detroit developed a penchant for late-inning heroics and walk-off victories. The groundskeepers boogied around the base paths with glee as they raked the Tiger Stadium infield.

The Yankees and Red Sox squared off in New York. As vendors walked the aisles in TAKE THE PEPSI CHALLENGE aprons, the high-kicking Righetti was all business, striking out 11 in the opener. The revived Jackson had 2 hits and made a diving catch in right field. Gossage came in to nail down the victory with 2 scoreless innings, his wild motion, limbs centrifugally trying to leave his body, baffling Boston hitters.

The following afternoon the Red Sox trotted out one of their young pitchers, Bobby Ojeda, who no-hit the Yanks into the ninth inning at the Stadium. Ojeda had saved himself with a superb play on a comebacker to the mound in the eighth, but Cerone doubled to lead off the next inning, ending Ojeda's bid for the record books. The Yankees romped in the finale: Bob Watson hit a gargantuan home run 417 feet to deep center field, Nettles dove every which way at third, and Jackson, again, made a stellar play in the field when he gunned down Jim Rice at third with a frozen rope from right. New York looked strong.

Days later, the two teams met again, this time at Fenway, with the Red Sox coming off a 4-game sweep of the first-place Tigers. After an opening loss, Boston fell behind 5–1 heading into the bottom of the eighth. Davis came in for Guidry and got two quick outs. On his way to shutting down the Red Sox, a funny thing happened. Carl Yastrzemski worked a walk and the Boston lineup exploded— single, walk, single, double, walk, single, and 3-run homer. The 7-run rally for an 8–5 victory was the greatest comeback Yaz had ever seen, and the unexpectedly poor showing of the Yankee relief corps gave Boston a series win.

The Brewers lost a 3-game series in New York, in which Gorman Thomas couldn't resist taking mammoth hacks at pitcher Dave LaRoche's high-arcing "LaLob" pitch, almost coming out of his shoes and mustache before tossing his bat in disgust. Quickly rebounding, the Brew Crew took 2 of 3 from Baltimore, New York, and Baltimore again. In Milwaukee, "Stormin' " Gorman beat Righetti with a huge home run, and soon after the Datsun bull-pen car dropped Fingers off at the mound, it was game over.

Though the Orioles were in the race, paced by Eddie Murray, who blasted 2 grand slams and drove in 33 runs in 33 games, and DeCinces, who stayed hot, attendance at Memorial Stadium had cratered, dropping nearly 30 percent. The second-half average of only 16,000 per game didn't tell the tale. Many games were played before fewer than 10,000 spectators.

A reported quote of DeCinces's may have contributed to the lack of fan interest. After the Yankees won two straight, impressively scoring 10 runs in each game, DeCinces was asked about the first-half leaders and the division races winding down. "We can only take care of ourselves, but if the Yankees keep scoring like that, then call in the dogs, put out the fire, the hunt's over." The Orioles needed to win.

When the papers came out the next day, the sports headline read, "DeCinces Says 'Hunt's Over.' " When he arrived in the clubhouse, he was called in to the manager's office by an irate Weaver.

"I never had an owner come in so pissed off," said the spunky skipper. "He wants me not to play you. He thinks you're a quitter."

Since the strike, Williams had not spoken with his former confidant, walking right by him in the locker room without so much as a hello. To Weaver's credit, he snooped around and discovered the full sense of DeCinces's remarks. DeCinces's life with the only team he'd ever known was becoming stressful.

The American League West was a mess. The Royals had straightened themselves out and, on September 15, were firmly in first, the only team in the division with more wins than losses. Even the Twins were in competition, having pulled off 7 straight wins. The A's weren't concerned. Martin, while in the dugout, signed baseballs from kids straining to reach him. Henderson was leading the league in hits, runs, and stolen bases and was near the top in batting average, while outfield partner Armas paced the circuit in homers and RBI. Norris got his 11th win, over Texas, after being stopped by a Coliseum security guard who wouldn't let him in the stadium. Finally proving his identity, Norris hurriedly suited up, ready to pitch with 15 minutes to spare. Martin was happy, even with his team trailing Kansas City.

The Astros had taken command of the National League West behind unhittable bull-pen pitching, 1 run allowed over 18 innings, and tremendous starting work by Ryan, Knepper, and Sutton, now hot after a slow start. Pacing the league with a 22–13 record that included a 9-game winning streak, Houston looked hard to beat as the weeks ran out. Richard watched sadly from the dugout.

With a healthy Bench clouting 4 home runs in his first four games back, including a game winner at home against the Padres, the Reds were trying to claw their way to the lead, desperately trying to make up for the split season that had punished them. When the Dodgers came to town, the Reds won the first two. It was Seaver against Valenzuela in the second of those two, but like many trumped-up pitchers' duels, it was a washout. Both were off their game, giving up 4 runs each in the 6 innings they pitched. Dodgers outfielder Rick Monday smacked two over the wall. The Reds pulled it out in extra innings for their fifth 1-run win of the week.

The next week, Cincinnati went to Los Angeles. Bench was sent up to pinch-hit in the ninth against Dave Stewart. It was only the third time the veteran had faced the young reliever called Smoke, and Stewart had made him look bad on sinkers. Bench fouled off seven pitches before getting a fastball left up in the strike zone that he sent out toward the mountains for a 2-run homer and the Reds victory. The Dodgers, who had climbed to 2 games behind Houston, went into a tailspin.

Feeling much better, Templeton returned on the 15th after nearly three weeks. Profusely apologizing to the fans for the behavior that resulted in a one-game suspension, a $4,000 loss in salary, a stint on the disabled list, and some hospital time, Templeton said it was depression, not drugs, that led to his outburst. His father's illness had caused added stress.

The Cardinals welcomed him back. They'd gone 9–7 in his absence, maintaining a slim lead over the Expos, and as fate would have it, "Tempy" returned for a huge 5-game series in Montreal, including back-to-back doubleheaders. In his first game, Templeton smacked 4 singles and made two fine plays. The next night he added 3 more hits in the opener. In the week of his return, the chastened shortstop hit a staggering .452. It took two days of apologies and the obligatory discovering of God to put Templeton back on track. "When you find the Lord and get Him in your heart, everything is fine," said the new acolyte.

Fanning's fatherly concern for his players took on laughable proportions. At Olympic Stadium the dividing line between the field and the dugout was a painted white line on the track, not a real physical demarcation that a catcher, staring up at a foul pop, could feel. Fanning watched Carter circle under a ball and inch perilously closer and closer to the camera well.

"You've got room! You've got room!" he shouted, hoping he could help his catcher, going full tilt, avoid another injury. As Carter got near the dugout, preparing to catch the ball, he bumped into Fanning, who had wandered out into the play to reach out and protect his man. When the ball fell, the bench erupted in laughter.

Fanning's initial rocky start was seemingly behind them. After the St. Louis series, the Expos won 8 of their next 9.

Neither the Cardinals nor the Expos could deliver the explosive knockout right that "Sugar" Ray Leonard delivered to the head of Thomas "the Hitman" Hearns in the fight of the year at Caesars Palace on September 16. Rose rooted for the two teams to wear each other out. The Phillies were out of it, and all they could do was hope their first-round playoff opponents were tired. Not all was peaceful for the team from the City of Brotherly Love. Rose, though used to the heckling of fans outside Philly, took exception when a St. Louis fan spilled beer on him. (Maybe Templeton was right about that crowd?) Seeking to scare off his harassers, Rose smacked the handle of his bat on the visiting-dugout roof, allegedly hurting a fan's hand. The police got involved, issuing a summons for "individual peace disturbance" when charges were pressed.

Fan anger toward players had been growing. In San Francisco, Reggie Smith was ejected after going into the stands to fight a heckler who had thrown a batting helmet at him. The Dodgers outfielder was fined $5,000 and suspended for five games by NL president Feeney. In Atlanta, Astros outfielder Cesar Cedeno climbed the fence into the fourth row to get at three fans chanting, "Killer, killer, killer." Cedeno had never been able to live down his December 1973 conviction for involuntary manslaughter after shooting—accidentally, he claimed—a young woman in the Dominican Republic. Feeney tried to suspend Cedeno, but it was lifted after an appeal. Whether staying away from the ballpark or taking it out when there, the fans were acting out, and the players responded. The owners had no public face. There were no repercussions for them.

While his teammates (and others) got in trouble, Steve Carlton was on a strikeout tear, fanning 15, 12 (putting his career total past Bob Gibson's for the all-time National League record), and 11 in his last three September starts. In 1969, Carlton had tied the all-time single-game strikeout record with 19 in a loss to the Miracle Mets. In the 15 K game, the Mets beat him again. The Mets, no matter who wore the orange and blue, gave Carlton fits. He was 25–28 against New York over his career, 261–173 against everyone else.

Even as their slim hopes for October faded, the Mets played tough, sweeping St. Louis to the benefit of Montreal. Hubie Brooks and Mookie Wilson made for a promising future. The veterans were the problem. Valentine was hitting .207, Mazzilli .228, and Kingman .221. The fiery Stearns criticized them publicly, exhorting them to try harder, or at all. He came back from his harangue to find his locker completely trashed, the contents taken out and strewn on the floor while he warmed up on the field.

At the close of play on September 21, with two weeks left in season, the Mets were still in the running. Their overall record was 37–54, horrendous by any standard, yet they were $2\frac{1}{2}$ games behind first-place St. Louis. The four pennant races were tightly packed, no second-place team more than 3 games behind the leader. On the surface, the split season was working, but it was a thin surface.

If the season had been played in full, the races would have been more exciting and grounded in reality. The Cardinals would still be in first, $3\frac{1}{2}$ past the Phillies, 4 ahead of Montreal. The Reds would have received full credit for their National League best record, a half game atop the Dodgers. The A's would have maintained their grasp on first, and the Royals, now looking like the fall team to beat, would have been mired in fourth place, 6 games below .500. The Yankees and Tigers would have been deadlocked with Boston, Milwaukee, and Baltimore no more than $1\frac{1}{2}$ games behind, a five-team race!

It was a missed opportunity, great pennant runs with the rightful teams, but that would have done nothing to satisfy ABC and NBC, who demanded assurance that there'd be divisional playoffs. Kuhn had asked the networks before the strike ended if they'd be interested in a three-tier playoff system. They both said yes. Had they said no, it was unlikely there would have been a need for divisional series. The 1979 television contracts with the two networks paid approximately $5 million to Major League Baseball and contained a clause on a three-tier system. It had already been considered. What was good for TV was good for baseball? It was hard to be sure.

What was certain was that Reggie Jackson was back. The dynamite of the immense pressures upon him all year finally blew on September 23. Jackson, his average up around .240, a huge second-half surge from his .199 at the strike's start, was again a force to be feared. The Indians' John Denny knew it.

After singling in the first, Jackson swaggered to the plate in the second. Denny delivered a fastball, high and tight, which sent Jackson sprawling to the ground. Springing up from the dirt, Jackson headed toward the mound and the benches cleared. After striking out, Jackson was hauled away by teammate Bobby Brown to prevent a brawl.

"If you throw at me, I'm coming after you!" yelled Jackson, a few curses added for good measure.

In the fourth, Jackson, always able to supply the drama, stepped up and powered a tremendous shot into the right-center-field bleachers. Relishing the moment, Jackson trotted around the bases, waving his helmet at the adoring Yankee Stadium crowd, oblivious of Denny, who had made his way to the dirt near home plate. There was no avoiding a confrontation now.

The two wrestled to the ground, Jackson putting Denny in an armlock as both dugouts spilled onto the field. Jackson was carried off by Brown and Gamble, smiling and clapping his hands with glee. When he got to the dugout, he pulled off his jersey and charged back at Denny, this time to be restrained by Bobby Murcer. Jackson was a happy man and the fans loved him, the money-throwing craze now a form of tribute rather than mockery, a plea for him to stay a Yankee rather than a commentary on greed. He'd already collected about $200.

"I need about another two million dollars," he said, laughing. The game was fun again.

It was thrilling too. The next night, Baltimore, struggling to stay close to the front-running Tigers, arrived in New York. It was Palmer vs. Guidry, Jackson and Winfield vs. Murray and DeCinces, but any chance of a pitching duel was dashed when Guidry had to leave after two innings with two bruised toes on his left foot.

There was almost a replay of the Denny-Jackson incident when, in the seventh, Palmer threw a high, inside heater that made Jackson hit the deck. The Yankee rooters howled in protest, but the pitch wasn't as close as it seemed from the stands. When DeCinces led off the eighth, the game was in the bag for the Orioles, Palmer in charge of a 5–1 lead.

From the moment DeCinces sent a low liner to left and ran hard toward first, he only hoped the ball would stay up. He knew he'd tagged it, but wasn't sure it had enough height to leave the stadium.

Winfield saw the ball screaming toward him and broke toward it at full speed. Lemon had watched him before games preparing for hits like these, charging into the wall, digging his right spike into the padding, using the makeshift rung for lift as he climbed the wall. He timed it right, leaping with the ability that made him a collegiate basketball star, the glove on his left hand extending four rows deep, his armpit resting on top of the eight-foot wall. His right forearm, used for additional leverage, was cut as he pushed hard to maximize his elevation.

DeCinces was not quite to first base when he glanced up to see Winfield coming out of the stands, holding the ball aloft so the umpires would see he'd made the grab. DeCinces stood in disbelief. Some called this phenomenal catch the greatest in history. (For years, Major League Baseball would run it in an ad that pitched the slogan "Baseball fever, catch it!" Each time he saw the commercial, DeCinces would cringe.)

At the end of the inning, Winfield ran in, smiling. "I'm catching everything you hit down here," DeCinces told him.

Nobody hit anything when Nolan Ryan took to the Astrodome mound for the Saturday *Game of the Week* outing against the Dodgers. It wasn't much of a contest. After walking 3 Dodgers in the first 3 innings, a problem for "the Express" (he'd broken the career mark for bases on balls in early June), Ryan, mixing fastballs consistently in the high 90 mph range and knee-freezing curveballs, retired 19

in a row. The only scare came in the seventh inning, when Mike
Scioscia, who'd struck out twice, hit a deep shot to the warning
track in right-center field. Ryan craned his neck roofward, watching the ball soar, then saw Terry Puhl, a streak of red, orange, and
yellow stripes, stick out his glove hand for a backhand catch.

Two quick outs in the ninth, including Ryan's 11th strikeout,
and up to bat came Baker, considered by many the toughest out in
the lineup. He drew two quick balls, the crowd quietly murmuring
in anticipation, on their feet with mild claps of encouragement, the
mascots, Astrojack rabbit and the Astrodillo, nervous and sweating
in their foam heads.

The moment Baker sent an easy grounder to Art Howe at third,
it was a lock. As Howe threw to first, Ryan watched the play se-
dately, then raised his hand in the air as the entire team came to
mob him. He'd lost a no-hitter three weeks earlier, taking a gem
into the seventh inning against the Expos, but this one was a keeper.
For the 34-year-old Ryan, it was his fifth, a new major league record, breaking the tie he'd held with Sandy Koufax.

"Shoot, I don't get emotional about these things anymore," he
twanged. "This is probably the one I'll cherish the most. I did it at
home, on national TV, and my mother was here. This is the first one
my mom has seen." No other pitcher had the luxury of picking from
a handful of no-hitters to choose a favorite.

Houston kept their hold on first place, their pitchers on a roll.
Ryan and Knepper had the league's lowest ERAs, and Sutton piled
up wins. At the moment, they had the Dodgers' number.

Numbers were on Billy Martin's mind too, the kind connected
to dollar signs. With the postseason drawing near, the A's manager
announced that he'd be taking his coaches to the Arizona Instructional League instead of the division playoffs because no provisions
were made for managers and coaches to get a share of extra playoff
money.

"It wasn't our idea to strike and we shouldn't be penalized. If
my coaches are not paid for the playoffs, then we will not participate," said Martin. The managers and coaches had been paid during

the strike, unlike the players, and Marvin Miller felt the division money should offset player losses.

Earl Weaver pointed out that for all Martin's grandstanding, back in 1968 Miller had hoped the union could bring everyone into the fold and sent a letter to coaches offering them full membership rather than their present dues-paying, nonvoting status. The owners said these people were management, but the players wouldn't agree to that in writing and left it open. When only 30 percent responded to his offer, Miller dropped it. Still, coaches, managers, and trainers all received full benefits (pension, insurance), though they were not covered under the Basic Agreement. As a result, managers and coaches received two and a half times their dues in licensing dollars.

A's management decided they'd pay their five coaches, two equipment managers, trainer, and travel secretary out of the club's share of the division playoff pool. Martin's contract excluded him from pay.

The Brewers were not looking to boycott the playoffs, fighting desperately to notch a second-half crown. The Tigers' cubs had kept a thin grip on the lead. Jack Morris paced the solid starting staff. Milwaukee couldn't compete with that; they were next to last in pitching, but they had an ace in the hole, or the bull pen.

Fingers was unhittable, keeping games under control as the Brewers surged. An eighth-inning home run by Ben Oglivie put Milwaukee in first on the 26th. The two teams would face off in the final weekend, a 3-game series that the *Milwaukee Journal* was pushing fans to embargo. The lingering soreness of the strike wouldn't fade away, and the paper urged the faithful to stay home. "Now is not the time for disgruntled baseball fans to give in. Now is not the time to return to County Stadium. Now is the time, more than ever, to boycott major league baseball."

The editorial was the talk of the ballpark on Friday night. Brewers owner Bud Selig was disappointed that, on the eve of the team's first postseason appearance, the newspaper would punish them. The city listened somewhat, only 23,000 coming out for the first game of the stretch run. The 44-degree October night might have had something to do with that.

After taking the opener convincingly, an 8–2 shellacking, the Brewers were poised to finish things off on Saturday afternoon. With the Friday loss, the Tigers were now 2 games back, the Yankees 1, and a Milwaukee win would knock them both out of the second-half title. Tiger DH and part-time gravedigger Richie Hebner drove in the only run of the game, reaching safely, as Gibson scored, on a Cecil Cooper misplay at first base. The Brewers then had the daunting task of facing a red-hot Morris the next day, already leading the league with 14 wins.

Molitor walked to lead off the bottom of the eighth, igniting an inning of bunts, ground outs, and walks that scratched out 2 runs for the lead. With Fingers already in the game, brought in for the final out of the top half of the inning, the crowd went wild with expectation. Fingers was a sure thing that year, truly Milwaukee's finest.

In the second half, Fingers, with a newfound mastery of his forkball, was involved in two-thirds of all the team's wins, his ERA well under 1 run per game. "Maybe I get better with age. Maybe I'll be better next year," he reflected. "I doubt it," he added realistically. This was a career year.

Fingers got two quick outs as the 28,000-plus rose in ecstasy. When the last batter, Lou Whitaker, whiffed on a fastball, Fingers shook his fist twice and then watched as catcher Ted Simmons thundered his way to the mound. "I hope he's not as hefty as he looks," Fingers thought. Fingers grabbed the leaping catcher, locking him in a hug.

"I love you, I love you," Fingers repeated, now on his way to postseason baseball for the first time since his glory days with Oakland in 1975.

The affection Jim Fanning had for his players had changed the atmosphere in Montreal. After Raines broke his right hand, and the team dropped 3 of 5 to the Cardinals in the great Templeton comeback, the manager advised his players to look inside and ask if they were playing up to their extraordinary ability.

"Everybody had to look at themselves. That's thought provoking, and that can be action provoking," commented Rogers. The action provoked was 8 wins in their next 10 games at Olympic Stadium. The Cardinals had dropped out of the lead after a 9–4 loss to Philadelphia, the first time since August 19 that they weren't setting the pace. The Expos kept ahead for a few days, expanding their lead to 2½ games, seeing it shrink to a mere half game after losing to St. Louis 6–2 at Busch Stadium. The Cardinals regained the top spot by the slimmest of margins after an 8–4 win the following night. There were 5 games to go.

St. Louis lost, won, lost, and won again. The Expos kept winning on the road, first in Pittsburgh, then in New York. Everything was on the line on Saturday, October 3, Montreal 1½ games ahead. St. Louis needed to win its last two and needed the Expos to lose their last two for the Cards to win the division.

Rogers had shut out the Mets on Friday, putting to bed his reputation for not delivering in crunch time. The next afternoon the scoreboard at Shea Stadium showed the Cardinals off to a monstrous early lead over Pittsburgh. As if that weren't bad enough, the Mets charged to a 3–0 lead after three. The Expos, late-season losers in both 1979 and 1980, felt their past creeping up on them. One run in the fifth eased the pain, and in the sixth, with Raines pacing the dugout in his blue satin jacket, a plastic cast on his fractured hand, Carter provided the spark with a home run to bring Montreal within 1.

Bill Lee was finishing up two innings of shutout relief. Despite his losing record, Lee's sparkling ERA showed his true value. A Wallace Johnson triple in the seventh put Montreal ahead for good, and despite the Cardinals also winning their Saturday game, the Expos clinched their first postseason berth, winning the second-half East Division title. The Cardinals, with the best overall record in the division, were heading home.

Valenzuela's second-half fade, from 8-0, 0.50 ERA, to 5-7, 3.68, concerned the lagging Dodgers. With LA fading, the Astros were fending off a Big Red Machine in full gear. The Reds were hot, 11–2 in their best road trip in nine years, but none were more scalding than Seaver. On his way to a 14–2 record, the best winning percentage for a National League starter in three decades, Seaver was an imperturbable pitching marvel, going 7–1 in each half-season and winning league pitcher of the month for September. After a 2-game split series in Cincinnati between the two top teams, the division came down to the wire.

The Astros headed to Los Angeles, losing the opener 6–1. Worse news for the Astros came in the top of the third when Sutton stepped up to the plate to face ex-teammate Reuss. Squaring around to bunt, hoping to advance the runner on first, Sutton was too set to get out of the way of Reuss's errant pitch. His fastball slammed flush against the Astro pitcher's left kneecap and shattered it. Sutton was finished for the season. The Reds squandered the opportunity to pick up ground, losing to the Braves and Gaylord Perry, who got his 297th career victory.

Los Angeles kept handing Cincinnati their chance, walloping the Astros again the next day, but the Reds couldn't get past Atlanta, even with Seaver on the mound. The score was tied after seven innings when Reds relief man Tom Hume came out of the bull pen. Powerful Braves third sacker Bob Horner, who had already homered twice in the game, singled immediately, moved to third on another single and scored on an error. The manufactured run was all that was needed to beat the Reds and end their season. Dick Wagner's nightmare came true. The Reds, who finished the first half of the season one half game behind the Dodgers, came up $1\frac{1}{2}$ games short of Houston in the second half. The team with the best record in all of the major leagues was done, unable to make it through the absurdity of the split season. Wielding a homemade pennant, the Reds ran onto the field to the applause from an appreciative Riverfront crowd. The act cried defiance—"We don't need your stinkin' flag!"—but they did.

"We were cheated," cried manager John McNamara. Seaver, ever the diplomat, was measured: "You can moan all you want, but we had our chances." In St. Louis, where feelings were equally hard, Cardinals infielder Dane Iorg summed things up: "That's Bowie Kuhn's great split season."

It took the Royals until the last day of the season to clinch the West. A 9–0 win over Cleveland put them a game ahead of the A's, having played four more games than Oakland in the second half. They were the only two West Division teams to play winning baseball over the poststrike months. For the full season, the Royals lost 3 more games than they'd won, yet here they were, undeservedly on their way to the playoffs. The second game of the Kansas City–Cleveland doubleheader was canceled due to irrelevancy.

It was time for recrimination and recapitulation. The split season was an artistic bomb. Abbreviated pennant runs were nothing compared to what could have been; actual records would have created a five-team race in the American League East, the Brewers at the apex with the Orioles, Yankees, Tigers, and Red Sox all within $2\frac{1}{2}$ games of the lead. St. Louis would have finished 2 games ahead of Montreal, and, right behind them, Philadelphia. The Reds would have been convincing champs, the Dodgers 4 games to the rear, and the A's would have outlasted the Rangers by 5 games.

The teams that had unwittingly clinched a playoff position in the first half couldn't muster up any enthusiasm to play hard. The Dodgers went 27–26, the Phillies 25–27, and the Yankees, sixth-place finishers, 25–26. "The Yankees play their best when they have to win," said the astute Piniella. Only Martin drew fire, as the A's played slightly better than even at 27–22.

It was a financial fiasco as well. Attendance was weak. The first half in the American League averaged 20,865. In the second half, it plummeted to 17,751. In the National League, attendance dropped from 21,015 to 19,034 per game. The split season was a failure in fairness and in ginning up interest, but TV got what it wanted. Was that enough?

The split season removed all the momentum of the regular schedule, taking all credibility with it. That the Mets and the Mariners, two of the most awful teams in all of baseball, stayed in contention, ridiculed the game. Even the Toronto Blue Jays were close enough to a second-half division win that they printed playoff tickets, even though their full-season record was 36–65. The Cubs came close, leading Herzog to pull at his blond hair. "You can talk about the Cubs being a contender, but if they [went] to the World Series, it would be a mockery." Martin also expressed his scorn. "Whoever devised it isn't a baseball man. It must have been the commissioner's lawyer, some guy from Dartmouth." Quickly realizing that A's president Eisenhardt was an alum, Martin panicked. "I mean some guy from Yale." And he wondered why he got fired so often.

The now-detested season drew criticism from owners who had created it. Williams went back to the source: "Every time I think of what that guy did . . . ," he said of Grebey. That man forced the strike, said the unforgiving Williams, and the owners made it worse with the split.

In the midst of the turmoil, Grebey wasn't defensive, aggressively touting the PRC as a full-service body, not merely a negotiating force, but a year-round organization to assist the owners in grievance and arbitration procedures. His take on the strike, after all that had happened, was that the players were more divided than the owners and he was around to stay, with an automatic two-year extension of his contract at the end of the calendar year. The players' association thanked Miller with a monthlong trip to anywhere in the world. There'd be no gifts for Grebey.

The World Series was set to begin October 28, six days later than originally scheduled. With weather delays, it could become the first to stretch into November. In 1976, Kuhn sat in near-freezing temperatures at Riverfront Stadium for the Reds-Yankees Series. Determined to make his own reality, Kuhn refused an overcoat, pretending it wasn't cold after all. That particular delusion had stuck with the commissioner ever since.

"If you've studied October weather patterns as I have," pronounced Kuhn, "you know that, historically, the weather does not change from week to week." Back on earth, Allen Lewis of *The Philadelphia Inquirer* studied weather in the nine cities that could've hosted the World Series in each of the last five years. He found a dramatic drop in average temperatures between the third and fourth weeks of October. On October 22, 1969, Montreal saw a foot of snow.

John McNamara, still smarting for his cheated Reds, hoped "this thing would end up on Halloween in Montreal, with the baseball powers that be up to their butts in snow." McNamara said Kuhn should wear a mask, but of whom?

Chapter 8

The new era of division series began in Kansas City on the day Egyptian president Anwar Sadat was assassinated in Cairo during the annual parade celebrating Egypt's crossing of the Suez Canal. With the world in shock, the A's and Royals were set to start a best 3-of-5 short series. In Game 1, Norris delivered a steady stream of screwballs and off-speed pitches. Royals second baseman Frank White derided the soft stuff as slop, but it was pretty good slop, at least good enough to hold the Royals to 4 hits in a 4–0 shutout.

The next day was more of the same. McCatty, the league ERA champ, was stellar. Armas doubled in a run in the eighth inning for a 2–1 victory. After a travel day the teams arrived in Oakland, where the A's finished the sweep 4–1 behind Langford.

In this deserved trouncing of a team that never belonged there, no one cried for the Royals except George Brett, 2 for 12 in the series to end a miserable year of injuries, altercations with the press, hometown booing, and attacks of frustration on unsuspecting locker-room toilets. "I was horseshit," Brett analyzed. In the A's clubhouse, the celebration was in full swing. "This could be the year of the A's," boasted beer-soaked A's shortstop Fred Stanley.

The Dodgers began their series against the Astros in Houston, old-man Ryan against young-idol Valenzuela. Ryan's confidence was at a high; he'd just no-hit this team in his home ballpark. What could they do this time around?

Nothing. Ryan blew Los Angeles away for 6 scoreless innings until Garvey, recently separated from his wife, Cyndy, after ten years of marriage (she'd left him for songwriter Marvin Hamlisch), fought through his tangled emotions to blast a solo shot to tie the game at 1. It was Ryan's only mistake of the game.

Valenzuela was equal to his elder, allowing a single scratch run through 8. Hoping for a rally, Lasorda sent up pinch-hitter Jay Johnstone in the top of the ninth, but Ryan retired the side in order. Dave Stewart came in from the bull pen to keep the game under control, putting down the first two Astro batters before giving up a single. Alan Ashby, a .271 hitter for the entire year but Houston's hottest in the final month, dug in.

Ashby saw one pitch and deposited it over the right-field wall for a game-winning home run. Ryan, who'd given up 2 hits, while facing 29 batters and tossing 104 pitches, earned a stunning win.

Game 2 was a repeat pitchers' duel. A long banner reading AS-TROS, WATCH YOUR KNEECAPS hung from the stands, reminding the home team that Reuss was on the mound. Unperturbed, he shut out the Astros for 9 innings as Joe Niekro blanked the Dodgers through 8. Stewart, brought in for the 11th, gave up a single to Garner and another to Tony Scott, before being yanked by Lasorda. There was no time for patience. Two pitchers and four batters later, the Astros had won again. Pinch-hitter Denny Walling cracked a bases-loaded liner into the right-center gap off Tom Niedenfuer, handing the hard-luck Stewart his second loss in as many days. Lasorda furiously threw his shoe against the wall.

Houston was one game away from advancing. "We would hate to let 'em get their heads above water in their own park," Garner said with a mixture of assurance and concern. It was off to LA and, Houston hoped, a trip to the next round.

Lasorda predicted that his team would win three in a row. Normally, that was bluster and pep talk, but the Dodger skipper had seen enough to know that the Astros had problems in Los Angeles.

It was impossible that Houston, though two games ahead, wasn't also aware and slightly uptight.

From the get-go, Game 3 was different. The Dodgers put a trio of runs on the board in the bottom of the first, Garvey, seeing Hamlisch's face on the ball, tattooed another home run, this time scoring 2. Hooton kept the Astros in check, and the Dodgers romped to a 6–0 win. Houston sorely needed Sutton, who underwent extensive knee surgery that day.

The Astros were still one victory away from ending the series when they faced Valenzuela in Game 4. In a reversion to the first two pitching-dominated matches of the division series, Valenzuela and Astro starter Vern Ruhle each went the distance, but Fernando in October, pitching like Fernando in May, came out on top, 2–1. Valenzuela, like Ruhle, surrendered only 4 hits, his screwball bewildering the Astro batters. He fielded well and had a perfect sacrifice bunt. It was Fernandomania redux, pure pandemonium when the game was over. The series was tied.

One year earlier, when the Astros beat the Dodgers in the single-game playoff at Dodger Stadium, they thought they'd shaken the LA jinx. Game 5, with Ryan on the mound, gave them an added shot in the arm. In his last two outings against the Dodgers, Ryan had dominated—one no-hitter, one 2-hitter, and 18 strikeouts. But those gems were hurled in the climate-controlled Astrodome.

"The Dodgers aren't going to beat me," boasted the flame-thrower, but he had never won at Dodger Stadium. Ryan put that out of his mind, but 55,979 rabid rooters weren't going to let him forget.

Astros manager Bill Virdon received much criticism for not pitching Ryan the day before, when the late shadows and glare of a 5:00 p.m. start would have made Ryan more unhittable than he'd been of late. Virdon backed off from the idea, explaining that Ryan hadn't pitched with less than four days' rest all season.

At first it didn't seem to matter. Ryan was throwing goose eggs, but Reuss was matching him inning for inning. Suddenly Ryan fell apart in the Dodger sixth, when a combination of walks, errors, and base hits put him behind by 3 runs. While Ryan shook, Reuss was firm, continuing to shut down the Astros lineup. Garvey tripled in another run in the seventh, and it was all over, a 4–0 shutout. The Dodgers became the first team to come from a 0–2 deficit to win a 5-game series. Garner's worst fears were realized, and Ryan, now 0–6 lifetime in Los Angeles, was wrong. Lasorda, smiling, knew it all along.

Like the Astros, the Expos jumped to a 2-game series lead against the Phillies. Montreal weather was brisk, in the mid-40s, and Kuhn was without his overcoat, donning a sweater instead. The commissioner found it quite warm. True, he was under the heat lamps in the owner's box, but still.

Rogers continued his clutch pitching with a 3–1 mastery of Carlton in Game 1. In Game 2, starter Bill Gullickson shut down Philadelphia for 7⅔ before Fanning brought in Reardon. Ordering his top reliever to intentionally walk Mike Schmidt, putting the winning run on but taking the bat from his hands, Fanning, with beginner's luck, made the unconventional work when Gary Matthews hit a foul pop to end the inning.

The Phillies avoided a sweep with a convincing 6–2 win at the Vet. Game 4 was a masterpiece, the stars shining, the two teams trading blows like heavyweight fighters. The Phillies took a 2-run lead in the first when Schmidt punched one out of the park. Carter began the Expos charge in the fourth with a round-tripper of his own, his 15th in Philadelphia. In the sixth, Montreal tied it at 4. Shortstop Chris Speier, the unlikely hero of the first two Expo wins with a pair of game-winning hits, tremendous fielding, and a .400 average, was in the thick of the rally. Matthews propelled a homer over the left-center fence off 41-year-old Woodie Fryman leading off the sixth, but Carter got the run right back with a double to center in the seventh. It stayed knotted at 5 until the tenth inning.

Dallas Green sent up George Vukovich, a part-time outfielder, to face Reardon, a full-time stud, who'd already saved the first two games of the series, his fastball hard to hit, even for the regular-lineup guys. It was a mismatch.

Ahead in the count after two straight balls, Vukovich was sitting on a fastball. When he saw the pitch, down and in, and connected, he thought his heart stopped. As he watched the ball sail out, giving Philadelphia a 6–5 win, tying the series, his heart nearly burst out of his chest. One more game, Rogers vs. Carlton, would decide it all.

Rogers never felt better so late in the season. The 50 days off from the strike provided much-needed rest for his tender shoulder. He was thankful to be on the field, uplifted by his recent performance, and ready to nail things down.

Carlton came out strong by striking out the side in the first inning. He was not planning to be beaten again. Rogers was not as dominant, giving up singles to Rose and Schmidt before getting out of the jam when Matthews grounded into a force-out to end the opening frame. That was all the Phillies could muster as Rogers set down the next 9 in a row.

With 2 out in the fourth, Matthews pulled a single to left. Manny Trillo drilled a long single to center. Knowing it would take a perfect throw to nab him at the plate, Matthews streaked toward home. It took two perfect throws—the first from Dawson to second baseman Jerry Manuel, the second from Manuel to Carter—to tag out Matthews, who attempted to score standing up. It was a devastating play.

The Expos pushed back in the fifth, loading the bases for Rogers. Not a great hitter—"whaling and bailing" he called his style, which produced a .145 season's average and 2 RBI—Rogers seemed like an easy candidate to ground into a double play to end the inning.

It was a bad time for Carlton to miss on his slider. With a 1–1 count, "Lefty" put one down and in, but it wasn't down enough, hanging there for Rogers to make contact. The ball skipped past the mound and into center field for the first 2 runs of the game. Dawson would drive in another tally in the sixth, and Rogers took it from there, besting Carlton for the second time in five days. It was gratifying, proving to the doubters that he could come through when it counted most.

"Our bar-mitzvah year," said owner Charles Bronfman happily as his team finally came of age. For the Phillies, it seemed to be the end of an era, with Green rumored to be heading to the Cubs and Carpenter close to selling his team.

Each of the four division series started off 2–0. For the Yankees, behind Guidry and Righetti, their two wins were on the road in Milwaukee. Again there was a quasi-boycott of County Stadium, crowds of only 35,064 and 26,395 came to see the inaugural playoff appearance of their Brewers, nowhere near the 53,192 capacity. The Yankees jumped on starter "Moose" Haas in Game 1 with 4 runs in the fourth, Gamble's home run with a man on base and catcher Cerone's double the two big blows.

Yankee killer Mike Caldwell took the mound for Game 2, replacing Pete Vuckovich, scratched due to strep throat, tonsillitis, and a fever of 102.8. Righetti, who fell $1\frac{2}{3}$ innings short of winning the ERA title in his rookie year, dominated the potent Milwaukee lineup, fanning 10 in 6 innings of work. Ron Davis nearly blew the lead, loading the bases in the seventh, until Gossage came in to put out the flames over the next $2\frac{2}{3}$. Jackson made the rest of the Brewers sick with a 2-run clinch homer in the ninth. It was back to New York to nail down that final victory, but as expected with the Yankees, nothing came easy and emotions were raw.

Before Friday night's Game 3 at an overflowing Yankee Stadium, Steinbrenner had an important question to ask his starting pitcher: "What would you think of Travis throwing out the first pitch?"

Tommy John was touched and agreed, but since he would be in the bull pen getting warmed up, he'd need to find someone to escort Sally and Travis to the mound. There was only one person to ask.

"Tom, I would love to," Jackson choked out, tearing up as he spoke. "But why me?"

"Because you're a friend and Travis loves you." Jackson had visited the boy many times in the hospital, never failing to be warm and wonderful to him. Few ever saw that side of Jackson.

"This is one of the greatest honors of my career," Jackson said in accepting.

When it was time to walk out to the deafening cheers and silent tears of over 56,000, Jackson took Sally's arm and Travis's free hand,

and the unlikely threesome started to the mound. Reggie pointed to the boy's picture on the giant scoreboard screen.

"That's you!" Jackson exulted, the happiest he'd been that entire year.

Cerone stood a few yards from the mound. Holding in both hands a little white ball, lightweight with red stitches painted in nail polish by his mother, Travis looked over to check a nonexistent runner at first, then threw a heater for a strike to the Yankee catcher. To the huge ovation, Jackson lifted Travis to his shoulder. Jackson was criticized for elbowing his way into the spotlight, but John put the reporters in their place, explaining what had happened and why, that Jackson was truly and sincerely involved with the trials of the John family during a season when Jackson had so many troubles of his own.

On this emotional night John pitched well enough to win. He didn't, losing 5–3 to the combination of Randy Lerch, another substitute for the still-ill Vuckovich, and Fingers. In the bottom of the sixth, with the Yankees leading 1–0, a rally was extinguished when third-base umpire Mike Reilly called Winfield out at second on the lead end of a double play. The fans howled in disapproval. In the top of the seventh, a drunk ran out on the field and jumped on Reilly. John said he wasn't rattled, but he gave up a single to Cecil Cooper, and after botching a hit-and-run play with a foul ball, Ted Simmons sent a forkball into the seats to put Milwaukee ahead.

The Yanks tied it against a shaky Fingers, but Molitor homered beyond the outstretched, leaping Winfield, and the Brewers wouldn't give up the lead.

Vuckovich was well enough to start Game 4, a Saturday day game and a close one, marred by sloppy play, terrible baserunning, and weak hitting by the New Yorkers. "Vuke" slogged through 5 innings, and after three relievers filled the gap, Fingers secured the series tying win, 2–1.

Steinbrenner was seething. He stormed into the clubhouse, adorned in his daily outfit of blue suit, white shirt, and Yankee tie (Jackson thought the owner must have had closets full of these in

New York and Tampa). Out of control, on a tirade, Steinbrenner set off screaming, threatening to break up the team if they didn't shape up.

"Stupid, stupid baserunning. It was that way the whole damn ball game." His fury mounted as he shouted. "Mental mistakes! I'm sick and tired of goddamn mental mistakes. Do you know what it's like for me to have to look Bud Selig in the face after you embarrass me like you did today?" The shipbuilding Steinbrenner couldn't face losing to a car salesman like Selig. "We're gonna blow this thing. It will be the worst and greatest disaster in Yankee history. It's not just me you're embarrassing. You're embarrassing the fans. You're embarrassing New . . . York . . . City." Jackson hollered to the clubhouse man to shut the door.

Calm, seated in his rocking chair, Murcer said quietly, "Now is not the time, George. Now is just not the time." The veteran club was down on itself. They didn't need this kind of help.

"It is the time, goddamnit! You guys're playing like shit."

From the rear of the room, Cerone fumed. Cerone had struggled all year: the arbitration war with Steinbrenner, the aches and pains, the thumb injury that ruined his second half. He knew he was playing badly, well aware that he'd struck out in the bottom of the ninth with two men on base to end the game. He didn't need Steinbrenner screaming at him, it was too much.

"Fuck you, you fat son of a bitch," Cerone exploded.

Steinbrenner spun around to face the challenge. "You're gone next year. Nobody talks to me that way."

"Fuck you, George! You don't know what you're talking about. You don't know a fucking thing about baseball." Cerone was a New Jersey tough guy, and he wasn't going to take the malicious bullying. By standing up, Cerone made Steinbrenner stand down. His teammates cheered Cerone, backslaps and smiles all around. He had the nerve to express in words, salty ones, what they'd been feeling. The press suspected a new controversy, but Jackson defused it, taking the heat on himself and speaking to the eager reporters for hours.

Jackson trudged to Steinbrenner's office a few hours later, defending his teammate. This was the dichotomy of Reggie Jackson, selfish and selfless, individual and team leader.

"He's a gamer, and he's been playing hurt most of the year. We need him."

That night Jackson checked in with Cerone. "You okay?"

"I'm fine, Reg," a tired voice replied. "I'll be there tomorrow."

The next day Jackson, serving as peacemaker, went to Steinbrenner's office and tried his best to explain how ballplayers went about their business, how much they tried and how demoralized they were when they failed, telling Steinbrenner how good Cerone really was. The owner gave him a letter to hand to Cerone. Jackson didn't read it, surmising it was an apology for the Boss's losing his cool.

"And when are *you* going to start hitting?" Steinbrenner said with a grin.

Before Game 5, Jackson went third person. "I'm interested in finding out how much of this Reggie Jackson crap is true. Everybody is always saying I come through in the big game. Well, if I'm ever gonna do anything, it'll be tonight."

In the fourth inning, Steinbrenner and Brewers starter Haas found out. Jackson, after a near home run in his first at bat, tattooed a forkball in his second, standing in the batter's box as he watched it, a tracer of a line drive soaring to the right-field upper deck. Haas was shaken by the prodigious blow by "Mr. October" and served another gopher ball to Gamble. Cerone hit a 2-run homer to clinch it in the seventh, tempted to sardonically tip his cap to Steinbrenner. Prudence won out, as Cerone realized that showing up the owner might backfire.

In his suite after the 7–3 romp, Steinbrenner paid tribute to Jackson and Cerone for their marvelous work, no doubt a result of his inspirational postgame harangue.

Billy Martin vs. George Steinbrenner, Billy Martin vs. Reggie Jackson, the Oakland A's vs. the New York Yankees. It was an American League Championship Series dream match. The twice-fired-by-Steinbrenner Martin had the chance to beat both his former boss and his ex-outfielder, both of whom had given him so much trouble on and off the field. The hype was huge, but the three played it cool for the press—no hard feelings, we respect each other—but the nasty truth found its way to the surface.

When asked about Jackson, Martin couldn't conceal his contempt. "We're not afraid of him. Mr. October?" said Martin, the World Series hero of 1952 and 1953, whose fielding and hitting paced the Yankees to wins over the Dodgers. "I was Mr. October before him." Reflecting on the most recent Steinbrenner outburst, Martin heralded Cerone's insight that Steinbrenner didn't know a thing about baseball. When Martin managed in New York, it took him weeks to soothe his Yankees after another tantrum from the owner. "I think George believes it helps," Martin said, trying to be understanding, "but I don't agree with what he's doing."

While Martin was yapping to the reporters on the prowl for some controversy, Steinbrenner was working behind the scenes, visiting MacPhail on the eve of the playoff, urging him to have the umpires crack down on the season-long use of illegal pitches by the A's staff. Martin took umbrage. In May, Steinbrenner had castigated Norris for throwing spitters, and New York had cameras shooting video of the Oakland pitchers, the owner harping on the umpires so much that they focused on Martin's hurlers to the point of harassment.

Of more concern was the state of the starters. Even in a short season, with time off and fewer innings pitched, the A's staff had been taxed since Martin took the helm for 1980. Martin would say he had no choice but to go the distance with his starters, that they were producing. With a weak bull pen, Martin felt he had no other options. The Yankees sensed that their opposition was wiped out.

Still, Martin saw a win in the offing. His pitchers were better than theirs, his hitters were stronger than theirs, and he had Henderson. "Rickey is a once-in-a-lifetime player. You see very few Rickey Hendersons. You might not see another one for fifty years." The A's were confident.

While Norris warmed up in the visitors' bull pen on the night of October 13, he heard a noise like a helicopter, a loud whirring followed by a crash. Immediately he hunched his shoulders, pulling his head in, turtlelike, to avoid being hit by a half-filled bottle of Southern Comfort hurled his way from the stands. It shook him up enough that he gave up 3 quick runs in the first inning. Nettles hit a Norris screwball off the end of his bat, the ball twisting away in left center between Henderson and center fielder Dwayne Murphy, for a double that cleared the bases for the only runs of the game and a Yankee win behind John.

The Yankees notched a single tally in the first inning of Game 2, Jackson driving in a run on a groundout, but it was in the top of the second that Oakland's fate was sealed. Armas, the league's leading home-run hitter, belted a Rudy May offering straight at Winfield in left. There was no angle to play and the sun made it hard to see. All he could do was run toward the fence. At the base of the wall Winfield planted and jumped, right cleat dug into the padding, chest parallel to the fence, turning his head to follow the spinning ball. His left arm went up, high above the wall silhouetted against the white shirts in the bleachers. Simultaneously, he felt the crash of the wall and the ball in the glove's webbing. Regaining his footing, Winfield tossed the ball back to the infield, behind him a broken fence with a huge flap drooping down. Even Martin had to admit that it was one of the greatest catches he'd ever seen.

Still, the A's were leading 3–1 in the fourth inning of Game 2, in control A's style—Henderson tripling, McCatty, their victory leader, on the mound. Even better, Jackson had left the game in the third inning with left-leg pain, the area between his Achilles tendon and calf knotting up. That was, until the bottom of the fourth.

It started innocently enough with a Nettles single. Then, after Bob Watson flew out to left, Cerone trotted to first after his helmet was lightly hit by an errant toss. A Willie Randolph single, a Jerry Mumphrey walk, and Dave Beard was called in from the bull pen Martin blanched at using. For good reason; by the time it was all over the Yankees had sent 12 batters to the plate, Nettles getting 2 hits, Piniella homering, and Winfield blasting a double as the Bronx Bombers put 7 runs on the board on their way to a 13–3 blowout. It was so bad that Martin sent his pitching coach out to switch pitchers in the seventh inning. "The game got out of hand. When that happens, I think Billy loses interest," explained Piniella.

The Yankee relief corps was unbeatable. This time it wasn't Davis and Gossage, but George Frazier, a journeyman who, like so many before him, shone as soon as he put on the pinstripes. Frazier had an ERA of 1.63 during the season and blanked the A's over 5⅔ innings for the win. Heroes and goats are made in the short and stressful postseason, and on this day, Frazier was masterful, debuting a forkball in the tense setting of a playoff game. From the rafters fans sang, "Good-bye, Billy, good-bye, Billy, good-bye, Billy, we hate to see you go," and though Steinbrenner insisted that there was nothing to celebrate, going to Oakland for Game 3 would be purely a formality.

"Krazy" George Henderson, rabid A's fan and rooter, realized that his team needed something to perk them up, down 2–0 in the series and facing elimination at their home park. He'd been working on an idea since he was a cheerleader at San Jose State and was ready to unveil it at the Coliseum on the afternoon of the 15th.

Henderson organized three sections, explaining and gesturing his instructions, pointing to the fans to rise to their feet, raise their hands in the air, and holler in a rolling fashion, one group rising, then falling as the next stood up. It took three or four tries until everyone understood. When it grabbed hold, going around the entire stadium, over and over, the crowd more frenzied with each rotation, the wave was born.

Righetti and Keough paired off, exchanging zeroes for 5 innings until Randolph put the Yankees ahead with a solo home run. That was all it would take. By the ninth inning, Murphy and Henderson were injured, the Yanks had scored 3 more times, and the series was over. Nettles was named Most Valuable Player, hitting .500 with a record 9 RBI. Winfield did little beyond his phenomenal snag, knocking 2 hits in 13 at bats in his first league championship. The Royals' sweepers were Yankee swept, quietly. It was after the series that the fireworks began.

Now that there *was* something to celebrate, a return to the

World Series after two years away, Steinbrenner booked a party at Vince's, an Oakland restaurant, and invited players and their families. Others, outside the two categories, came. It wasn't a strict list. Even the press were invited, but they had to file their stories of the final game and then fly home. They missed quite a party.

Nettles, the star of the moment, arrived with his wife, Ginger, their kids, plus his father and brother. The family picked a table and headed for the buffet. Ginger left her fur coat and purse on a chair to reserve their seats.

From their table, where they sat with Howard Cosell and Raiders owner Al Davis, Tommy and Sally John saw Jackson enter with a huge entourage. Oakland was Reggie's home base, and with him were his sister, her husband, some friends, some family. The Jackson party of six saw the vacant table where the Nettleses had been and grabbed it.

Ginger returned to the table with her 3-year-old asleep in her arms and her 12-year-old in tow. As she went to sit, one of Jackson's group told her that the seat was taken.

"We were sitting here. Will you please move?" she argued. Then, seeing that her bag was missing (it had been moved to the floor), she grew agitated. "Where's my purse? My purse is gone?"

Jackson's niece felt accused of stealing and sensed a racial overtone in the misunderstanding, and when a member of the Jacksons said something that upset Mrs. Nettles, she went to find her husband.

Nettles and Jackson had never got along. Nettles didn't like Jackson, not his bragging, not his spotlight hogging, not his poor fielding ability, and, from the very beginning, not his dismissal of friend and teammate Thurman Munson. The Nettles-Jackson relationship was adversarial from the very beginning.

Jackson tried to make Nettles like him, always acclaiming Nettles's baseball IQ and admiring his quick wit, but Nettles didn't care. He wasn't interested in liking Reggie Jackson. More often than not, Nettles returned Jackson's praise with scorn, followed by ethnic and racial jokes that Jackson hated. Nettles was already needling Jackson, telling Mr. October that, based on Nettles's recent showing, he had the month covered this time.

Jackson was at the buffet, oblivious of the events, but by the time Nettles found him, Jackson was up to speed.

"I have no beef with you, but your friends, who don't even belong here, told my wife she couldn't sit at their table," said Nettles, beer bottle in hand.

"Hey, man. Why the hell did your wife think we stole her purse?" Jackson, a few beers into the night already, laid into Nettles.

"What the hell are you talking about, Reggie?" yelled an exasperated Nettles. "Your people took my family's seats." Nettles was gesturing with his beer bottle to make his point.

Jackson flashed back to his time with the A's, a team constantly fighting among themselves on the way to three World Series titles in a row. He remembered a brawl when one player got cut by a beer bottle, had seen this play out badly before and wasn't about to see it happen to him. He slapped the bottle out of Nettles's hand.

Not privy to Jackson's internal flashback, Nettles reacted to the sudden, violent move, punching Jackson in the mouth, an undeniably large target. Jackson was pushed back on his heels and fell against a chair behind him. Though he went down, Jackson quickly came to his feet, ready to wrestle. Watson, Gossage, and Winfield hopped from table to table to break it up. Murcer, who had hurt a finger breaking up a 1974 fight, did it again breaking up this one.

Steinbrenner, in the hallway when the melee broke out, came rushing into the room when he heard the noise. He immediately blamed Jackson. "Goddamnit, Jackson! What the hell are you doing? You're disgracing me again. You're degrading the Yankees," yelled Steinbrenner.

Jackson screamed right back. "I ain't liked that dude for ten years. I don't care if I play in the World Series. I don't have a contract. I can go anywhere. I ain't drunk. I ain't gonna take this stuff anymore."

"You should get out of here," ordered Steinbrenner.

"You'll pay for this," Jackson said as he left.

"I've had it up to here with him," said Steinbrenner after his sullen star had skedaddled. "He's got to be the boss of everything.

He has to be the big shot and run everything. Well, he's not going to get away with it anymore."

When all calmed down, Nettles was embarrassed, Jackson remorseful. On the bus the next day, the two sat together. "Whatever we think about each other," Jackson told his teammate, "fighting at cocktail parties isn't my style."

All the Yankees could do now was sit and wait it out.

Game 1 at Dodger Stadium looked bad for the Expos and was. Montreal had lost 9 straight there, 18 of their last 19, and their chances were slim. After Burt Hooton employed his knuckle curve to shut out the Expos over 7⅓ innings, Montreal had their 10th straight defeat. Ron Cey, who'd had his left forearm broken by a September 9 pitch, had found a light plastic shield that protected his arm and allowed him to play. After over one month away, Cey doubled in Garvey in the second inning. The Expos had injuries of their own, Raines still nursing his broken right hand. The Dodgers found themselves in a rare place—leading a series.

It wouldn't be that way for long. The next afternoon Ray Burris, who'd bounced from the Cubs to the Yankees to the Mets before signing as a free agent in February, outpitched Valenzuela 3–0. Fernando performed well enough to win, but not well enough to beat Burris, who went the distance.

Back in Montreal, the American League series now over, Rogers continued his amazing pressure run. With a 4–1 complete-game triumph over his Missouri high school rival Reuss, Rogers had all but obliterated the notion that he was weak in the clutch. It had been an incredible year on and off the field. The strike and negotiations had helped him mature, forced him to separate emotions from the task at hand in order to be effective. That experience "played a part in how I approach everything else," he confided. "I think it has helped me." It also put the Expos one win away from their first World Series appearance, the first for any team outside the United States. Over 54,000 crazed fans sang, "Val-deri, Val-dera, Val-deri,

Val-dera-ha-ha-ha-ha-ha." (Their favorite tune was "The Happy Wanderer," in French.)

After checking out of the hotel and packing their bags in case of elimination, Lasorda erupted.

"Listen, you . . ." He began spitting out curses and invective to his players in a pep talk of sorts. He wasn't going to stand for this team to be beaten. "Okay, bussie"—he turned to the driver—"let's go." At Olympic Stadium, he gave another rousing speech that had the team roaring as they ran through the tunnel to the field.

Hooton was on, again, as he was in Game 1, but so was his Game 4 opponent, Bill Gullickson. It was the Expos bull pen that gave it away, 6 runs in the final two frames, including a Garvey 2-run home run that had his teammates bursting into a mocking chorus of *Valderis* and *Val-deras*.

Bull-pen stopper Reardon, who had been terrible in the opener, warmed up, trying to fight his way through a strained back muscle. Fanning said his relief star was ready, that, in fact, he was at 100 percent. But clearly that wasn't the case or Fanning would have used Reardon in a pinch. Instead, Fryman blew the game wide open. Fanning had no good options other than starters such as Burris and Rogers going the distance. One last game would decide who would face the Yankees.

Sunday the 18th was the kind of day Kuhn assured everyone couldn't happen. Gray, rainy, 37 degrees, with intermittent snow—it was miserable. Lasorda knew this weather well; he'd spent nine years with the Montreal Royals and played in Jarry Park, the first home field of the Expos. Had the real records set the playoff teams, the day's game would have been in relatively balmy St. Louis. No official rain delay was announced for hours, Major League Baseball being so afraid of facing the NFL head-to-head that management waited until the day's football games were over to start the most important game of the NL season. As the teams waited, Dodgers outfielder Johnstone stuffed some padding under his jersey, flipped up the brim of his cap, and did his best Lasorda waddle. Expos outfielder Terry Francona dove headfirst on his belly, sliding on the wet tarp. Finally, at 7:30 p.m., the PA announcer at Olympic Stadium gave the news: the game was postponed.

Game 5 temperatures were no better, in the 30s by the 4:00 p.m. starting time. Dawson kept himself warm with hot ointment and baby oil. Valenzuela, with an additional day's rest, was matched against Burris, the hero of Game 2. Raines opened the Expos' half of the first inning with a double to center. After being sacrificed to third—making it when Valenzuela threw too late to nab him—Raines scored when Dawson hit into a double play, driving in the first run. That would be all. The refreshed Valenzuela had a little extra oomph on his pitches, and the Expos were unable to pose another threat.

Burris was equally fine, holding the Dodgers down until the fifth. Rick Monday singled to start the rally. Guerrero singled, and with a line out and a Burris wild pitch putting Monday on third, the Dodgers got their first run when Valenzuela drove Monday home with a grounder to second. With Burris in trouble, Fanning had Rogers warm up in the bull pen. In any final game, it's "All hands on deck;" everyone's available when there's no next day. Fanning told Rogers, who'd only had two days' rest, to be ready. Fanning wouldn't put his best starter in late, but in a tight game, he needed Rogers ready for the middle innings. Despite Reardon's assurances that he was healthy, Fanning was worried about his reliever's back.

The Expos threatened in the seventh when third baseman Larry Parrish doubled with two outs, but Valenzuela escaped the jam. Burris went easily through the eighth inning. With the Expos up, Fanning had a tough decision. With one out, Burris was due up.

Having gotten eight innings and a lot of pitches out of his surprise star, Fanning knew he needed to give his team a chance to get out ahead. Ambivalently turning to Tim Wallach, who had only 4 home runs that year but had a better shot at hitting one out of the park than Burris, Fanning made his call. Burris was gone. When Wallach grounded back to Valenzuela for the out, it seemed questionable. The early concern over Fanning's inexperience was back, in the stands and on the bench.

Rogers was warming up again. "Hey, Yak Yak," Rogers asked the usually silent Reardon, "how do you feel?"

"Okay." But Reardon wasn't going to get the nod. It was to be Rogers in the ninth.

As he approached the mound, Rogers's adrenaline was pumping hard. He hadn't come in, in relief, since 1978. Usually Rogers had great stuff on the second or third day after a start. A top-down pitcher whose mechanics were geared to throwing with power, Rogers lived and died by his sinker. If he was right on, he'd get ground balls all day long. If he overthrew, batters would get the ball in the air. A great finisher needs to keep a lid on his emotions, and he was having a difficult time keeping himself calm.

Garvey led off and popped up to second. Rogers had always got the Dodgers first baseman out with a sinker or slider. Garvey's out was an out, but it was sent skyward. Rogers knew he was off. Though he was driving through the mound toward home, he was throwing too hard. His sinker wasn't there.

Cey blasted a hanging sinker to the base of the wall in left that Raines ran down. Two outs, and Monday, a left-hander, was the next batter. It was the ideal time for Fanning to thank his good fortune and bring in Reardon. Instead, he left Rogers in. Reardon may have been ready, but Rogers was Fanning's best.

Rogers fell behind before throwing a strike that Monday smoked, a towering shot to right field, foul. Another ball put the count at 3–1. Carter called for a sinker, and Rogers threw. The pitch, supposed to break down and away, hung in the air. It was thrown too hard, a physical, not a mental, mistake.

When Rogers released the pitch, he knew it was going to be hit. When Monday hit it, he lost sight of its path. When Dawson saw the ball, he got a bead on its path, going back, onto the warning track, until he ran out of room. When Monday saw the outfielders turn their backs to the wall, he realized it was a home run, leaped in the air, and raised his left arm in celebration. He almost fell between second and third. Monday was taken out for defensive reasons in the bottom of the ninth, but Valenzuela remained, retiring the first two batters before Carter drew a walk. Then Parrish did too. That would be all for Fernando, who had been brilliant over 8⅔ innings of 3-hit ball and an RBI.

Lasorda turned to one of his starting pitchers, the fastball-throwing Bob Welch. Jerry White swung at the first pitch, sending a bouncer to Lopes at second for an easy out. The Dodgers poured out of the dugout, Lasorda jabbing both fists in the air.

Dawson sat in the dugout, shattered, his head buried in his hands. Next to him sat Cromartie, downcast, grimacing sadly as he put his arm around his distraught teammate, holding Dawson's powerful right bicep in his hand. For the third year in a row the Expos had seen their hopes vanish.

"Fuck, who cares. Who wants to win a pennant during a split season, anyway?" thought Bill Lee.

Chapter 9

The New York Yankees and the Los Angeles Dodgers had the great-est rivalry in sports, the roots of it spreading back to 1941 when the Dodgers were still in Brooklyn. In 8 of the 10 times they'd faced each other, the Yanks prevailed.

This was back in the Golden Era, the postwar baseball glory days of Mickey Mantle and Yogi Berra, Jackie Robinson and Pee Wee Reese. New York–centric in the extreme, the purported glory days were a false construct. From 1947 to 1958, the Yankees, Dodgers, and New York Giants won 18 of 24 pennants. Ask a fan in Pittsburgh, Chicago, or Boston how golden that period was. In this tarnished wasteland for most of the country, nearly all the successes focused on three boroughs of one city. New York ruled and no one else had a chance. The complete absence of competitive balance was a hall-mark of the time, the old way that the owners had wished to pre-serve when they fought to pull back on free agency.

Since the Dodgers' westward move, the two storied opponents had met three times. Sandy Koufax guided his troops to a 1963 sweep of Mantle and Roger Maris. More recently, the Yankees had dominated, winning in 1977 and 1978. The modern versions of the ancient franchises reflected their owners.

The Yankees, under Steinbrenner's reign, were entering their fourth Fall Classic, as chaotic and schizophrenic as their headline-grabbing boss. The Dodgers, once under Walter O'Malley and now under son Peter, were stolid and workmanlike, no flash, no hullaba-loo. Fernandomania was a wholesome endeavor compared to the daily tribulations in the Bronx. Steinbrenner had gone through eight managerial changes since his 1973 purchase; the Dodgers had gone through one. They'd only had two managers since 1954—Walter Alston and Tommy Lasorda. And there was no meddling. "Tommy knows what I want. There's nothing I can add," said O'Malley. Steinbrenner may have thought that his pressure worked, but the Dodgers were entering their fourth World Series, same as the Yankees in the same time frame.

The Yankees had had five days' rest after they'd decimated the A's; the Dodgers had none, only enough time to get from Montreal to New York. It was also enough time for Kuhn to make another poor decision.

Jimmy Cagney had returned to the big screen in *Ragtime*, his first feature film in two decades. The nation reveled in the reemergence of the fast-talking, smart-alecky New York native. Though long past his days as a light-on-his-feet hoofer, Cagney still had that twinkle in his eye, and his comeback was surprising and joyous. Who better to throw out the first pitch before Game 1 at Yankee Stadium? The commissioner found it beneath the game's dignity to have actors do such ceremonial honors. Kuhn ruled that Cagney was out, to the outrage of the sporting public and the Yankee Doodle Dandy himself.

"So what! I'm going to the game anyway," said the 82-year-old firebrand from his farm in upstate Dutchess County. "I'm a Yankee fan and I love baseball. George Steinbrenner was kind enough to invite me, and I am going." The commissioner wasn't going to ruin Cagney's triumphant return, which included the World Series opener on the night of October 20. After that, on Sunday, he was slated to visit another actor, one now residing in the White House, for a private screening of Cagney's new movie.

With the growing indignation at his shabby treatment of an

American icon, Kuhn recanted, permitting Cagney to participate in Game 2. For the first game, Joe DiMaggio got the call.

On the fourth pitch of the game, Lopes scorched one to third base. Nettles acrobatically hit the dirt, sprang to his feet, and pegged a tracer to first, just nailing the speedy runner. The last time these two teams met, Nettles had been spectacular with the glove. On the bench, Tommy John told Righetti, "This is déjà vu. I've seen this before." John, then a Dodger, had been on the losing end in both 1977 and 1978.

This year's World Series had no designated hitter, and with Jackson out with a sore left calf, Watson had to provide some power. He did, with a 3-run home run off Reuss in the bottom of the first. It was another sign that this night belonged to New York. Stellar defense and solid pitching by Guidry put the game away until the eighth.

Guidry came out and Davis came in to start the inning, walking two before getting the hook. Gossage was brought in to tamp down the flames, but a single by Johnstone and a sacrifice fly by Dusty Baker, who had earlier in the night dodged soda bottles raining down at him from the left-field seats, brought the Dodgers within 2 with Garvey batting. Working the count to his advantage, up 3–1, Garvey drilled a line drive to that man at the hot corner.

Nettles timed it perfectly, diving fully horizontal toward the foul line, to snag the bullet. It took the steam out of the Dodgers, the rally, and the game.

"I get sick to my stomach," groaned Lasorda when asked about Nettles's phenomenal plays. For the big-bellied, pasta-loving manager, that was a lot of sick.

From the commissioner's box, Cagney, in black glasses and buttoned blazer, belatedly threw out the first pitch to ring in Game 2. To his right stood Kuhn, beaming at the actor with the thick, gray hair under a Yankee cap. The pitchers that night, John and Hooton, were old friends and former roommates. During his time in Los Angeles, John had rejuvenated his career, undergoing a revolutionary surgery that moved a tendon from his right forearm to his left, a surgery that now bore his name. John knew the hitting habits of his former team, and they knew him equally. He wasn't worried. After his arduous year, he was simply happy to be on the mound.

When a smoke bomb went off in right field when the Dodgers came out, chants of "An-i-mal! An-i-mal!" were aimed at the culprits from the rest of the crowd. That was all the heat generated in the first half of the game, as both lineups were masterfully contained by the two starters. The Yankees went ahead in the bottom of the fifth on a double by Larry Milbourne, the kind of player who comes out of nowhere to shine in a World Series and leave a mark in the history books.

Steve Howe, last season's Rookie of the Year, relieved Hooton and put two runners on base, who both scored after Howe was pulled. Gossage came in to get his second save in as many games, and the Yanks won their sixth straight. The series seemed firmly in hand.

The Dodgers were familiar with the spot they found themselves in. For the third time in a row they had fallen behind. "Now we've got them where we want them," Garvey joked. The team was loose.

Steinbrenner was in heaven. He hadn't criticized Lemon once, and the team was winning with Jackson out of the lineup. Feeling pretty good about the state of things, he okayed a victory party at trendy disco Xenon. But under the surface there were problems. Nettles had sprained his left thumb when he'd landed awkwardly on his glove hand diving for a stop. Jackson's health was questionable, and Winfield was hitless. They were leaving New York for California, where the rumblings would emerge.

Palm trees swayed and the ground shook on the morning of Game 3. Two minor earthquakes could be felt throughout Southern California. Everyone felt the tremors save for one Yankee coach. "It must have bypassed me," said Yogi Berra.

The Dodgers were happy to be home, laughing and chattering as they took batting practice. On the mound was Koufax, 45, who had returned to the organization in 1979 as a roving pitching instructor. Koufax, the pitcher of his era, the symbol of Los Angeles Dodgers' success, had retired at age 30 to preserve his damaged arm into old age. Garvey, Baker, and Cey stepped in to face the still-lean left-hander, looking as if he'd never left his home on the mound.

He threw 11 pitches, all swings, all misses. Fastballs entered the batting cage; none came out until Guerrero got up and took one deep into the stands. Garvey stepped back in and flipped his wrist, requesting a curve. Koufax obliged with a knee trembler that dropped from 12 to 6. Again, Garvey, Baker, and Cey missed or, if lucky, fouled off, 13 more pitches. Embarrassed looks were exchanged. The Dodgers hitters, less than an hour from taking the field, were becoming demoralized in a series in which they were already down 2–0.

A Dodgers coach ran out to the hill and said something to Koufax, who nodded his head, realizing that what he'd been doing wouldn't do. He walked off the mound and a new BP pitcher grooved pitches in an attempt to rebuild a shattered lineup.

Jackson was raring to go. He felt a sweep coming and couldn't wait to hit against Valenzuela, whose screwball tailed inside to a left-handed batter. Jackson went over to Lemon in the dugout. "Just wanted to let you know I'm ready to go, Meat," Jackson excitedly offered. "Man, I can't wait to get a shot at Valenzuela."

Lemon stared out to the field. "Ummm, I don't think you should play tonight, Reggie." Lemon didn't believe Jackson was up to facing the best left-hander in the National League.

"What are you talking about?" Jackson said in disbelief. He saw the hand of Steinbrenner at work here, not allowing the manager to play whom he wanted. It was "Lemonbrenner" who was keeping him from playing. Jackson was eager to get into Fernandomania and call it out, but sat instead. "He's so determined to take me down," Jackson thought about the owner, "now he's even taking October from Mr. October."

Jackson was benched and Nettles was out too with a sore thumb. Koufax threw out the first pitch, this time gently, and Valenzuela took center stage in front of a record crowd of 56,236. He struggled from the outset, walking Randolph and Winfield before getting Piniella to end the inning with a double-play grounder.

It was worse for the other star rookie, Righetti. (This was only the fourth time two rookies had started a World Series game.) Coming off one week of rest, "Rags" was rusty and in immediate trouble, putting two on base before Cey, his arm better, popped a 3-run homer. Righetti was gone after 2 innings, replaced by Frazier. Behind Watson's round-tripper and Milbourne's RBI single, the Yankees clawed their way back to 3–2. In the third, Cerone put the Yankees ahead with a 2-run shot. Though the Yankees had pulled ahead, Lemon's moves were baffling. Two times, in the third and the fifth, Lasorda walked the now-dangerous Milbourne to face the pitcher. Both times Lemon had the pitcher hit, and both times he struck out, only to be replaced the following inning. It made no sense.

Valenzuela was struggling, and from his seat on the pines, Jackson knew that if he'd only been given two at bats, he would have put the game away. Instead it stayed close, and in the bottom of the fifth the Dodgers eked ahead with two tallies, both charged to Frazier, who was pulled with the bases loaded. Lasorda was planning to send Reggie Smith to pinch-hit for Valenzuela, but when catcher Scioscia, who'd stayed in after hitting for starter Steve Yeager in the third, grounded into a twin-killing, scoring Cey, Lasorda changed his mind. Good thing.

Valenzuela settled down, more comfortable with Scioscia behind the plate, allowing base runners but no further scoring. Aurelio Rodriguez, in for Nettles, started the top half of the eighth inning with a single to left field, followed by a base hit by Milbourne.

Lasorda darted from the dugout to calm his young starter. On the mound, Lasorda told him, in Spanish, "Listen, Fernando, if you don't give the other team any more runs, we'll win this game."

"Are you sure?" he replied in English.

With men on first and second and nobody out, Lemon sent up Murcer to pinch-hit and gave the veteran specific instructions: bunt for a hit, not for a sacrifice. Murcer tried, hitting a hard pop toward third base. Cey saw the ball headed foul and sprawled into a forward dive, made the catch just on the foul side of the line, and popped up to make a quick throw to first base over a crouching Valenzuela. Milbourne had broken hard for second on contact. From his vantage point the ball looked as if it would drop fair. He was doubled off, a huge mistake.

From two on and none out the Yankees were left with two out and Rodriguez still at second. A runner in scoring position was still a runner in scoring position. Rodriguez learned nothing from what he'd just seen, and when Randolph chopped a grounder to Cey, Rodriguez took off to third. "The Penguin" could never have thrown out the quick Randolph on such a slow-moving ball. He didn't have to. Rodriguez was nearing the bag and Cey waited, ball in glove, and tagged him for the third out. An unwritten rule in baseball was to never make the first or third out of an inning at third base. Rodriguez's blunder killed the Yankees.

It took 145 pitches for Valenzuela to complete the game and get the win, a gritty performance that turned the whole series around. Nettles would be out for the next two games, and Winfield, now hitless in 10 attempts, 2 for 23 going back to the series against the A's, was absent in his own way. The Yankees led the series 2–1, but suddenly it didn't feel that way.

An irate Steinbrenner sensed it and met with Lemon, insisting that a change, any change, was needed. If Steinbrenner had to tinker with the lineup himself, so be it. The owner decided that the slumping Jerry Mumphrey would have to sit. Winfield would start in center, Piniella in left, and Jackson in right. Mumphrey was shocked. He'd played well defensively and wasn't the only one not hitting, but Winfield, at his price point, was not going to be benched.

At first Game 4 seemed like a return to form, as New York scored 4 unanswered runs. Steinbrenner thought himself a whiz for the increased offense he helped create with the lineup change. Jackson, in his first game back, was proving himself at the plate—two singles and a walk in the first 4 innings—but in the sixth the momentum switched.

The Yankees were leading 6–3 when Johnstone homered, driving in 2. Lopes then skied one to Jackson in right. The Dodgers outfielders knew that it was impossible to see in right field at that time of day. Losing track of the fly ball in the glare, Jackson flubbed it, Lopes reaching second on the error. "Reg-gie! Reg-gie!" the fans mocked before erupting as Lopes scored on shortstop Bill Russell's single to tie the game. Lemon brought in Frazier to nail down the side.

Rodriguez singled to center starting the seventh, but in recklessly trying for a double made his second mental mistake on the base paths. He was nailed by Guerrero, a meaningful opportunity squandered.

Baker reached safely to start the Dodgers seventh, then Monday sent a liner to Bobby Brown in center field, which Mumphrey formerly patrolled so well. Brown misplayed the out into a double, putting the potential winning runs on second and third. Frazier, again the victim, intentionally walked Guerrero before being replaced with Tommy John. John, not Gossage. Exiting the bull pen, John shrugged at Goose. It was another remarkably bad move by Lemon. That gut he listened to was giving him bad advice and indigestion. After Yeager's sacrifice fly and Lopes's single, the Dodgers were up 8–6.

It took a Jackson home run in the eighth to shut up the Dodgers fans. His 10th overall in World Series play, it tied him with Lou Gehrig. (Mickey Mantle was number one with 18.) Steinbrenner may not have liked it, but Jackson was definitely in the pantheon of Yankee greats. The 1-run game would remain that way, Howe the winner in relief, Frazier the loser for the second day in a row. Torn napkins fell like confetti when Howe got Randolph for the final out of a grueling game, 3:32 worth of lead changes, home runs, bad baserunning, atrocious fielding, and lousy hitting. The Dodgers were happy to take it. They'd come back to deadlock the series. Lemon was heavily criticized for his dreadful decision making, though Steinbrenner had nothing but praise for the increase in runs he saw as proof of his astuteness. After the loss, he instituted a 10:00 p.m. curfew. It wouldn't help. The Yankees couldn't sleep this off.

Early to rise for the Sunday afternoon game, the Yankees got off to an early lead, for the fourth time in five games. Jackson doubled sharply down the left-field line to start a second-inning rally, advanced on Lopes's first error of the day (he'd get 3, tying a single-game World Series record), and scored on Piniella's single. Reggie, now a perfect 4 for 4 since he'd returned, was giddy. Reuss, the Dodgers starter, was less so, but he bore down, casting aside the scouting report that said to throw curves. He relied on his fastball instead; he had to. Guidry was mowing down Dodgers hitters with an array of fastballs and sliders. The 1–0 lead held.

The besieged Winfield, still hitless, morosely made his way to the plate in the fifth. The press had been all over him for his failures, Steinbrenner too. "The guy we depend on isn't producing one bit," he chafed. The World Series was turning out not to be much fun, even after he tagged a Reuss pitch to left field, a looping pop that dropped in front of Baker for a hit. It did little to break his mood. Some levity seemed in order.

Winfield stopped the game to ask for the ball. Reuss was baffled, but both benches erupted in laughter. They saw the irony in Winfield's bit of self-mockery, pausing to celebrate his futility. Watching as the pricey star made a joke out of his poor performance, Steinbrenner, grim faced, thought it was disgraceful.

Guidry kept rolling, as did Reuss, and New York was holding on into the bottom of the seventh. As Baker struck out, the ninth victim of the day, coach Manny Mota told the next hitter, Guerrero, to stand back in the batter's box to give himself a longer look at Guidry's pitches. "And don't swing so hard!" Guerrero had taken a mighty swipe in the fourth inning, nearly coming out of his shoes and missing by a mile.

Guerrero looked at a first-pitch strike and leaned back, his bat on his shoulder. He paused, for a brief moment, before stepping back into the box. After a practice swing he called time, just as Guidry was set to pitch. Instead Guidry tossed the ball to his catcher, who returned it to the mound. It was enough to break his stride. Guidry hung a slider, and, bam, the score was tied, the poor pitch finding a new home in the left-field bleachers. Yeager was up next. He'd received the same spiel from Mota, but was having difficulty executing.

"Nice easy swing, Steve, nice easy swing," Lasorda exhorted

from the dugout, his pleas echoed from the bench. Yeager couldn't hear. He half-swung at Guidry's first offering. Strike one. The home crowd was still buzzing from Guerrero's blast.

Guidry's second pitch was a ball, then once again, as he was ready to deliver, time was called, this time by the third-base ump. Guidry walked off the mound toward second base and, fully composed, got Yeager to weakly swing for a second strike.

Now Yeager remembered Mota's advice, and taking a deep breath, he dug in as far back in the batter's box as he could, reminding himself to take it easy, to relax. It worked, and Yeager muscled a 1-2 fastball for another home run. Lasorda ran out to hug his catcher. Steinbrenner, standing in a luxury box, scowled behind dark sunglasses.

Guidry got through the inning, but the damage had been done. Gossage was brought in for the eighth inning. Cey was the fourth hitter, coming to bat with Lopes on first.

In the on-deck circle, Baker heard it, a cannon shot. On the mound, Gossage had yelled, "Oh, God, look out!" at the instant the 94 mph fastball left his right hand.

Cey had seen it coming, tried to stay with the pitch for as long as he could, but once he realized it was too close and getting closer, he tried to get out of the way, but the ball followed him like a heat-seeking SAM, crashing into his Dodger-blue helmet, the ball thudding above his left ear. It felt like a slow-motion trip toward the ground.

"Get up, get up," Gossage pleaded from the mound to the motionless, but not unconscious, Cey. Lasorda and others ran out to gather around the fallen hitter.

Cey could see their faces and asked, "What do I look like? Am I all right?" The crowd was stunned into silence, watching, waiting. After a seemingly interminable time, Cey rose to his feet, walking off on his own, Lasorda and the trainer on either side of him, and Baker behind with a look of alarm. Cey, up but not out of his stupor, held his drooping head in his hand. Everyone in the stadium was relieved to see him move.

Fran Cey was waiting for her husband in the clubhouse. "I thought you were dead," she cried. On the diamond, Reuss was closing a complete-game 5-hitter, putting the Dodgers up 3–2, but Cey was the prime focus. Gossage visited the Dodger clubhouse to find out how he was and finally exhaled when he saw Cey moving around. The fleeting nature of a ballplayer's career, that it could end in the millisecond it took an errant pitch to crush against a man's skull, was a prime driver of the union's cause, at the heart of why they fought to protect their members.

Dr. Frank Jobe, the team physician and surgeon who had saved Tommy John's career, examined and x-rayed Cey. Except for dizziness caused by a slight concussion, he was fine. If he wasn't dizzy before the next game, he could play. Cey, with an ice pack on his forehead, pondered his fate. Between his arm and his head, he wondered if he was being tested from above. It had been so important to him when he woke that morning that the Dodgers win and take the World Series lead. By the time he returned home, sitting with his wife and kids, he realized what mattered more was that he was alive. He tried to sleep that night, but Fran was under instructions to wake him every few hours.

Steinbrenncr wasn't able to settle down either. He was out of control, his team now behind in the series, his big-money guys failing, opportunities squandered. It was enough to make a man punch a wall in frustration, and maybe he did.

Later that evening, Yankees publicity director David Szen was fast asleep in his suite at the Hyatt Wilshire when his phone rang. "Come up to my room," Steinbrenner ordered. When Szen arrived, he saw the team trainer, Gene Monahan, working on the owner, creating a makeshift cast for his broken right hand. As he was tended to, Steinbrenner told Szen to get the press together.

The reporters arrived at the owner's 11th floor suite at eleven thirty, way past deadline in New York. The Boss opened the door himself, bandaged, his upper lip bruised and swelling, a knot growing on his head. In a plaid shirt, with obligatory blazer, Steinbrenner regaled the half dozen scribes with his battle over the honor of his team as they jotted down notes.

Dick Young, in his robe and a bit tipsy from the red wine he'd imbibed at the hotel bar, stumbled to the phone in the center of the room. "This is Young; get me rewrite right now!" He began dictating.

"What are you doing, Dick? I told you this is just a briefing. This isn't to be written," shouted Steinbrenner amid the press he had assembled. What did he expect them to do, keep a secret?

"A thing like this you don't keep out of the paper." Young, knowing this was big news, kept talking. " 'George Steinbrenner, president of the Yankees—' "

"Wait a minute! I'm not the damn president. I'm the owner!"

Exasperated, Young went on, " 'George Steinbrenner, the principal owner of the Los Angeles Dodg—"

"The Yankees! Principal owner of the Yankees! Not the Dodgers."

The constant interruptions were getting on Young's nerves, but he preserved. " 'Early this morning in the hotel where the Dodgers are staying—' "

"The Dodgers? What's wrong with you? We're staying here—the Yankees!"

The travesty so far was nothing compared to the story about to be told. Steinbrenner was heading down to meet his wife and a few friends and team officials for an 8:00 p.m. dinner. He was alone in the elevator, stewing over the day's loss, when two young men entered on the seventh floor. They had been drinking. One still had a bottle of beer in his hand; the other wore a Dodgers cap.

"Steinbrenner, right?"

"Yeah, that's right." Cue the spaghetti-western sound track and quick-cut close-ups on the eyes.

"Why don't you go back to those fucking animals in New York and take your choke-ass players with you?"

Steinbrenner was horribly offended at the attack on his players. Chivalrously he fired back, "Go fuck yourself."

One dude hit Steinbrenner on the head with the bottle. Steinbrenner countered with a left-right flurry of punches. The first drunk fell, the second connected with a rap to Steinbrenner's mouth. Steinbrenner hit back, knocking out a couple of teeth. When the elevator door opened, Steinbrenner walked out, leaving one on his knees, the other crouched in the corner. Calmly the Battling Boss went to the bathroom to wash the blood from his hands and face and headed for the evening meal. The reporters couldn't stifle their guffaws, it was that absurd. Young got the scoop. The *Daily News* headline read, "Steinbrenner KOs 2 in Brawl."

The next day Nettles wondered why so many cameras were there to watch the Yankees bus leave Los Angeles. He and Ginger sat in the next-to-last seat and giggled uncontrollably when Steinbrenner boarded, his hand wrapped, his head sporting a Band-Aid.

Nettles slumped in his seat, hoping not to be seen. It didn't work.

"Where were you when I needed you?" Steinbrenner asked his third baseman, himself bandaged and unsure whether his thumb would heal enough to play Game 6.

"George, I was in bed. You told us all to get our sleep."

Bob Weddle, "the Singing Bus Driver," entertained during the 45-minute ride to the airport, crooning "Yankee Doodle" and "Over There" ("the Yanks are coming, the Yanks are coming," and all that).

Nettles chirped, "Hey, bussie, how about dedicating a song to George? Do you know the words to 'Rocky'?"

On the plane home, Jackson did a spot-on Howard Cosell impersonation. Billy Martin sent a telegram to Steinbrenner expressing great, and likely sarcastic, sympathy. No one believed the tale of pugilistic prowess. There were no witnesses. John, a caller into Bud Furillo's KABC radio show, said he and his friend Paul were the two kids involved. Curses were exchanged and George threw a punch that crashed into the elevator wall. Ringo was nowhere to be found.

When the rains came in New York, Game 6 was pushed back a day to Wednesday the 28th, the latest date for a World Series game ever. The extra day was enough to give Cey, who'd been examined by a neurosurgeon and cleared to fly, and Nettles, whose x-rayed thumb showed an incomplete fracture and was still sore and throbbing, the rest they needed.

Hooton, who'd pitched solidly in Game 2, was squaring off against John. The two were figurative lights-out. When electrical breakers outside Yankee Stadium were tripped, causing a third of the vapor lights to literally go out, it took 10 minutes to bring the power back in the ballpark, and another half inning to bring it back to the home team. Randolph put New York ahead with a solo shot in the bottom of the third. In the bottom of the fourth, Nettles doubled. After the second out, Milbourne came up.

"They're gonna hit for Tommy," coach Monty Basgall told Lasorda. There was no way Lemon would take out his starting pitcher, especially one who had only given up 1 run in 13 innings, not so early and not with the game tied. At least that's what Lasorda thought until Basgall pointed to the action in the bull pen. Lasorda had Milbourne intentionally walked to see what Lemon would do.

Lasorda had no idea what had already occurred. Before the last loss, Steinbrenner had sat with Lemon. Playing Connie Mack, Steinbrenner, acting as owner and field leader, explained that Guidry seemed to be less effective after 6 innings and should be pulled. Lem didn't listen and Guidry gave up 2 homers in the seventh. Before Game 6, Steinbrenner met with his manager and coaches and told them straight-out, "Let's get a lead and then let's go to the bull pen and hold it." The Yanks didn't lead, but with John about to hit, Lemon wasn't taking any chances.

"I'm pinch-hitting for you."

"You're what?" said a flabbergasted John.

"We're going to try to get a run."

"You got to be kidding me."

"Nope. I'm going to the bull pen," said Lemon.

"Who're you gonna bring in?"

"I'm bringing in Frazier."

"Frazier? I can't believe it. He's lost two games already."

"Damn it"—an angry Lemon had reached his limit—"I'm going to the bull pen. That's what I'm going to do. End of discussion."

"That's the worst move I've ever seen in my life."

John stomped to the end of the dugout, leaning against the

wall. The TV cameras captured his disgust, the shaking head, the words he spoke to himself in disbelief. Pinch-hitter Murcer flied to right, just shy of the warning track, to end the rally and the inning.

Celebrating the gift given him, Lasorda clapped his hands and urged his team, "Now let's start scoring runs!"

Which they did, pronto.

Lemon still had confidence in the snakebitten Frazier, who had become the first pitcher in 40 years to lose two World Series games in succession. Cheap hits had victimized the Yankees middleman, not lack of ability. Still, two losses are two losses, and with the World Series on the line Frazier seemed like a bad choice.

Lopes singled to lead off the fifth and advanced on a Russell sacrifice bunt. Garvey flew out to Winfield in left, and Cey, still in recovery, hit a soft grounder up the middle that hit the edge of the grass and, taking a strange hop, eluded Randolph. Lopes streaked home for the go-ahead run. Baker then singled.

Before Game 6, coach Mota had reminded Guerrero to stay down to see the ball better; he'd been standing too straight at the plate. Mota's advice had worked before. It worked again. Guerrero crushed the ball over Mumphrey's head in center field for a triple, and a 4–1 Dodgers edge. "I can't believe this is happening," Cerone thought from behind the plate.

Frazier was done for the day after finishing the inning. He went to the manager's office to watch the rest of the game he'd just blown wide open and found Murcer, John, and coach Johnny Oates already tuning in.

Frazier sat down and Oates quickly moved away. "I don't want to sit next to you the way you're going. The roof might fall in on me."

They all laughed. There wasn't much else they could do as they saw Ron Davis get pounded for 4 runs, putting the game, and the World Series, beyond reach. The mighty Yankee bull pen had fallen. Adding injury to insult, Nettles reinjured his thumb in the sixth inning.

Steinbrenner found nothing to laugh about. He summoned Bill Madden of the *Daily News* to his office and handed him a press release on Yankee stationery that Steinbrenner had typed himself: "I want to sincerely apologize to the people of New York and to the fans of the New York Yankees everywhere for the performance of the Yankee team in the World Series. I also want to assure you that we will be at work immediately to prepare for 1982. I want also to extend my congratulations to Peter O'Malley and the Dodger organization—and to my friend, Tom Lasorda, who managed a superb season, playoffs and brilliant World Series. Sincerely, George M. Steinbrenner." The game wasn't even over yet!

Hooton gave up a single run in the bottom of the sixth, giving way to Howe. The Yankees couldn't catch up with his four-seam fastball and went down meekly until the ninth. Even after Randolph walked and, two outs later, Jackson reached on Lopes's error (breaking the World Series record for second baseman), no one believed they could summon the strength to come back from a 9–2 deficit.

Watson skied the final out to center field to put an end to the game that had been lost in the fourth inning. Howe, exultant, leaped into Yeager's arms; Garvey held his glove hand high in celebration. In the clubhouse, Bob Uecker interviewed the Dodgers first baseman, incorrectly reported as the series MVP. It was fitting that the award should be shared— Cey, Yeager, and Guerrero the actual recipients—in a total team effort. In the Year of Fernando, the Dodgers seemed destined to come out on top. Lasorda, a tower of shaving cream swirling on his head, beamed. Crowed Lopes, "You don't know how sweet it is to beat New York in New York."

The Yankees had failed miserably. Every facet of their game fell apart after the first two victories. The bull pen, except for Gossage, who never gave up a run, was inept. Davis's ERA was 23.14; Frazier's, 17.18. Not since "Lefty" Williams in 1919 had a pitcher lost three games in a World Series. (Unlike Frazier, Williams had eight games to accomplish his notorious record, and as a member of the "Black Sox," he was trying to lose!)

Their hitting was no better: 55 men were left on base in 52 innings, breaking the record for a 6-game series set in 1980 by the

Royals. Winfield, Cerone, and Jackson were 0 for 12 in the final game, but Winfield's futility was the story. One hit in 22 times at bat, an average of .045. His failure in the World Series would live with him forever. "Mr. May" was born.

Steinbrenner performed the worst of all. The benching of Jackson at the start, the elevator fight, the interfering with his manager, the apology, his utter disregard for his players as human beings, hurt the club he so wanted to help. "Find out how much he charges for a pep talk," Lasorda mocked.

The apology rankled most the veteran team of prideful pros, who had, after all, made the World Series. Gossage was repulsed and began thinking about leaving when his contract expired in two years. Jackson had nothing to apologize for. He played hard, when given the chance, and hit well, batting .333.

The day following the loss, Jackson drove up Madison Avenue to Yankee Stadium, the same path he'd taken since signing with the Yankees in late 1976, the same drive he took when he was the hero of New York, hitting 3 homers in Game 6 to beat the Dodgers in 1977, so far past it seemed. Clearing out his locker, taking his sweet time as the press watched and teammates chattered, Jackson eventually said his good-byes.

"See you down the road," he said, heading to the elevator that took him upstairs to Steinbrenner's office.

"You need a ride to the airport?" the owner asked.

Jackson replied he was sticking around for another day, then noticed the newspapers, headlines ringing about Steinbrenner's apology, not of the team, not of Reggie Jackson.

"Same old stuff, right?"

"Same old stuff," said Jackson, but it would never be quite like it again.

Ten thousand fans waited at LAX for the Dodgers to land. For five hours they cheered, danced, and sang in delirious joy for their comeback kids. The players waded through the crowd to the limos waiting to take them home. Lasorda, for the first time in his life, was speechless, hoarse from cheering the night before. Mayor Tom

Bradley announced that the following day would be a special day of celebration for the new champs, and 75,000 to 80,000 would show, the freeways emptying, office workers spilling out into the streets. On the eve of Halloween, in the near 80-degree warmth of the sun, Dodger fans and costumed revelers—clowns, doctors, buccaneers, and chorus girls—screamed for Valenzuela, Cey, Garvey, as they rode by.

The split season was over, unloved by some, unforgettable to all.

Chapter 10

BEYOND THE SPLIT SEASON
NOVEMBER 1981–PRESENT

The end of the most untraditional season saw the beginning of the usual practice of firing and hiring managers. In Atlanta, Bobby Cox was fired, though still admired, by Ted Turner. "Bobby would be a candidate for the job if he wasn't the guy I was firing," Turner explained in his peculiar logic. Turner first offered the post to Hank Aaron, who wisely declined, then set his sights on Joe Torre.

On the last day of the season, Mets manager Torre had asked to meet with his general manager. Torre had one year left on his contract, his coaches none, and he asked whether his staff would be returning.

Upon receiving his answer, Torre left the front office and returned to his own, adjacent to the locker room. He called the five coaches in and they each took a seat.

"We're leaving," Torre said. "We're leaving. We're going to be replaced." Then the ex-manager went out to tell his shocked players that he, along with his staff, were gone.

He wouldn't be out of work long. Turner snatched up the 41-year-old ex-Met. He's "not real old and he doesn't have a drinking problem," pronounced Turner, his head back, cigar tilted upward, part-FDR, part–Groucho Marx. (Torre was an excellent choice; he'd lead the Braves to the playoffs in 1982.)

In the pick-up-sticks world of baseball managers, where the

umber of Type A (top 20 percent) free agents—Guidry,
en Griffey of the Reds, Ed Farmer of the White Sox, Dick
the Cubs—whose signing would now result in professional
ion and an amateur draft choice with the losing team re-
50,000, had already dwindled. Garner resigned with the
inbrenner had seen the World Series loss and decided the
the Yankees problems was more meddling. He planned
he team on speed and worked out a deal with Cincinnati
nine days before the draft. In the Type B category was
s, another swift outfielder that the Boss would ink on
3. It was bye-bye Reggie.

, who could have been locked up before the draft took
$1 million per year asking price (Steinbrenner had of-
illion over three years), was chosen by 18 teams, guar-
price would rise. Jackson was chosen by eight and was
courted by Turner for the Braves. "He can be club
e can be general manager," claimed Turner. With the
ing no plans for Jackson, it was anyone's guess where
d up. Jackson was eager for a new start, saying he'd
t base, be a team player, and any other thing he'd re-
There was much to be said for Atlanta, with 150 games
ion WTBS, a cozy ballpark conducive to home runs,
to win, and, of course, Turner himself.

rious free agent negotiations began, Grebey floated a
should offer more than three years guaranteed. A memo
clubs, asking them to consider the data that multiyear
an effect on player performance and to balance the rate
laries with the rate of revenues. That was, if any con-
ed at all; there seemed to be a freeze on signings.

n't know for sure if a plan was in place, but all indi-
l as public statements by management, backed up the
collusion. If this was the case, it would be a violation
greement, which stated clearly that neither players
allowed to work in concert with their peers.

Japan on an exhibition trip with the Royals, denied

same assortment is shaken and realigne

Bamberger joined the Mets (announc

World Series in a futile attempt to ste

kees), Cox was swooped up by the Blu

over the Padres. Jim Fanning was

Montreal, the *interim* tag removed.

By year's end, rumors were th

and replaced by, wait for it, Gene M

(Instead, Steinbrenner waited a full

shove Lem off the stage and bring b

be fired after 86 games].) Asked wh

ings of a manager, Michael wasn'

does, I want to be the owner." As

be the laser cannon than the alien

The long-speculated departur

to Chicago came to fruition, when

lion deal to become executive vic

the Cubs. Not a squawk was hea

aries nor cries of compensation f

leader.

In other Phillies news, Bill

bid by a syndicate offering $2

chise for over $30 million. Gile

general manager of the Reds ar

the October 29 press conferer

since he was 15, achieving v

dream of. In baseball his enti

ters chose him instead of the

Phillies all year long, from

nounced he was considering

The main postseason fd

draft for free agents. Repres

tions in the Baroque Room

Diego stayed home). The dr

in the open, began at 11:00

The

Garner, K

Tidrow of

compensa

ceiving $1

Astros. Ste

solution to

to rebuild

for Griffey

Dave Colli

December 2

Guidry

place at his

fered $2.5 n

anteeing his

immediately

president. H

Yankees hav

he would er

DH, play firs

sisted before

on Superstat

the potential

Before se

plan: no team

was sent to al

contracts had

of increased sa

tract was offer

Miller did

cations, as wel

rumors of tacit

of the Basic A

nor clubs were

Grebey, in

any conspiracy. Clubs were simply relating contract terms to player performance. It was only coincidental that they were all doing it the same way. If the "Grebey plan" wasn't a crime, the burglarizing of the players' association office while Miller was on vacation certainly was. Twice in a five-week span, small electronics were stolen, and important papers had been scattered about. Building security surmised that the theft of a few calculators could have been a cover for the real mission, to search through files. In Chicago, writer Jerome Holtzman, now with the *Tribune*, wrote the story. Kuhn was appalled, not by the theft, but by the reporting.

"Extremely irresponsible story by Holtzman," he noted. "It makes his ridiculous suppositions look like facts. Somebody should talk to the Cubs." The commissioner, formerly a lover of liberty, was willing to have the Cubs pressure their parent company to quash the free press.

"Free" was becoming a thing of the past in the Windy City when the White Sox announced they were moving 112 games to pay TV in 1982. Co-owner Einhorn, no longer willing to enrich the Tribune-owned WGN—60 games were broadcast on the channel in 1981, with WGN making 80 percent of the money—was taking his product to cable's Channel 60. For $21.95 per month, a Sox fan could get a scrambler and tune in. The package included 26 Sting soccer games, 56 Blackhawks games, and 56 Bulls games. That wasn't so appealing in the days before Michael Jordan.

After 11 years with the Sox, Harry Caray couldn't abide the lower exposure and high price tag of the move to cable. He had his constituents to think of, the cabdrivers, the diehards, the shut-ins, and the barkeeps that depended on free television. Instead of accepting a one-year pact to work on the South Side, Caray headed north of the river to Wrigley to become the Cubs' top voice in the booth. Seventy-seven percent of Cubbie rooters were displeased that they'd be subject to Caray's blathering, with irate fans phoning the Cub switchboard to lodge a protest. That would all change in time.

There may have been a conscious halt to inking the marquee names, but players *were* on the move. Two of the four negotiators were sent packing—Boone sold to the Angels, Belanger, let become a free agent after blasting manager Weaver in the press, signed by the Dodgers. Rich Gale was sent to the Giants, leaving Kansas City, and the Hyatt, far behind.

Garry Templeton's request to be traded, asked of Herzog when the shortstop was in the hospital, was granted when a mammoth trade sent Tempy to the Padres and Ozzie Smith to the Cardinals. Bartering an all-around player such as Templeton for the light-hitting, though fine-fielding, Smith? It didn't seem like a good deal for St. Louis.

The day the Cardinals began their 1980s ascent with the acquisition of Smith, the two leagues met in Hollywood, Florida. In the American League, Edward Bennett Williams took a place on the Executive Council, which controlled any changes in the power structure, and everyone knew Williams was gunning for Grebey and looking to overhaul the PRC. With Eddie Chiles, his firm ally now on the PRC, a more businesslike setup was on the horizon. No longer would Grebey, or someone like him, be able to criticize their employers. Chiles went one further, looking for a board and chair structure, with an owner as chair. Lee MacPhail thought that impractical. How would one club owner make impartial decisions over his competitors or for the other league? (Bud Selig, a staunch Kuhn supporter, would become just that, owning the Brewers while simultaneously serving as acting commissioner in the 1990s.) The loose cannons were dug in.

In the National League, the bloody coup began. Five clubs sought to dump Kuhn immediately. In the early-morning hours, O'Malley asked everyone to cool down, reminding them that Kuhn's renewal could not be discussed under baseball rules prior to 15 months before his seven-year term expired on August 12, 1983. Talks could begin, at the earliest, on May 12, 1982, but since any four owners in the NL could boot him, Kuhn was doomed as of this moment. He had eight months to fix things.

The league meetings merged into the 80th annual Winter Meetings. A local newspaper urged Kuhn to step down and allow Walter

O'Malley to assume the commissionership. O'Malley, dead since 1979, was unavailable for comment. Williams was: "We already have a dead man filling the job."

Now the lamest of lame ducks, Kuhn set up a committee to look into restructuring. As he watched the American League plead with the National to allow for three divisions, Kuhn decreed that he had the power to stop the AL from implementing their plan if the other league vetoed it. Was he that unaware of what had just happened to him? Did he not see that his days were numbered? Whatever power he always thought he had, that he was the overseer of the entire game with full authority to employ his interpretation of the "best interests of baseball," had been shattered by the strike. He was merely the owners' man, and now it was made plain to all but himself that most didn't want him around anymore.

One year after his 1980 speech that gave the union all the proof they needed that the owners were going to force a strike and their claims of poverty would have to result in the crushing of free agency, Kuhn gave his state-of-the-game speech. He pumped the late-season success of the split-season plan and the added playoff. (Though attendance in the divisional playoffs was disheartening overall, especially in Philadelphia and Montreal, and ratings were so weak that NBC expressed disappointment and was not advocating for more. In fact, ratings for the prime-time LCS games were dramatically lower, and the three showcase World Series games were down from 1980, even though New York and Los Angeles were the two largest media markets in the country.) And Kuhn saw the strike as worthwhile, that it resulted in meaningful compensation that was sure to strengthen competitive balance.

"I'm an optimist, and I see bright things in baseball's future. Inevitably, there will be those who prefer to focus on negative aspects. I think that's shortsighted."

The shortsightedness of the owners, led by Kuhn and Grebey, had provoked a strike. They fought to pull back free agency, which had, in a few short years, driven baseball to unprecedented heights of popularity, while providing a new competitive equity that had never before existed. Now a team didn't have to wallow in the cellar forever; they could turn it around with a free agent or two.

There was reason to be optimistic for sure. The players had made it so by going on strike and saving the game from the owners themselves. By end of first week of December 1981, over a million tickets had been sold for 1982.

Jackson met with Turner at the Disneyland Hotel in Anaheim for three hours. It was Angels country, but the Braves owner felt he had the inside track. They were meant for each other, finding connections as they discussed morals, Turner's theory on molecules and why they were the reason so many home runs were hit at Fulton County Stadium, and the possibilities of their future together. "I've always dreamed of talking to someone who understands my crazy ideas. Today, I did," Jackson said of his new soul mate. Only on the new space shuttle, tested throughout 1981, could Jackson hit more dingers, said Turner.

The Turner hard sell wasn't enough. Jackson met with the Angels later that same day and signed with them on January 22.

When Belanger departed, Earl Weaver had his eye on the greatest infield in the big leagues. Despite the strike, the manager respected DeCinces for what he did, for the principle he stood for, and assured him he was the starting third baseman for 1982. The kid, Ripken Jr., would move to short. DeCinces and the Ripkens went back a long way, to the minors in Asheville, where Sr. managed him and treated him like a son. Once, when a wild rifle shot whooshed past them as they played pepper in center field, DeCinces grabbed a young Cal and carried him off the field. Weaver counted on the two being together again, until Williams called and told him he was trading DeCinces to the Angels.

"Don't trade him! I'm putting Ripken at short and we'll have the best infield in the league," shouted Weaver. It was too late; the deal, sending DeCinces back to Southern California for Dan Ford, corked bat and all, was in the works.

Two hours later, Weaver called his soon-to-be-ex third baseman, making sure DeCinces knew it was management, not the manager, who wanted him gone, but it wasn't to happen so quickly. Ford's contract caused a snag, and days went by without consummation.

On the third day, Williams called his former friend and confidant. "I just want you to know if this trade doesn't go through, you're my starting third baseman." Williams tried, with no success, to make it seem as if he weren't behind the whole thing.

"You'll trade me somewhere else," answered the hurt and angry DeCinces. "I treated you with respect, and you treated me this way. Make the trade." It was finalized on January 28.

The 1982 Angels were packed with union leaders—DeCinces, Boone, Jackson, Don Baylor, Steve Renko—much to the displeasure of their union- and Miller-hating manager, Gene Mauch. California, behind a rejuvenated Jackson, who led the league in home runs, DeCinces, who had a career year and finished third in the MVP race, and Boone, who guided the pitching staff, made the playoffs. They jumped to a 2–0 lead against the Brewers before Don Sutton, traded from Houston in the stretch run, turned the series around with a Game 3 victory. The Brewers came back to win the series and earn Milwaukee an appearance in the World Series against St. Louis.

The 1982 season would be Steve Rogers's best. Winning 19 games, leading the league in ERA, starting (and winning) the All-Star Game, second behind Carlton for the Cy Young Award, Rogers was in the rarefied air of the pitching elite. Though the Monday home run took the luster off 1981, foremost of his memories were his late-season run and the legacy of leadership of the players and what they accomplished. It had been the most productive year of his life. At the top of his game, Rogers couldn't know he was a few short years from the end, finished by 1985, his career-long arm problems finally insurmountable. For the Expos, 1981 was their final shot—they'd never make the postseason again. In 1994, the Expos, with the best record in baseball and a commanding lead in their division, were denied a playoff spot when the season ended with another strike.

The Japanese Seibu Lions offered the Phillies $500,000 to release Rose after 1982. If they did, the Lions would gladly pay Rose $1.5 million for one year. The money was tempting and Rose was all about the numbers, but the number he set his sights on was the all-time, good-old-American career-hit record held by Ty Cobb. After breaking Musial's league record, Rose was asked about breaking Cobb's. "I am forty years old now, and Cobb's record is still 560 hits away. At my age it's pretty difficult to think of matching that one. But given a few more good seasons, who knows? If I get close enough, I certainly would make a try for it." He would best Cobb in 1985, at 44, back as player-manager of the team he'd loved the most—his hometown Reds. Rose's fairy tale turned grim when, in 1989, he was handed a lifetime ban from the game he'd played so well, but gambled on while playing and managing. But the Pete Rose of 1981, the man-child whose on-field style, skill, enthusiasm, and humor kept fans galvanized, is the one to remember best.

At the East Los Angeles annual Christmas parade, 250,000 screamed, "Fernando, Fernando," over a three-mile route through the Latino community. Valenzuela, the grand marshal, was riding out front, exactly where he should have been. Having brought the Dodgers their first World Series championship since 1965, Valenzuela was now looking for a big payday. In addition to his $42,000 salary, about $10,000 over the minimum, Valenzuela made an extra $300,000 or so—$140,000 for a Mexican bank commercial, $75,000 for a US fruit juice commercial, $50,000 for the poster deal—but the Dodgers had made so much more, and now he was both the Cy Young winner and Rookie of the Year (the Dodgers' third in what would be a four-year string).

What did the Dodgers get? Eleven sellouts in 12 starts, averaging 48,323, 13 sellouts on the road, averaging 33,273. Over 1 million came out to see him. Nothing in the Basic Agreement or the strike settlement would take some of that money and send it his way. What would he want?

"He wants Texas back," Lasorda quipped, but he was fearful of losing his main attraction. The Dodgers were already in transition. They broke up their long-running infield quartet, trading Lopes to Oakland. Johnstone, important off the bench and more important for keeping the club loose with his wisecracks, was released. Reggie Smith was allowed to test the free agent waters. As the old stars were leaving, it was crucial to keep the new one happy. Valenzuela demanded $750,000 for 1982; the Dodgers weren't going to give it to him, so he held out, refusing to report to spring training, damaging the team's hopes to repeat and killing innocence. That Valenzuela turned out to be human, a man looking for his due, instead of a cartoon to be used as seen fit by the Dodgers and baseball, turned off fans who needed the fantasy. Valenzuela settled for $360,000 and went on to win 19 games.

Over the coming years, Valenzuela went from phenom to superstar to injury-riddled journeyman to legend, but nobody could forget that enchanted year of 1981. The Baseball Project, a supergroup of 1980s and 1990s indie-rock giants—Steve Wynn (Dream Syndicate), Scott McCaughey (Young Fresh Fellows), Linda Pitmon (Zuzu's Petals), and Peter Buck (R.E.M.)—remembered him wistfully in 2008. Written and heartbreakingly sung by Wynn in Spanish, "Fernando" speaks to that year and the checkered history of the Dodgers, the Latino community, and the boy who shot uncomfortably to fame when baseball itself seemed more simple.

> *The people say, "Go back where you came from."*
> *And why, when we've lived here for so many years?*
> *But in 1981 they loved me!*
> *And now, what has changed?*
> *I want to know.*
> *Fernando, we need you now.*

. . .

"I'll take Manhattan," Winfield crooned at the Macy's Thanksgiving Day parade. Even with its ups and downs he loved playing that year, though he found it hard to fit in. Rumors had emerged that Winfield went to Steinbrenner's office to apologize for his World Series performance a few days after the final game. Winfield denied it. Regardless, the love affair between Steinbrenner and Winfield was over.

The David M. Winfield Foundation sued Steinbrenner in 1982 for failing to make contributions to the charity. By mid-decade, Steinbrenner was publicly wishing for Reggie Jackson and disparaging Winfield. "Where is Reggie Jackson? We need a Mr. October or a Mr. September. Dave Winfield is Mr. May!" (Winfield redeemed that reputation in 1992, knocking in the winning runs to clinch a World Series win for the Blue Jays.) By the end of the '80s, Steinbrenner had hired Howie Spira to dig up some dirt on Winfield, resulting in the owner's getting himself banned from day-to-day operations of the Yankees.

Steinbrenner's hands-on moves for 1982 were a disaster. The Yankees finished in fifth place in the first of 13 years of roaming the no-playoff wilderness. Guidry, who signed for the nearly $1 million per year he wanted, was good, not great, though it was impossible to garner many wins with such a lousy team. Collins was a washout, Griffey not much better, and Righetti, the American League Rookie of the Year, suffered through the sophomore jinx. Tommy John, embroiled in contract issues with Steinbrenner, got traded to the Angels in August.

When the Angels came to town at the end of April for the first game after Lemon's firing and the return of Jackson, the crowd was on edge. Jackson, off to another slow start, faced Guidry to start the seventh inning. He connected with a soaring home run, smiling ear to ear as he trotted the bases.

The crowd erupted in disgust. "Steinbrenner sucks! Steinbrenner sucks! Steinbrenner sucks!" they jeered violently, turning their gaze to the man himself, sitting in his box behind home plate.

That George Steinbrenner was forgotten when the Yankees started winning again in 1995. His frequent characterization in *Seinfeld,* starting in 1994, did much to transform his image from that of a malicious megalomaniac into a lovable, paternal figure.

The complete breakdown of the 1982 A's pitching staff was laid at the feet of Billy Martin. He'd overused them, wore them down, and now they were ruined. His pitchers defended him—Keough said it was "horseshit" to blame Martin; McCatty, still devoted, "would run through a brick wall for the guy." But the fact was, all five starters were finished.

Martin came home to Yankee Stadium after being fired as the A's skipper at the end of 1982. He made it through the entire season before being canned. And he was hired for 1985 after Steinbrenner fired Yogi Berra after 16 games, only to be fired after fighting with his pitcher Ed Whitson, in a brawl that started at the Cross Keys Inn bar in Baltimore and ended up in the parking lot. And he was hired for 1988, lasting less than half the season before getting flattened in a topless bar and being removed in favor of Lou Piniella.

Only death could keep Martin from managing the team he loved for the sixth time. During a Christmas Day ice storm in 1989, he was killed in a one-car crash north of Binghamton.

Despite his efforts to professionalize the owners' negotiating style, the scars of 1981 assured Grebey's exit from the game. On Easter Sunday, 1983, Grebey was home in Connecticut, enjoying a peaceful holiday, when the phone rang. A reporter from the Associated Press was following up on a Chicago-based story that Grebey had been fired after a Good Friday assembly of the Player Relations Committee.

"That's complete news to me. They didn't even meet Friday," Grebey, in no mood for an interview, angrily replied.

He was right, they hadn't met. Instead they held a conference call to do their dirty work. Grebey was soon asked to resign, and he did, to be replaced by MacPhail. Baseball, which Grebey adored, had served him so poorly, even at the home of his beloved Cubbies. Once, attending a game in the bleachers at Wrigley Field with his old friend Bill Veeck, the PA announcer introduced Grebey as "the man who caused the '81 strike." The crowd lustily booed.

Grebey thought back to his beginnings at Inland Steel. During the strike of 1949, when a settlement was near, Grebey asked his boss a question, hoping to understand what he'd witnessed.

"How could you settle after a long strike and still get along with the union?" the young trainee asked the executive.

"Well, what we do is we pick someone and say, 'He's to blame for all this.' Then the union blames the same guy. This way we both protect the industry."

Such is the story of Ray Grebey, scapegoat. When he died in August 2013, his obituaries blamed him for the strike. It was all he was remembered for.

Kuhn lasted slightly longer than Grebey. In November 1982, Kuhn got the three-quarters majority he needed to stay in office from the American League, but he couldn't get through the National. There, the Cardinals, Mets, Reds, and Astros voted no. He decided to stay out his term through August 12, 1983, and ended up hanging on through the 1984 campaign. At the end of his tenure he tried to revise history, telling none other than Murray Chass that he had tried to forestall a confrontation, that he had moved behind the scenes to cajole owners into making concessions. He thought the owners' toughness put some balance in the game. Supporters such as O'Malley defended Kuhn, citing him as the one who had kept the owners flexible, who kept the strike from lasting even longer. It was a hard characterization to swallow.

"Given the roles [in the strike] of both, I feel this was a kind of retribution wreaking on them," Miller gloated about the demise of Grebey and Kuhn.

Unlike the two leading management figures, Miller was still

desperately wanted by his people. Though he went through with his promised retirement, Miller soon returned to the union. His replacement as executive director had been none other than Ken Moffett, the mediator whose experience during both 1980 and 1981 allowed him to get a running start. Miller was kept on as a consultant, to ease the transition, but Moffett didn't want him around, hiring his own people, almost losing Don Fehr. The tension was immediate. By November, the union had decided to fire Moffett and coaxed Miller back. Reluctantly, he returned—"Marvin, you've flunked retirement," his wife said—and stayed on briefly until Fehr was named acting executive director.

With time on their hands, the two old foes Kuhn and Miller set to writing. Kuhn's 1987 autobiography, *Hardball*, emerged first. In this exercise in score-settling and vitriol, his former enemies were lambasted with invective on page after page. Miller's *A Whole Different Ballgame* followed four years later. Forthright, often biting, this incisive work described the monumental progress the players had made under Miller. Both books reflected the men behind them.

Kuhn went from writing back to lawyering, forming, with corporate lawyer Harvey Myerson, Myerson & Kuhn in 1988, to great press ballyhoo. Two years later, the firm filed for bankruptcy. Personally liable for $3.1 million in loans to Marine Midland Bank, as well as for other firm obligations, Kuhn suddenly relocated from New Jersey to Florida, some said to keep his home and $2 million investment account from being taken from him by creditors, not allowed under his new home state's laws. For a while, Kuhn was nowhere to be found. Miller kept articles on Kuhn's ouster and downfall, proof to himself that the former commissioner was always guilty of malfeasance.

The 1981 strike was not the last labor problem to hit the national pastime. Two days of play were lost in 1985 over salary arbitration. Also, in 1985, the owners asked for the pool system to be removed. Though they, and Kuhn, had trumpeted it as effective, it was a disaster for them.

Case in point: White Sox owners Reinsdorf and Einhorn, along with general manager Roland Hemond, gathered on January 23, 1984, to read through the Teletype list of unprotected players. The Sox were entitled to a selection after losing middle-of-the-road pitcher Dennis Lamp to Toronto. They scoured the names and, to their disbelief, saw Tom Seaver's. Seaver, who had triumphantly come back to New York in 1983, was left unprotected in a Met effort to keep their young hopefuls and key position players. They never dreamed anyone would pick a 39-year-old past his prime. The White Sox could never have made a trade this good—Lamp for Seaver.

"How can you take my player?" Mets president Fred Wilpon hollered at Reinsdorf on the phone.

"Why'd you leave him unprotected?" Reinsdorf said, countering with the obvious. Every time he picked a player from the pool, the Chicago owner lost a friend. In this instance, even Kuhn was badgering the White Sox not to pick Seaver.

Seaver himself was furious, mad at the Mets for cutting him loose, angry at the White Sox for snagging him.

"What would you do if you could pick Tom Seaver?" Reinsdorf asked. Seaver understood.

From 1985 to 1986, the owners engaged in wholesale collusion to keep players on their teams by prohibiting interest from others. It took Andre Dawson, in early 1987, to break through. His knees destroyed from years on the rock-hard artificial surface at Olympic Stadium, Dawson simply had to play on the grass lawn of Wrigley Field to save his career. He handed Green a blank check, asked him to put in what was fair. Dawson took the risk that Chicago would sign him for something and, if they didn't, show the public that the owners were in cahoots. Green was cornered and offered Dawson a deal with the Cubs. Dawson energized the city in an MVP first year. (In September 1987, an arbitrator found the owners guilty of collusion in 1985; in July 1988 they were found guilty of collusion in 1986. The total settlement—lost salaries and damages—was reached on December 21, 1990. It cost management $280 million, millions more than they'd hoped to save by breaking the rules.)

A 1990 lockout kept the players off the field for 32 days over salary arbitration and the salary cap. Then came 1994.

Miller stayed a strong voice for players' rights throughout his retirement. As money in the game grew to astounding levels, Miller warned that healthy finances shouldn't trump rights. In 2002, during the controversy surrounding steroid use, Miller warned all who would listen that players had civil rights regarding privacy when it came to drug testing, and it would be wrong to relinquish them. Others felt the real moral issue was the drugs themselves. The players bucked Miller's opinion and paid for it. When Alex Rodriguez's "anonymous" drug test was leaked in early 2009, Miller was again proved correct. Unlike in the early days of the union, when the biggest stars sacrificed for the well-being of the group, now the players association was selling out some of their own to protect their larger economic interests. Performance-enhancing drugs did what the owners never could, splintering the union into factions.

As the years unfolded, Miller was increasingly heralded for his instrumental role in the evolution of baseball, but it was Kuhn who would gain entrance to the Baseball Hall of Fame in Cooperstown in December 2007, nine months after his death. At the July induction ceremony, Kuhn's son proudly proclaimed that his father "had a long-term vision of what was good for the game" and toiled to create "a working cooperation with the players." Baseball's growth, though, came despite Kuhn's efforts. It was the planning and tenacity of Miller, coupled with the strength and determination of the players he represented, that brought the game to the heights it now enjoys.

A campaign to induct Miller gained momentum but was dashed two years later when Miller was passed over again. Though it seemed a long shot that Miller would be voted in to the Hall, he garnered growing support. From his Stamford home, Grebey, in his 80s, his left eye lost to cancer, though, like his former adversary full of energy and solid of memory, wrote a letter of support that implored the Hall's Board of Directors to ensure Miller's election, "an honor he has earned and deserves."

Grebey explained, going even further, and deeper, into his own personal history, "No other individual played a more prominent role in creating the structure and process within which today's game is played. To those who did not vote for Marvin's election to the Hall in yesterday's voting, I say put the animosity aside, look at the record. I took my share of criticism and insults, but the history of the game must prevail." This beautifully noble letter was a touching tribute to his former opponent.

Miller claimed not to care, but he sounded hurt in his protests. His life was always about the cause, about justice. He knew he'd done the right thing, just like those garment workers on the picket line. None of them had made the Hall of Fame either. Miller, 95, died in Manhattan in November 2012.

Though a 1994 strike over a salary cap and revenue would do what the 1981 strike couldn't—cancel the World Series and stretch over two seasons—today's baseball business is marked by labor peace. In the long run, Marvin Miller won. Today's players no longer have to beg owners for scraps. They are partners, in a very real sense, with management, overseeing a business that generates over $8 billion in revenues and allows individual players to sign contracts worth hundreds of millions of dollars. The players association is every bit as interested in keeping the status quo as the owners.

In that way, Bowie Kuhn won too.

Acknowledgments

A direct line leads to this book and its point of origin is Michael D'Antonio.

In early 2008 I got a call from Michael asking me about the Kansas City A's. He was looking for clarification on a letter he'd turned up researching his forthcoming biography of Dodgers owner Walter O'Malley, *Forever Blue*. Here was a member of a Pulitzer Prize–winning team of reporters, a bestselling author of scads of nonfiction works, ringing up the author of a small-press baseball book, looking for answers. That's what makes Michael so good. It was the beginning of a wonderful relationship, him serving as guru, me as willing apprentice. A pure gift I was lucky to receive.

Michael introduced me to David Groff, a gifted poet and editor. David and I worked on a book proposal about how my wife and I raised our oldest son, Nate, who is high-functioning autistic, and changed our life as a result. David challenged me to raise my game as a writer, and hopefully I did. I thank him for that.

David is affiliated with Rob Weisbach Creative Management, and though he never guaranteed that our work on the Nate book would result in my signing with the agency, through David I met my agent, Erin Cox. We met for lunch at the Standard Hotel, under the High Line, and hit it off immediately. Though the Nate book didn't sell (it will!), Erin and I continued to explore my other ideas. Her belief in me, sans bullshit, is exactly what I need, as is her quick understanding of my minor neuroses. Not a day goes by that I'm not thankful for her.

Big thanks to Rob Kirkpatrick at Thomas Dunne Books. From the moment he extolled Jerry Grote and Grote's 7 RBI game for the Royals in the summer of 1981, I knew he was the editor for me. His attention to detail made both the book and its author look better.

Back in 1981, when I was a heartbroken, almost-19-year-old fan, it never entered my wildest fantasies that I would speak with and meet the principals of the day. That kid would have thought the very idea he'd become the one who told the tale quite unbelievable, and talking to your idols is the strangest thing. Thanks to all of them for making it so easy and comfortable: John Castino, Ron Cey, Murray Chass, Don Fehr, Phil Garner, Clark Griffith, Jon Matlack, Jerry Reinsdorf, and Andy Strasberg. I also had the chance to spend time with Ray Grebey and Marvin Miller. Grebey asked me to come to his Connecticut home, and we spent the whole day talking. On my way out he gave me a cigar for the road, which came in handy during traffic on the Rip Van Winkle Bridge. I spoke with Miller on three occasions and was dumbstruck at how exact his memory was. I was looking at 30-year-old clippings and he was reciting what was in them. Truly amazing.

Extra thanks are due to Steve Rogers, who spent hours on the phone with me explaining the ins and outs of the negotiating session. Steve's ultracompetitiveness is still there. He had no problem setting me straight if I'd interpreted something incorrectly. (Thanks to Scott Crawford from the Canadian Baseball Hall of Fame and Museum for getting me to Steve.) A huge, huge thank-you goes to Doug DeCinces. Doug and I skyped, talked, and e-mailed over many months as I worked my way toward getting the story right. It meant a lot to him that I did—he, like Steve, was in the trenches in a stressful time—and it meant a lot to me that he was available.

Some good people who have helped and read along the way: Rick Angell, Howard Bryant, Alan Cantor, Jim Caple, Paul Dickson,

Jonathan Eig, Doug Glanville, Kevin Guilfoile, Tom Guilfoile, Steve Jacobson, Kostya Kennedy, Paul Lukas, Bruce Maxson, Reed Metzger, Ken Moffett, Rob Neyer, Chip Northrup, Darren Rovell, Billy Sample, Jimmy Seidita, Tom Shieber, Rusty Staub, Rick Telander, and Steve Wynn. Also, thanks to the helpful staff at the Tamiment Library/ Robert F. Wagner Labor Archives at NYU, where Marvin Miller's papers reside.

Living in Cooperstown means I can walk to the greatest baseball library in the world. The National Baseball Hall of Fame and Museum is not only a world-class institution, but has a staff that is professional and hugely helpful, and over the years many have become pals. Thanks to Tim Wiles, Freddy Berowski, Claudette Scrafford (who guided me through Bowie Kuhn's papers), Jim Gates, Tom Shieber (again), and Bill Francis. A special shout-out to Hall president Jeff Idelson, one of the best people I've ever known and one of my first friends when I moved to Cooperstown.

My boys, Nate, Rob, and Joey, all have their unique strengths and interests, but collectively they never fail to crack me up or add something interesting and insightful. They give me a lot to be proud of. Plus, they all love going with me to record stores.

While this book is proof there was life before December 31, 1985, for me that's when it began in earnest. I met Karen at a New Year's Eve party in Scarsdale. Five months later we were engaged, five months after that we were married, and five months after that we moved to Chicago. Karen's always supported me in whatever I set my mind on, even when, in 2003, I wanted out of my day job of trading options and thought moving to Cooperstown was a great idea. She's the one that makes everything happen.

Sources

ARTICLES

Allen, Maury. 1981, July 29. "Doubleday: Miller's on the Run." *New York Post*.

"All-Time Greats: Strike Bad News." 1981, August 4. *Daily Star*, 14.

"AL West." 1981, July 18. *Sporting News*, 31.

Amdur, Neil. 1981, June 17. "Chicago Cubs Are Sold by Wrigley to Tribune Co. for $20.5 Million." *New York Times*.

Anderson, Dave. 1980, July 2. "Arm Ailment Imperils Tom Seaver's Career." *New York Times*.

Associated Press. 1978, February 15. "Big Leagues Hire Grebey."

———. 1981, April 18. "A's Playing 'Billy Ball.'"

———. 1981, May 29. "A Foul Wind for Mariners."

———. 1981, June 7. "2nd Threat on His Life."

———. 1981, September 25. "Martin's Boycott Shunned." *New York Times*.

———. 1981, October 8. "Astros Ax LA in 11th, 1–0."

———. 1983, April 4. "Grebey Unaware of His 'Firing.'" *Pittsburgh Post-Gazette*, 18.

———. n.d. "Miller Lambasts Kuhn." From National Baseball Hall of Fame Library.

Bisher, Furman. 1981, March 21. "Fans: Let's Strike, Beat Players to the Punch." *Sporting News,* 17.

Bodley, Hal. 1981, February 14. "Phillies' Paychecks Total $7 Million." *Sporting News,* 43.

—————. 1981, July 4. "180-Degree Turn: Ruly a Hard-Liner." *Sporting News,* 32.

Boyle, Robert H., ed. 1981, March 30. "Scorecard: They Said It." *Sports Illustrated,* 12.

"Braves: Aaron Worried." 1981, July 25. *Sporting News.*

Bunis, Dena. 1981, June. "Oops! Media Covers Iggy, Briefly." *Rochester Democrat and Chronicle.*

Carchidi, Sam. 2005, July 11. "Boone's Version of 'the Play' He Says Rose Messed Up Before the Famous 1980 Catch." http://articles .philly.com/2005-07-11/sports/25433833_1_bob-boone-phillies -history-mitt.

Caught on the Fly. 1981, March 14. *Sporting News,* 50.

—————. 1981, April 4. "Kuhn, Miller Labor Update." *Sporting News,* 51.

Chass, Murray. 1981, March 14. " 'No Choice,' Players Say After Strike Vote." *Sporting News.*

—————. 1981, May 23. "Secret Panel Seals Owners' Lips." *Sporting News,* 12.

—————. 1981, June 13. "Judge, Legal Batteries, Decide Baseball's Fate." *Sporting News,* 13.

—————. 1981, June 20. "Owners Reject Player-Pool Plan." *Sporting News,* 13.

—————. 1981, June 27. "Bargainers Fail to Halt a Strike." *Sporting News,* 2.

—————. 1981, June 29. "No Talks in View in Baseball Walkout." *New York Times,* C4.

—————. 1981, July 2. "Owners Shift Slightly in Talks." *New York Times.*

—————. 1981, July 3. "Talks Off for a Day; Owners Expected to Make a Move." *New York Times.*

————. 1981, July 4. "Owners' Stance Angers Players." *Sporting News,* 13.

————. 1981, July 13. "Owners Seem Close to Final Position." *New York Times.*

————. 1981, July 16. "Secretary of Labor Urges Negotiators to Step Up Talks." *New York Times.*

————. 1981, July 18. "Players Call Peace Report False." *Sporting News,* 21.

————. 1981, July 25. "Owners Shoot Down Moffett Plan." *Sporting News,* 2.

————. 1981, August 1. "Talks Move to Washington." *Sporting News,* 26.

————. 1981, August 5. "Both Sides Echo a Plea—'Let's Not Let It Happen Again.'" *Sporting News,* 2.

————. 1981, August 9. "Strike Over, Baseball Resumes." *New York Times.*

————. 1981, October 13. "Yanks, A's Stir Spitball Dispute." *New York Times.*

————. 1981, October 22. "John of Yankees Faces Ex-Mates." *New York Times.*

————. 1996, October 21. "Why Did Yankees Lose in '81? Ask Steinbrenner." From National Baseball Hall of Fame Library.

Cohen, Jim. 1981, June 21. "Selig's Cigar Smoke Is Heavy." *Milwaukee Journal,* 3.

Collier, Phil. 1981, March 28. "Upset Kroc Won't Sell Padres." *Sporting News,* 28.

DeArmand, Mike. 1980, November 29. "Porter Only Free-Agent Fish in the Sea for the Royals." *Sporting News.*

DelNagro, Mike. 1981, October 19. "The Gang of Four Shoots to the Top: Dodgers." *Sports Illustrated,* 44.

Durslag, Mel. 1981, May 2. "Big Salaries Generate Publicity." *Sporting News,* 17.

Durso, Joseph. 1981, May 9. "The Buildup for Valenzuela Annoys Some of the Mets." *New York Times.*

—————. 1981, July 29. "Owners' Session Called; Players on Coast to Meet." *New York Times.*

—————. 1981, August 3. "Wilpon Concerned About Fan Reaction." *New York Times.*

—————. 1981, October 6. "Torre's Cast Regrouping." *New York Times.*

—————. n.d. "Getting Their Act II Together." From National Baseball Hall of Fame Library.

"Fernando Saluted for Gritty Job." 1981, November 7. *Sporting News,* 16.

Fimrite, Ron. 1981, March 16. "The Trade That Made Milwaukee Famous." *Sports Illustrated,* 22.

—————. 1981, April 17. "Winning Is Such a Bore." *Sports Illustrated,* 18.

—————. 1981, August 31. "Baseball." *Sports Illustrated,* 74.

—————. 1981, October 19. "The Gang of Four Shoots to the Top A's." *Sports Illustrated,* 44.

—————. 1981, November 2. "The Series Was Up for Grabs." *Sports Illustrated,* 30.

—————. 1981, November 9. "A Last Hurrah for Los Angeles." *Sports Illustrated,* 28.

Flannery, Mary. 1981, June 3. "Billy Returning to A's amid Debate over Penalties." *Daily News.*

Fong-Torres, Ben. 1981, April 19. " 'Billy Ball.' " *Parade.*

Friedman, Mark. 1981, September. "Better Be Careful When You Knock Reggie Down." United Press International.

Galloway, Randy. 1981, May 30. "Chiles Never Ducks Issue." *Sporting News,* 8.

—————. 1981, July 4. "Chiles Opens Fire on Kuhn, Grebey." *Sporting News,* 27.

"Game Two Notes." 1981, November 7. *Sporting News,* 15.

Greer, Thom. 1981, August 11. "Pete Told Son: This Is It." *Daily News.*

Grimsley, Will. 1981, July 9. "Grebey Cast as Baseball's Villain." *Rochester Times-Union,* 4D.

Hummel, Rick. 1981, September 12. "Templeton Gets Psychiatric Help." *Sporting News,* 39.

———. 1981, October 29. "Yankees' Hard-Luck Frazier Smiles at Trio of Losses." *St. Louis Post-Dispatch,* 3C.

Insiders Say. 1981, May 9. *Sporting News,* 6.

———. 1981, May 23. *Sporting News,* 6.

———. 1981, June 20. *Sporting News,* 10.

———. 1981, August 1. *Sporting News,* 8.

Isle, Stan. 1981, July 11. "Pot Took Raiders Toll, Doc Recalls." *Sporting News,* 13.

———. 1981, August 15. "Johnny Mize Spoke with His Cigar." *Sporting News,* 7.

———. 1981, December 26. "Big Flow of Red Ink, Kuhn Worries." *Sporting News,* 35.

"It's Cooperstown's Big Weekend." 1981, August 1. *Daily Star,* 3.

Kaegel, Dick, ed. 1981, May 30. "Our Opinion: Editorial." *Sporting News,* 3.

———. 1981, August. "Cheers Ring Out for Hall's Heroes." From National Baseball Hall of Fame Library.

———. 1981, November 7. "Acrobat Nettles Unveils New Act." *Sporting News,* 14.

———. 1981, November 7. "Reuss Learns How to Chill Yanks." *Sporting News,* 14.

Kaplan, Jim. 1981, May 11. "Raines Really Pours It On." *Sports Illustrated.*

———. 1981, June 22. "No Games Today." *Sports Illustrated,* 17.

———. 1981, August 10. "Let the Games Begin." *Sports Illustrated,* 14.

———. 1981, October 5. "Retelling the Tale of Two Cities." *Sports Illustrated,* 32.

———. 1981, October 26. "All the Yankees Were Dandy." *Sports Illustrated,* 22.

Kirshenbaum, Jerry, ed. 1981, February 16. "The Continuing Saga of Dr. Mazza and His 'Good Friends.'" *Sports Illustrated,* 11.

———. 1981, June 8. "Needy—or Greedy?" *Sports Illustrated,* 20.

———. 1981, July 6. "Endangered Season." *Sports Illustrated,* 13.

———. 1981, July 6. "Strikeball." *Sports Illustrated,* 20.

———. 1981, July 13. "Scorecard." *Sports Illustrated,* 11.

———. 1981, August 3. "Divided Loyalties." *Sports Illustrated,* 14.

———. 1981, October 5. "A Disaster and a Mockery Followed by (Weather Permitting) a World Series." *Sports Illustrated,* 18.

———. 1981, October 13. "Scorecard." *Sports Illustrated,* 21.

———. 1981, November 2. "They Said It." *Sports Illustrated,* 25.

———. 1981, December 28. "They Said It." *Sports Illustrated,* 15.

Koppett, Leonard. 1981, June 1. "Yesterday." *Sports Illustrated,* 92.

———. 1981, June 27. "Keep Compensation Rule as Is." *Sporting News,* 11.

Kuhn, Bowie. 1981, July 18. "I Am Nobody's Agent." *Sporting News,* 20.

Lang, Jack. 1981, July 28. Unknown. From National Baseball Hall of Fame Library.

———. 1981, October 18. "Lasorda Pep Talk Packs a Wallop." *Daily News,* C28.

———. 1981, November 28. "Guidry Hottest Reentry Item with 18 Picks." *Sporting News,* 53.

Leavy, Jane. 1981, May 27. "Players Win Ruling by NLRB." *Washington Post.*

———. 1981, June 11. "Players Lose; Strike Imminent." *Boston Globe,* 65.

Leggett, William. 1981, January 12. "Top Banana at Tampa Bay." *Sports Illustrated,* 13.

Liff, Mark. 1981, June 27. Unknown. From National Baseball Hall of Fame Library.

———. 1981, July 24. "Take Heart, Fans, Baseball Is Near." *Daily News,* back page.

Lupica, Mike. 1981. "Reggie: The Fallen Idol." *Daily News.* From National Baseball Hall of Fame Library.

MacDonald, Ian. 1981, October 31. "Rogers Erases Big-Game Doubts." *Sporting News,* 42.

Madden, Bill. 1981, August 11. "Rose Gets THE Hit plus Call from the President." *Daily News,* C29.

Major League Flashes. 1981, July 4 and 11. *Sporting News,* 36.

Marley, Mike. 1981, June 22. "Players Will Sit Out Past All-Star Game." *New York Post.*

———. 1981, July 13. "Hatred Growing Between Bargainers." *New York Post.*

———. 1981, July 31. "Players Say Bitterness Will Linger." *New York Post,* 84.

Miller, Marvin. 1981, August 16. "Miller: The Union's Strength Is Established." *New York Times.*

"Miller Says Grebey Held Back." 1981, July 9. *New York Times.*

Montemayor, Robert. 1981, April 24. "From Mexico with Mystery." *Los Angeles Times,* CC/Part III.

Moran, Malcolm. 1981, July 30. "Vote Backs Miller's Effort." *New York Times,* D23.

Nack, William. 1981, March 2. "J.R.'s Pledge: I'm Going to Return." *Sports Illustrated,* 26.

Newsfile Memorandum. 1981, June 18.

Nightingale, Dave. 1981, August 8. "Crystal Ball Reveals, Fans, PRC and Kuhn Will Return." *Sporting News,* 16.

———. 1981, September 12. "Inside Story of Settlement: The Miller-MacPhail Deal." *Sporting News,* 2.

———. 1981, December 12. "Chances Dim for 3-Division Play." *Sporting News,* 39.

Ocker, Sheldon. 2006, May 15. "Pinnacle of Perfection." *Akron Beacon Journal.*

———. 1981, August 10. "Barker Turns Other Cheek on 'Kissing Bandit.'" *Akron Beacon Journal.*

Papanek, John, ed. 1981, July 20. "Scorecard." *Sports Illustrated,* 11.

Pepe, Phil. 1981, February 25. "Reggie Weighs Pitch." *Daily News.*

———. 1981, April 4. "Reggie-George Show Heating Up." *Sporting News,* 50.

———. 1981, May 7. "Reggie Crisis Looming over 'Half Player' Role." *Daily News.*

———. 1981, July 2. ". . . Till Doomsday." *Daily News.*

————. 1981, July 11. "Strike Could Be Good—or Bad—for Watson." *Sporting News*, 33.

————. 1981, August 18. "Righetti, Reggie and Goose Give Yanks Reason for Hope." *Daily News*.

————. 1981, October 15. "Yankees Humiliate A's, 13–3." *Daily News*.

————. 1981, October 17. "Reggie Warms Up for October Show." *Sporting News*, 19.

————. 1981, October 31. "Nettles, Reggie Never Friendly." *Sporting News*.

Pluto, Terry, and Tony Grossi. 1981, May 17. "Everything But . . ." *Cleveland Plain Dealer*.

Rappoport, Ken. 1981, July 16. "Baseball Strike." Associated Press.

Ray, Ralph. 1981, March 14. "A Strike? Players Must Act Fast." *Sporting News*, 13.

————. 1981, May 9. "Mediator Moffett Back in Bargaining Talks." *Sporting News*, 36.

————. 1981, May 16. "Gulf Is Growing Wider in Player-Owner Row." *Sporting News*.

————. 1981, May 23. "Phils-for-Sale Scares Owners." *Sporting News*, 15.

————. 1981, May 23. "A Pessimistic Strike Countdown." *Sporting News*, 11.

————. 1981, May 30. "NLRB Action Could Set Back Strike." *Sporting News*, 8.

"Reagan's NLRB Tips Toward Management." 1981, July 6. *BusinessWeek*.

Reidenbaugh, Lowell. 1981, October 17. "Reds, Cards: Best, Not First." *Sporting News*, 15.

Reusse, Patrick. 1981, July 11. "'What Strike?' Ask Twins Fans." *Sporting News*, 37.

Ringolsby, Tracy. 1981, March 7. "Maury Wills Fan Randle Hopes to Make the Feeling Mutual." *Sporting News*.

Robbins, Danny, and Jayson Stark. 1981, June 12. "Phils Just Plain Glum About Strike Prospect." *Philadelphia Inquirer*.

Roura, Phil, and Tom Poster. 1981, October 18. "People." *Daily News*.

"Settlement Is Thought-Provoking." 1981, August 15. *Sporting News*, 27.

Shalin, Mike. 1981, August 19. "Miller: Bowie Must Consult Players on Playoff Format." *New York Post*, 72.

Shattuck, Harry. 1981, July 4. "Lack of Fan Support Upsets Astro Players." *Sporting News*.

————. 1981, September 26. "Cedeno Is Fined; Goes After Fan." *Sporting News*, 23.

Slater, Chuck. 1981, June 5. "Billy . . ." *Daily News*.

Smith, Red. 1980, December 14. "The Prophet of Doom Is Heard Again." *New York Times*.

Stark, Jayson. 1981, June 13. "Owens, Giles Rue Timing of Strike That Turned into a Lost Weekend." *Philadelphia Inquirer*.

————. 1981, June 14. "Separate Tables." *Philadelphia Inquirer*.

Stier, Kit. 1981, October 24. "Up-and-Coming A's Frustrate Royals." *Sporting News*, 21.

Strauss, Michael. 1981, August 11. "Rose Breaks Musial's Career Hit Record." *New York Times*.

Strege, John. 1981, July 11. "Bavasi Still Optimistic, But . . ." *Sporting News*, 34.

Sudyk, Bob. 1981, May 30. "Perfecto—Barker First to Pitch Gem Since Hunter Did It in '68." *Sporting News*, 11.

Tucker, Tim. 1981, March 28. "Red Faced Turner Might Join Fan Picket Line." *Sporting News*, 28.

————. 1981, July 11. " 'We'll Play Again,' Murphy Tells Curious Braves Fans." *Sporting News*, 36.

————. 1981, August 1. "NL West—Braves: A Profit at Last." *Sporting News*, 38.

————. 1981, November 7. "Surprise! Torre Is Braves' Pilot." *Sporting News*, 22.

————. 1981, December 19. "Turner, Reggie Feel a 'Kinship.' " *Sporting News*, 46.

Vecsey, George. 1981, August 4. "Fame and Game at Cooperstown." *Washington Star*.

————. 1982, January 13. "Gaining Strength Through Losing." *New York Times*.

Voice of the Fan. 1981, May 30. "Editorial Reply." *Sporting News*.

————. 1981, July 11. "Commissioner's Complaint." *Sporting News*, 6.

Weiskopf, Herm. 1981, April 20. The Week. *Sports Illustrated*, 81.

————. 1981, June 1. The Week. *Sports Illustrated*, 58.

————. 1981, June 8. The Week. *Sports Illustrated*, 74.

————. 1981, June 15. The Week. *Sports Illustrated*, 58.

————. 1981, August 31. The Week. *Sports Illustrated*, 76.

————. 1981, September 28. The Week. *Sports Illustrated*, 57.

————. 1981, October 5. The Week. *Sports Illustrated*, 62.

Williams, Doug. 2013, February 27. "It's Settled: Where the Wave First Started." ESPN.com. http://espn.go.com/blog/playbook/fandom/post/_/id/18888/its-settled-where-the-wave-first-started.

Wulf, Steve. 1981, March 23. "No Hideaway for Fernando." *Sports Illustrated*, 26.

————. 1981, March 30. "Johnny Goes Job Hunting in a Tight Market." *Sports Illustrated*, 22.

————. 1981, September 7. "The Bounce, the Bench and the Boo-Birds." *Sports Illustrated*, 30.

————. 1981, September 21. "Will Inexperience Be a Great Teacher?" *Sports Illustrated*, 26.

————. 1981, October 12. "Milwaukee Spells Relief R-O-L-L-I-E." *Sports Illustrated*, 34.

————. 1981, October 19. "The Gang of Four Shoots to the Top: Expos." *Sports Illustrated*, 44.

Wynn, Steve. 2008. "Fernando." Recorded by the Baseball Project. On *Volume 1: Frozen Ropes and Dying Quails*. Yep Roc Records.

Young, Dick. 1981, March 24. "George: Reg Yanks' Best Bargain Ever." *Daily News*.

————. 1981, June 13. "Young Ideas—Class Not the Right Word for Bird." *Sporting News*, 5.

————. 1981, June 27. "Young Ideas—Now Players Must Pay the Piper." *Sporting News*, 9.

————. 1981, July 23. "George to Reggie: What About Me?" *Daily News,* C22.

————. 1981, August 1. "Garvey's Salary Plan Might Erase Agents." *Sporting News,* 5.

————. 1981, October 24. "Young Ideas—Reds Still Livid over Split Season." *Sporting News,* 5.

BOOKS

Angell, Roger. *Late Innings.* New York: Ballantine Books, 1984.

Barry, Dan. *Bottom of the 33rd: Hope, Redemption and Baseball's Longest Game.* New York: Harper, 2011.

Boswell, Tom. *Diamond Dreams.* Boston: Little, Brown, 1995.

Brinkley, Douglas, ed. *The Reagan Diaries.* New York: HarperCollins, 2007.

Carter, Gary, and Phil Pepe. *Still a Kid at Heart: My Life in Baseball and Beyond.* Chicago: Triumph Books, 2008.

D'Antonio, Michael. *Forever Blue.* New York: Riverhead Books, 2009.

Dawson, Andre, with Alan Maimon. *If You Love This Game . . .* Chicago: Triumph Books, 2012.

Deaver, Michael K. *A Different Drummer.* New York: HarperCollins, 2001.

Dickson, Paul. *Bill Veeck: Baseball's Greatest Maverick.* New York: Walker, 2012.

Flood, Curt, with Richard Carter. *The Way It Is.* New York: Pocket Books, 1972.

Gallagher, Mark. *The Yankee Encyclopedia.* New York: Leisure Press, 1982.

Gammons, Peter. *Beyond the Sixth Game.* Lexington, Mass.: Stephen Greene Press, 1986.

Golenbock, Peter. *Wild, High and Tight: The Life and Death of Billy Martin.* New York: St. Martin's Press, 1994.

————. *Amazin'.* New York: St. Martin's Griffin, 2002.

Grant, Jim "Mudcat," with Tom Sabellico and Pat O'Brien. *The Black Aces: Baseball's Only African-American Twenty-Game Winners.* Farmingdale, N.Y.: Black Aces, 2006.

Green, Dallas, and Alan Maimon. *The Mouth That Roared: My Six Outspoken Decades in Baseball*. Chicago: Triumph Books, 2013.

Helyar, John. *Lords of the Realm*. Norwalk, Conn.: Easton Press, 1998.

Henderson, Rickey, with John Shea. *Off Base: Confessions of a Thief*. New York: HarperCollins, 1992.

Herzog, Whitey, and Jonathan Pitts. *You're Missin' a Great Game*. New York: Simon & Schuster, 1999.

Hinz, Bob. *Philadelphia Phillies*. North Mankato, Minn.: Creative Paperbacks, 1982.

———. *Seattle Mariners*. North Mankato, Minn.: Creative Paperbacks, 1982.

Hollander, Zander, ed. *The Complete Handbook of Baseball, 1982 Season*. New York: Signet, 1982.

Jackson, Reggie, with Mike Lupica. *Reggie: The Autobiography*. New York: Villard Books, 1984.

James, Bill, and Rob Neyer. *The Neyer/James Guide to Pitchers*. New York: Fireside Books, 2004.

John, Sally. *The Sally and Tommy John Story: Our Life in Baseball*. New York: Macmillan, 1983.

John, Tommy. *TJ: My Twenty-Six Years in Baseball*. New York: Bantam, 1991.

Kuhn, Bowie. *Hardball*. New York: Times Books, 1987.

Lee, Bill "Spaceman," with Dick Lally. *The Wrong Stuff*. New York: Penguin Books, 1987.

Littwin, Mike. *Fernando!* Toronto: Bantam, 1981.

MacPhail, Lee. *My 9 Innings: An Autobiography of 50 Years in Baseball*. Westport, Conn.: Meckler Books, 1989.

Madden, Bill. *Steinbrenner: The Last Lion of Baseball*. New York: Harper, 2010.

Madden, Bill, and Moss Klein. *Damned Yankees*. New York: Warner Books, 1990.

Martin, Billy, with Phil Pepe. *Billyball*. Garden City, N.Y.: Doubleday, 1987.

Meese, Edwin, III. *With Reagan*. Washington, D.C.: Regenery Gateway, 1992.

Miller, Marvin. *A Whole Different Ball Game*. New York: Birch Lane Press, 1991.

Morris, Edmund. *Dutch*. New York: Random House, 1999.

Nettles, Graig, and Peter Golenbock. *Balls*. New York: Pocket Books, 1985.

Pluto, Terry. *The Curse of Rocky Colavito*. New York: Fireside Books, 1995.

Reeves, Richard. *President Reagan*. New York: Simon & Schuster, 2005.

Ripken, Cal, Jr., and Mike Bryan. *The Only Way I Know*. New York: Penguin Books, 1998.

Robinson, Frank, and Berry Stainback. *Extra Innings*. New York: McGraw-Hill, 1988.

Rose, Pete, and Roger Kahn. *Pete Rose: My Story*. New York: Macmillan, 1989.

Sahadi, Lou. *The L.A. Dodgers*. New York: Quill, 1982.

Schaap, Dick. *Steinbrenner!* New York: Avon, 1983.

Schoor, Gene. *Dave Winfield: The 23 Million Dollar Man*. Briarcliff Manor, N.Y.: Stein and Day, 1982.

———. *Seaver: A Biography*. Chicago: Contemporary Books, 1986.

———. *The History of the World Series*. New York: William Morrow, 1990.

Smith, Red. *The Red Smith Reader*. Edited by Dave Anderson. New York: Vintage Books, 1983.

Wilentz, Sean. *The Age of Reagan: A History, 1974–2008*. New York: Harper, 2008.

Williams, Dick, and Bill Plaschke. *No More Mr. Nice Guy: A Life of Hardball*. San Diego: Harcourt Brace Jovanovich, 1990.

Williams, Pete. *Card Sharks*. New York: Macmillan, 1995.

Winfield, Dave, with Tom Parker. *Winfield: A Player's Life*. New York: Avon Books, 1988.

Zimbalist, Andrew. *Baseball and Billions*. New York: Basic Books, 1992.

INTERVIEWS

John Castino

Ron Cey

Murray Chass

Doug DeCinces

Phil Garner

Ray Grebey

Clark Griffith

Tom Guilfoile

Jon Matlack

Marvin Miller

Jerry Reinsdorf

Steve Rogers

Billy Sample

Andy Strasberg

PAPERS

Harry Dalton Papers. BA MSS 40. National Baseball Hall of Fame Library, Cooperstown, N.Y.

Paul Degener. Hall of Fame Speech transcript.

In the Matter of: Major League Baseball Player Relations Committee, Inc. and Its Constituent Member Clubs and Major League Baseball Players Association. July 6–10, 1981.

Bowie K. Kuhn Collection. BA MSS 100. National Baseball Hall of Fame & Museum, Cooperstown, N.Y.

Memorandum of Agreement. July 31, 1981.

Marvin and Theresa (Terry) Miller Papers. WAG. 165. Tamiment Library/Robert F. Wagner Labor Archives. Elmer Holmes Bobst Library, New York University Libraries.

Daniel Silverman, Regional Director, NLRB vs. Major League Player Relations Committee, Inc. May 28–June 4, 1981.

VIDEO

Angeles, Cruz (director). *Fernando Nation*. 2010.

Major League Baseball Productions (producers). *This Week in Baseball*. 1981.

——— (producers). *The 1981 World Series*. 1982.

"Pete Rose Hits Milestones! 'Call from President Reagan!' and 'Is This Pete Rose? Please Hold.'" YouTube. http://www.youtube.com/watch?v=h70b9-dJzcc.

Shoemaker, Judy, Bill Veeck, and Tom Weinberg (producers). Don Voigt (director). *A View from the Bleachers: The Bill Veeck Show*. May 30, 1982, and January 1, 1983.

WEB SITES

Baseball Reference. http://www.baseball-reference.com.

Retrosheet. http://www.retrosheet.org.

Index